SEEING AND KNOWING

International Library of Philosophy and Scientific Method

EDITOR: TED HONDERICH
ADVISORY EDITOR: BERNARD WILLIAMS

A Catalogue of books already published in the
International Library of Philosophy and Scientific Method
will be found at the end of this volume

Seeing
and
Knowing

Fred I. Dretske

LONDON

ROUTLEDGE & KEGAN PAUL

First published 1969
by Routledge & Kegan Paul Limited
Broadway House, 68–74 Carter Lane
London, E.C.4

Printed in Great Britain
by Richard Clay (The Chaucer Press) Ltd
Bungay, Suffolk

SBN 7100 6213 3

Contents

To Brenda

Preface

This book was written in Florence, Italy. It would not have been written at all, much less in such pleasant surroundings, had it not been for a grant from the American Council of Learned Societies. To them I am deeply grateful for the opportunity I had to devote myself in the morning, every morning, for the space of a full year, to the unsolved problems of the preceding day. Whatever may be the case with others, and whatever may be the ultimate virtues of the product, I find the deepest and most enduring rewards of the philosophical enterprise in this process of sustained engagement.

In this connection I wish also to thank the Graduate School of the University of Wisconsin for their generous support of this project, both during the year mentioned above and during the preparation of the final manuscript.

The book was rewritten in London and revised again, and again, in Madison. During this time a number of individuals said and wrote things to me which I found valuable. Among my colleagues, Dennis Stampe and Bruce Freed read portions of the manuscript; critical of some parts, encouraging about others, they were always helpful and I profited greatly from my discussions with them. During the spring of 1967 I used the manuscript in a graduate seminar at Wisconsin. To the students of this seminar I am indebted for their levelling influence on a number of over- and under-sights. I must especially mention those whose remarks led me to make significant alterations: Hardie Jones, George Dicker, Judy Wilson, Al Mosley, and Gilbert Chambers. Several long discussions with Mr. Peter Brown were also extremely useful; his penetrating critique of crucial sections in Chapter III was invaluable.

And to my wife, Brenda, go thanks for her patience and receptivity; when there was so much to see, she willingly shared my passion for 'seeing'.

Madison, Wisconsin

I

INTRODUCTION

The variety of different verbs, and different constructions involving a single verb, which can be used to express what might broadly be called a visual state of affairs is, indeed, bewildering. We observe, study, perceive, watch, inspect, recognize, detect, identify, and discern the elements in our environment. We distinguish and discriminate between them; we glimpse, spot, notice, spy, and catch sight of them. Moreover, we see, or at least say we see, not only teapots and tigers, but what these things are, how they look, who they belong to, where they are located, what they are doing, that they have moved, whether they are nearby, when they arrived, and why they were late. We see under them, over them, the difference between them, the condition they are in, if they are in trouble, what caused it, and how to remedy it.

Nevertheless, impressive as is this diversity in our manner of describing our visual efforts and achievements, I believe there are just two fundamental themes which can be traced throughout the spectrum of differences, two fundamentally different, though not unrelated, ways of seeing things which can be found, either singly or jointly, in every distinctively visual situation. It is the purpose of this book to describe these two themes, to depict their most significant embellishments, and to integrate the results into a theory of knowledge.

My aim is primarily descriptive. I cannot bring myself to think that what I provide is a *theory* of perception; this word is much too pretentious to reflect my more modest aspirations. I do hope my description will be systematic, coherent, and thorough. There are many things which I make no attempt to describe in anything but an incidental way; the physics, physiology, and, to an appreciable degree, the psychology of these matters are of subordinate interest. My description concerns itself with those features of perception which have served, and continue to serve, as a touchstone for epistemological controversy. In a word, the topic is what we see and how we see in so far as the answers to these questions help us to get clear about what we know and how we know it. By virtue of their generality, most systematic descriptions of a complex phenomenon assume some of the characteristics of a theory. They provide some degree of unification and explanation; there is some assimilation of the puzzling and discrepant to the familiar and well-known. And if such results mark something as a theory, then, to this extent, the following pages embody a theory of perception.

Although this is not a psychological study, the investigations of practicing psychologists are certainly relevant to a number of the conclusions I reach. This is inevitable. For I am trying to say something about a human being's perceptual relation to his environment and, in pursuit of that end, something about his beliefs, dispositions, and behavior. Since these topics fall within the purview of scientific psychology, a degree of relevance is to be expected. This, however, is only to concede that what I shall be saying is frequently empirical in nature, the sort of thing whose truth depends on the way human beings are. But we already know a good deal about human beings, and when it is required, the evidential support for what I have to say comes primarily, almost exclusively, from that common fund of information which we all possess about ourselves and each other. The philosophy of perception is not, as I see it, a quest for new data; it is rather an attempt to assimilate the data already available and to describe it in a way which reduces or eliminates the philosophical problems which it, or various descriptions of it, inspire.

If this is not a psychological study, neither is it an exercise in English grammar or a meticulous cataloging of what ordinary people ordinarily say about what they see. Such linguistic matters will, of course, be of continuing interest, and a significant portion of this book is devoted to their discussion. One simply cannot talk about what people see or what people know and completely ignore the sorts of things people say, and refuse to say, about these things. But neither can one slavishly follow the ordinary use of a number of verbs and nouns. Even a brief glance at the way we use such verbs as 'to see' should convince one that a dogged adherence to its ordinary use will put one off the scent. We can *see* what a person means, but we share this ability with the blind. A man's eyeglasses do not help him to *observe* the rules, and it is not altogether clear what part one's eyes play in *seeing* how to solve an equation. If one is interested, as I am, in man's ability to see, in so far as this presupposes a certain visual endowment, in so far as it contrasts with the incapacities of a blind man, then not everything we say about what we see is relevant.

One of my chief interests is the relation of observation to scientific practice. There are, however, strategic reasons for developing a more broadly based examination. For unless one appreciates, in familiar settings and routine conditions, the sorts of variables which influence what we see and how we see, the role which scientific activity plays in this process will appear unique and isolated—and to that extent, for some people, implausible. Hence, I have confined my discussion of certain specialized issues, those which quite clearly belong within the philosophy of science, to the last chapter. What precedes it, in Chapters II–V, is a rather detailed examination of the more commonplace perceptual situations. The die is cast, so to speak, in these initial chapters, and the results are then applied to a cluster of interlocking problems in the philosophy of science. Chapter V is a transitional chapter; its examination of perceptual relativity presupposes the analysis which precedes it and, by extending this analysis, sets the stage for what follows.

To borrow a phrase, this essay was written for both the professional philosopher and the interested non-philosopher. It is not always easy to serve both audiences. I have attempted to do so, not by a compromise in rigor but by adherence to two expository guidelines: (1) I avoid, whenever possible, technical jargon whose currency is restricted to the philosophy seminar room, and (2) I forego those lengthy surveys which are designed to reveal the inadequacies of competing philosophical views. I have introduced several technical concepts of my own, but always, I hope, with adequate explanation. The absence of any lengthy polemic against alternative theories of perception may, perhaps, disappoint those who have advanced such theories, but the advantages to be reaped from a sustained development of the present approach are, I believe, entirely compensatory. If I am mistaken in what I have to say, an exhaustive inventory of the mistakes of others will hardly set things right.

II

NON-EPISTEMIC SEEING

There is a primitive visual ability which is common to a great variety of sentient beings, an ability which we, as human beings, share with our cocker spaniel and pet cat. It is an endowment which is relatively free from the influences of education, past experience, linguistic sophistication, and conceptual dexterity. The purpose of this chapter is to describe this fundamental visual capacity, not in any physical or physiological sense but in a way that will make clear its relation, or lack of it, to those perennial issues which have kept the philosophy of perception alive for hundreds of years. Only with a maximally clear account of this fundamental capacity is it possible, I believe, to render a coherent description of the other visual achievements of which man is capable and the relation which they bear to what he knows.

1. *Belief Content: A Negative Criterion*

A number of situations involving sentient agents exhibit a common negative feature. Since the way of seeing with which I am now concerned, the primitive visual ability mentioned above, falls within this class of situations, I would like to begin by discussing this feature. A variety of other situations, most of which are not visual in nature, also fall within this negatively characterized class. Nonetheless, this criterion, if not definatival, will at least help us to isolate this first way of seeing by contrasting it with other ways of seeing, ways of seeing which do not share this negative feature. A positive specification will be attempted in the following section.

4

Let S be some sentient agent, and let 'S . . .' be some statement about S: e.g. S is blond, S is asleep, S saw the parade, S stubbed his toe. Let us say that the state of affairs, activity, or condition which makes these statements true, if indeed they are true, has *zero belief content* if and only if there is no belief such that S's having or failing to have that belief is logically relevant to the truth of the state-ment. If the statement 'S . . .' entails that S has a particular belief, or set of beliefs, then we will say that the state of affairs expressed by this statement has a *positive belief content*. If the statement entails that S does not have some belief, or set of beliefs, then the situa-tion is one of *negative belief content*.

The terms 'logically' and 'entails' are brittle terms, but I think they will bear the weight I wish to put on them. Whether S is blond or not does not depend on what he happens to believe; at least the meaning of the predicate 'is blond' does not involve S's having a particular belief or lacking a particular belief. It is pos-sible, of course, that if S had not believed a particular thing, that he was confronted by a ghost, for instance, his hair would not be ashen white. In this case the color of his hair does happen to depend, perhaps causally, on a particular belief which he had. But the connection is not one of a logical nature; someone else might well have white hair without ever having held the same belief. Someone's hair is white if it passes certain visual tests, and if it passes these tests, his beliefs are a matter of total irrelevance. One does not understand what it means to have white hair if one ob-jects that a person's hair cannot be white *because* that person does or does not, happen to believe a particular thing.

S's having white hair, then, is a state of affairs which has zero belief content. S's stepping on a bug is similar in this respect. One can step on a bug without believing that one stepped on it; nor is there anything else which one must believe, or must not believe, in order to do this. On the other hand, consider what it means to wish one were six feet tall. This state of affairs is one that involves a belief to the effect that one is not six feet tall, or, at the very least, a failure to believe that one is six feet tall. If I believe I am six feet tall, I can scarcely wish I were six feet tall. I can, of course, *be* six feet tall and still wish I were this height; for I might believe, mistakenly, that I was only five feet ten inches. The statement 'S wishes he were six feet tall', therefore, describes a situation which has positive belief content (S's believing that he is not six feet tall), or, at the very least, negative belief content (*S*'s not believing that he is six feet).

Before attempting to apply this notion to visual matters, one word about the notion of belief. When I speak of *S* believing something, I wish this to be understood in a manner which does not prejudice the question of whether *S* *knows* that it (what he believes) is true. If we are of the opinon that *S* knows that so-and-so is the case, of course, we are not likely to say of *S*, simply, that he believes that so-and-so is the case. Nonetheless, I think there is a sense of the term 'believe' in which, if *S* knows something, that today is Monday, for example, then he believes that today is Monday. And in this same sense of the term he might believe that today was Monday without knowing that it was Monday (either because he is not entirely certain of it or, although certain of it, his grounds for believing it are conspicuously inadequate or, failing this, it is simply not the case that today is Monday). As I am using this term, a person (or animal) may know that something is the case and believe it (although, admittedly, it would be redundant to say the latter after one had said the former); he may also believe it without knowing it. It is a sense of the term which is interchangeable in some cases (but not in *all*—e.g. with an infant or an animal) with the locution 'accepts as true'.

So much for preliminary explanations. How does this help us to understand perception? It is related in the following fashion: the fundamental visual ability with which I am concerned in this chapter is an ability whose successful exercise is devoid of positive belief content. With respect to its positive belief content, seeing a bug in this fundamental way is like stepping on a bug; neither performance involves, in any essential respect, a particular belief or set of beliefs on the part of the agent. Nothing one believes is logically relevant to what one has done. *Purposely* stepping on a bug is something else again, and so is seeing *that* it is a bug, or *what* kind of bug it is. Both of these latter accomplishments, if I can call them that, have a positive belief content. But more of this in later chapters.

Our first task is to show that there is a way of seeing things which is devoid of positive belief content. To do this it must be shown that there is a way of seeing such that for any proposition, *P*, the statement '*S* sees *D*' does not logically entail the statement '*S* believes *P*'. If this can be established, it will have been shown

6

that this way of seeing does not have positive belief content. I shall have little to say about the presence of negative belief content. I will mention it, in passing, at several points in the discussion, but nothing I have to say will depend on how this further issue is decided.

Let D be any familiar object, person, or event—a book, a friend, or a sunrise. When we see D, although, normally, we frequently do identify what we see *as* D, and hence believe that it is D, this identification is not a necessary condition for our seeing D. This point is, perhaps, too obvious to labor. One can see a screwdriver without believing that what one is seeing is a screwdriver, without believing that there are any screwdrivers, without even knowing what screwdrivers are. If anyone needs to be convinced of this point, I suggest that they ask themselves whether they have never seen a maple tree, or an electrical capacitor, without realizing that it was a maple tree or an electrical capacitor.

The same is true of any of the more generic characteristics of D. That is to say, not only could S see his aunt and not believe that she was his aunt, but he might not believe that she was a woman, nor even that she was a human being. Depending on the lighting conditions, his attentiveness, and a host of other variables, he might mistake her for a mannequin, a shadow, or any one of a number of different things. Mistakes are not the only possibility, however. I shall go into this matter at greater length in a moment, but we are sometimes in the position of having to say, 'Well, yes, I suppose I did see it, but I was so busy at the time that I did not pay much attention.'

It might be thought that if D is some physical object, we must at least believe that it (where the 'it' is understood as referring to what we see) is some sort of object. If this means that one cannot see a physical object, such as a table or a typewriter, without believing that it is a physical object of some sort, the kind of object which other people can also see, then it is clearly false. The remark 'I don't know whether I really saw something or whether I imagined it' testifies to a state of mind which lacks the belief in question; yet, there is nothing odd about supposing that such an individual really did see something: e.g. a face in the window, a clown in the closet. Experiments have been performed in which the subjects were shown various colored shapes on the wall, but were led to believe that the shapes they were seeing were actually their own imaginative constructions.[1] The subjects were asked to describe these 'images of imagination', and

> ... after all the introspections had been recorded, the observer was asked whether he was 'quite sure that he had imagined all these things'. The question almost always aroused surprise, and at times indignation.[2]

This reflects a rather gross (but, given the conditions of the experiment, understandable) mistake in the classification of a visual experience. Nevertheless, the experimenters were not tempted to say that their subjects could not have seen the colored shapes on the wall. Of course they saw them; they simply mistook them for 'images of imagination'.[3]

People see flapping window shades and believe them to be ethereal spirits; some philosophers believe, or say they believe, that nothing they see, or anyone else sees, is physical. Are such beliefs at all relevant to whether window shades and water glasses are seen by the people who hold such beliefs? When an infant first sees its mother, whenever this may happen, must it believe that it is seeing a human being? A thing occupying spatial position? Some kind of publicly observable object?

The fact that we normally do believe something about the things which we see in this way is irrelevant. The point I am driving is that our failure to believe these things would not, in itself, prevent us from seeing what we see in this way. The bewildered savage, transplanted suddenly from his native environment to a Manhattan subway station, can witness the arrival of the 3.45 express as clearly as the bored commuter. Ignorance of X does not impair one's vision of X; if it did, total ignorance would be largely irreparable. This way of seeing a teapot or a tiger is consistent with one's believing that it is a visual hallucination, a mirage, a reflection, a part of one's own brain, a phenomenal gloss over an underlying reality, a mental image, or congeries

---

[1] 'An Experimental Study of Imagination', Cheves West Perky, reprinted in *Readings in Perception,* David C. Beardslee and Michael Wertheimer (eds.) (Princeton, New Jersey, 1958).

[2] *Ibid.,* p. 549.

[3] Care was taken in this series of experiments to rule out the possibility that the subjects *were* imagining various colored shapes and describing these rather than the shapes which they saw on the wall.

of such images. It is consistent, in other words, with any false belief one may care to mention about the generic character of what one is seeing. And since it seems obvious that it is also consistent with any true belief, it is logically independent of such beliefs.

Even if we concede this much, however, there still seems to be a difficulty. It has been suggested that whenever we see something we see it *as* something: 'All seeing is seeing as . . . if a person sees something at all it must look like something to him even if it only looks like "somebody doing something".'[1] This might, although it should not, be interpreted in such a way as to suggest that there is a rudimentary belief which is necessarily involved in every instance of seeing. It might be supposed, for example, that if we must, in seeing *D*, see it as something, then we must have some elementary belief about what we see: *viz.* that it looks such-and-such a way to us, or that something is appearing to us as such-and-such (where 'such-and-such' is an expression for what we see the thing *as*), or, finally, that something looks some way to us. And if this is true, there is no way of seeing things which is devoid of all positive belief content. I think this conclusion mistaken although I am quite prepared to accept a version of the main premise. Indeed, in the following section, I shall adopt a view somewhat similar, in expression if not in substance, to that embodied in the above quotation. What I wish to reject is the move from (1) *S* sees *D* as *Y* to (*a*) *S* believes himself aware of something *Y*-like, (*b*) *S* believes something looks *Y*, or (*c*) *S* believes something is appearing as *Y*. I am quite willing to admit that, in a certain sense, *D* must look some way to *S* (*not* to be read as: must look *like* something to *S*) in order for *S* to see *D*, but I do not think it is a necessary consequence of this admission that *S* must thereby believe something of the form (*a*), (*b*), or (*c*), or any modification of these. For *S*'s seeing *D* as something, in so far as it follows from *S*'s seeing *D*, must *itself* be understood as lacking positive belief content. I would agree, for instance, that whenever it becomes true to say of an infant that it can now see its mother, or of a rat that it can see the lever, it also becomes true to say of the infant and the rat that they see the mother and the lever as something—the

---

[1] G.N.A. Vesey, 'Seeing and Seeing As', *Aristotelian Society Proceedings*, 1955-6, Vol. LVI, p. 114.

mother looks some way to the infant and the lever looks some way to the rat. Must the infant believe, however, that something is a dark figure on a light background (if, indeed, this is the way we wish to describe the mother as looking to the infant), or that something looks like a dark figure? What *must* our experimental rat believe about the lever which it sees? I, personally, have no idea what the infant or the rat believes, or whether they believe anything, but I do think that the sort of beliefs described above imply an unusual degree of sophistication on the part of the creatures to whom they are ascribed. The questions to ask are: Does the child fixate on its mother? Does it move its eyes and continue to fixate as the mother moves about? If one insists that the child would not fixate unless it believed that something was appearing to it, I suggest that this is tantamount to urging that the child would not suck on its nipple unless it believed something elemental about the nourishment to be derived therefrom.

Let us consider an adult case. The difficulty in finding examples here is enormously increased by the fact that adults have spent years learning to identify, classify, and sort out the things which they see. Hence, the occasions on which an adult sees something without having some beliefs, however primitive they might be, about what he sees is correspondingly rare. Nevertheless, examples can be found; how persuasive they are will depend, to some extent, on the reader's own experience. It must always be remembered, though, that what I am trying to establish is a logical independence, not a *psychological* independence. It may be that adult human beings, by virtue of their past experience, cannot see a candle-stick holder, under any conditions, without at least being brought to the belief that they are visually aware of something. But this fact, if it is a fact (and I do not think it is), would not tend to show that it is logically inconsistent to say of someone that he saw a candle-stick holder without believing himself visually aware of anything, that seeing a candle-stick holder involves, as part of its meaning, the percipient's believing something of this sort. If I could show you that no adult human being can watch himself being attacked by an angry lion without a significant alteration in pulse rate, I would have shown you something about the make-up of adult human beings, but I would not have shown you anything about what we mean by 'seeing ourselves attacked by an angry lion'. And what I am now trying to do is tell you, in a negative way of course, what we mean when we say of some sentient being that he saw a candle-stick holder.

Assuming for the moment that you, the reader, have read one or two of the preceding pages, it might be asked how many distinct letters you saw while reading page six. I am *not* asking how many different letters there are to which you paid sufficient attention to detect, say, a misspelling. This is quite a different question. I am asking how many distinct letters you saw in the same way in which you might have seen *all* the books (every book) on the shelf but were too distracted, too hurried, or saw them under such conditions that you were unable to tell whether any of them were, say, upside down. Now I think that the likelihood is that, if you did read the entire page, you saw hundreds of different letters. It is possible that you did not see this many; perhaps your attention had strayed so much that the words were a blur and no distinctions between their constituent letters were made. But if we set this possibility aside, there seems to be nothing extraordinary in saying, of each of the many letters on the page, that you saw it.

What, then, are the necessary consequences of these hundred or so different statements about what you saw? Does each one entail that you had a certain belief about the way that letter looked to you? During the time that it took you to read the page, did you acquire hundreds of distinct beliefs about the assorted letters you saw? Granted, each letter that you saw must have looked some way to you, in some sense, but does this mean that you had to believe this? Can you remember believing anything of this sort?

I have occasionally been in such a preoccupied state that as I walked down the street I was, in the only way I can think to describe it, unaware of everything around me. It was only after I snapped out of the 'fog' that I realized I had been seeing certain things without being aware of it; that is, I can remember having seen things, but I cannot remember being aware, at the time I was seeing them, that I was seeing something or that things were looking a certain way to me. One could, I suppose, continue to insist that I was believing something at the time about the things which I saw, but that I simply can no longer remember the fact. Or, alternatively, one could insist that in such a preoccupied state I did not really see anything. One could cling to this view, but why? Is there something logically incoherent about saying, 'I must have seen it, but, at the time, I was totally unaware of anything but that pain in my foot'? Does this statement stand self-accused, on internal grounds alone, of being false?

Should one accept such illustrations as showing that there is a way of seeing that is devoid of positive belief content,[1] one is still left with the question of whether it is also devoid of negative belief content. I have already indicated that I shall not pursue this independent question; an answer to it is not relevant to any of the conclusions I shall be drawing. It may be of interest, however, to point out that there seems to be several types of situation, isolated and rare to be sure, which indicate that this way of seeing also lacks negative belief content: i.e. that for any proposition, P, S's not believing P is not entailed by his seeing D (in this way). Superficially it would seem that if S sees D he must, as a minimal requirement, not believe that he is not seeing anything. And if this were so, it would show that this way of seeing has a negative belief content. But if we take such phenomena as subliminal perception seriously, it would seem that we could say of the percipient, S, that he saw (in some sense) the lettering on the screen ('Eat popcorn') despite the fact that he does not believe he saw anything—or, to put it in the proper form, despite the fact that he believes he saw nothing at all. Or we might think up somewhat extraordinary cases in which a person was made to think he was in the dark and, hence, made to believe that he was not seeing anything, when, in fact, he was allowed to see a surrounding dark envelope. This sort of example may strain one's powers of imagination, but there does not seem to be any 'conceptual absurdity' in supposing that a person might be fooled in this way.

I do not wish to be committed, one way or the other, on the question of whether this way of seeing possesses negative belief content. But I am committed to its lacking positive belief content, and if the remarks I have so far made on this question fail to be persuasive, I can only ask the reader to delay his judgment until the discussion in subsequent sections. Aside from the question of what it means, positively, to see an object or the occurrence of an event in a manner which is devoid of positive belief content, there is also the question of when it is appropriate to say of someone that he saw such things. That is, one must disentangle

[1] I shall argue the point at greater length in the following section when I attempt to provide a positive specification of this way of seeing.

what we in fact say about these matters, what we find it inappropriate, misleading, or irrelevant to say, and what it is true to say. I shall suggest, in Section 3, that a confusion of this sort is partially responsible for obscuring the fact that we do see objects and events in the manner now being discussed. For the present I wish to emphasize only one point. One may find it extraordinary to suppose that anyone, especially an adult human being, should see another person or an automobile accident without believing something about what he saw and, perhaps, a good many true things. But I am not quarreling with this fact, if it is a fact, about human psychology. All I am suggesting here is that the possession of no particular belief, or set of beliefs, constitutes a logically indispensable condition for the individual's seeing what he does see.

There are, of course, other ways of seeing things, ways which possess a positive belief content. *S* cannot see that the lights are on without believing that the lights are on. Neither can one see how a person is dressed, where he is going, what he is doing, whether he is pretending, or who he is without (thereby) possessing some determinate belief about what is seen. If you see what a person is doing, that he is performing a trick, for example, then it follows that you know that what he is doing is performing a trick. But these are matters for later chapters. The way of seeing now in question must be carefully distinguished from these other achievements; in the way of seeing that I have specified one can see a man performing a trick without being able to say what the man is doing or whether it is a man at all.[1]

There are also a number of abstract nouns which, when used to describe what is seen, carry with them the implication of a positive belief content. For example, one can hardly be said to have

[1] Warnock illustrates the same, or a closely related, distinction by the contrast between seeing that White's bishop is dangerously exposed and seeing White's dangerously exposed bishop ('Seeing', *Aristotelian Society Proceedings*, Vol. IV, p. 214). In this excellent article Warnock distinguishes a way of seeing which is close, if not identical, to the one being discussed in this chapter, and I often rely on his discussion in the following sections. Also compare Roderick Chisholm's distinction between propositional and non-propositional seeing in *Perceiving: A Philosophical Study* (Ithaca, New York, 1957). My account differs markedly from Chisholm's however, and this should become increasingly apparent. More recently, J. F. Soltis, in his book *Seeing, Knowing and Believing* (London, 1966), isolates a way of seeing, 'simple seeing', which he defines as having 'no implications with respect to the truth or falsity of beliefs acquired by the observer', p. 65.

seen the problem (the mistake, the solution, the trouble) unless one believes, minimally, that there is a problem (a mistake, a solution, or some trouble). To the extent that this is true, one cannot see the problem or the solution in a way that is devoid of positive belief content. Nonetheless, such abstract nouns may be interpreted in alternative ways, some of which permit us to say that one can see the problem (mistake, solution, etc.) in a way that is devoid of positive belief content. As Robert B. Lees points out,[1] such abstract nouns may appear in copula sentences opposite both nominalizations *and* concrete nominals. We can say that the problem is *that his tonsils are inflamed*; but we can also say that the problem is, simply, *his tonsils*. In the former case it would seem that one could not see the problem *unless* one believed that his tonsils were inflamed; in the latter case, however, one might wish to say that the problem (i.e. his tonsils, or his inflamed tonsils) could be seen without any particular belief. Such subtleties must be kept in mind when one is trying to demarcate those cases of seeing which are devoid of positive belief content.[2] If we wish to say that a problem or a mistake can be seen in a way that is devoid of positive belief content, we must understand that this is simply another way of saying that a person can see that event, state of affairs, situation, or thing which may be referred to as the problem or the mistake without an appreciation of the fact that it *is* the problem or the mistake (or a problem or a mistake).

Several of my previous examples suggest something which I should now like to make explicit. Not only can books, cats, trees, automobiles, buildings, shadows, and people be seen in the way I have just depicted, but also such items as battles, departures, signals, ceremonies, games, accidents, stabbings, performances, escapes, and gestures. That is, to speak in broad category terms, events as well as objects (and such things as shadows) can be seen

---

[1] *The Grammar of English Nominalizations* (Bloomington, Indiana, 1963), p. 14.

[2] There is a class of nominalizations which display this sort of ambiguity. E.g. 'what was on the table' may be taken as a relative clause nominalization —the *x* which was on the table—or as an interrogative nominal, nominals which are used when speaking of the answer to a question, a piece of information, a datum, or a fact (see Lees, *op. cit.*). Seeing what is on the table can occur in a way that is free of positive belief content only when the nominal is understood as a relative clause nominal. I shall discuss the interrogative nominals in Chapter IV, Section 4.

in this way. I shall offer no elaborate support for this point now; this must await the discussion in the next section. One or two remarks, however, may help to dispel some of the initial doubts one may feel about the possibility of seeing an event in this fashion. Events are happenings or occurrences; they involve a movement or a change of some sort. Although we may not pay particular attention to a stationary man, we do tend to notice him when he moves. The person who is fidgeting in the back row is the one to whom our eyes keep wandering. We may not particularly notice a creature until it scurries away. In other words, events are just the sort of thing which, if seen at all, tend to be noticed; and *noticing* them does seem to involve, minimally, an appreciation of the fact that something is happening.[1] Consequently, the occasions on which we see an event take place without at least appreciating the fact that a change of some sort is occurring are exceptional. Once again, though, one should not mistake this psychological connection between what adult human beings see and what they believe, or tend to believe, for part of what we mean when we say that they saw something of this sort. Consider an officer who, from his point on the reviewing stand, takes the salute of a company of passing soldiers. I can think of a variety of things which might be 'running through his mind at the time', but I cannot bring myself to suppose that whether he saw a score or more distinct events (the individual salutes) depends on his sudden acquisition of a score or more particular beliefs, or even on one particular belief. Nor can I bring myself to believe that what the company mascot, Rover, saw as the men saluted depends on what he believes. Whether Rover saw the men saluting (not: saw *that* the men were saluting) seems to depend on the excellence of his visual apparatus, the distance of the men, the physical conditions under which he saw

[1] Somewhat paradoxically one tends to 'notice' them even before one sees them. In discussing the relative sensitivity of various parts of the retina to movement, R. L. Gregory says: 'The very extreme edge of the retina is even more primitive: when stimulated by movement we experience nothing, but a reflex is initiated which rotates the eye to bring the moving object into central vision, so that the highly developed foveal region with its associated central neural network is brought into play for identifying the object. The edge of the retina is thus an early-warning device, used to rotate the eyes to aim the object-recognition part of the system on to objects likely to be friend or foe rather than neutral' (*Eye and Brain: The Psychology of Seeing* (New York, 1966), p. 91).

them.[1] It does not seem to depend on what Rover believes.

It is sometimes suggested, although the claims are by no means unambiguous, that there is *no* manner of seeing things in the way I have just described. D. W. Hamlyn, for instance, ties seeing to identification: 'Anyone who can see things *must* be able to identify them in a number of circumstances. Otherwise we should not allow them the claim to see things at all.'[2] Or again:

> When we say that someone sees something we do not imply merely that he has certain experiences (even if such experiences are pre-supposed). We imply also that he knows something about the object and we indicate the source of his knowledge (i.e. the use of his senses).[3]

If this is taken to mean that one cannot see a cat without believing or knowing that it is a cat, it is simply false. But it is not altogether clear that Hamlyn means this; perhaps one must only know something about the cat, that it is an animal, or that it is a furry thing. This, of course, I would deny. Or it may be that Hamlyn's statements should be interpreted to mean, not that we cannot see a cat without knowing something about it, but that our *saying* of someone that he saw a cat implies that the person knows something about the cat.[4] I shall discuss this possibility in Section 3 of this chapter. D. M. Armstrong expresses a similar point of view: ' . . . Hence it seems that, whenever we talk about perceiving things in our environment or talk about perceiving features of things, we can also talk of acquiring knowledge of particular facts about these things.'[5] The use of the verb 'to perceive' helps to

[1] Constructions such as 'Rover saw the men saluting' are particularly ambiguous. I have here taken it to mean not only that Rover saw the men *who* were saluting but also that he was in a position to see *their salute(s)*. This distinction, and several other sources of ambiguity, will be discussed at length in later sections.

[2] *The Psychology of Perception* (London, 1957), p. 71.

[3] *Ibid.,* p. 110.

[4] In a later book Hamlyn concedes that there is a sense of the verb 'to see' in which one could see something without identifying it, but he goes on to say that this use is derivative: ' . . . in that primary use perception and identification must go hand in hand' (*Sensations and Perception: A History of the Philosophy of Perception* (New York, 1961), pp. 195-6). I shall argue that this use of the verb is fundamental, although, epistemologically, it carries very little direct significance.

[5] *Perception and the Physical World* (London, 1961), p. 108.

cloud the issue here, but, once again, if this means that we cannot see something without knowing something about it, without acquiring some true beliefs about it, then I think it is simply false. Certainly we are expected to learn something about the things we see, and in the vast majority of cases perhaps we do learn something; but our failure to do so would not imply that we did not see anything.[1] Total ignorance is not a sufficient condition for total blindness.

I have chosen to speak of 'one way' of seeing things, and this choice of words may be unfortunate in one respect. For it suggests that I am interested in such questions as: whether a thing is seen clearly or not, through what kind of medium, and under what circumstances. That is, we see things under the influence of drugs, through a window, in a mirror, from a good vantage point, and so on. In one respect these adverbial modifiers reflect different ways of seeing things. Yet, they are ways of seeing which cut through the category I am trying to isolate. As I have characterized (negatively) this fundamental way of seeing, we can see a tiger from the branches of a tree, by sneaking up behind it, or through the bars of its cage. The circumstances under which one sees the tiger may change, but the way of seeing it with which I am concerned may remain invariant.

It seems, then, that we may conclude, tentatively at least, that our negative criterion does isolate a primitive sort of visual achievement, a way of seeing which is logically independent of whatever beliefs we may possess.[2] The fact that this criterion is negative, however, leaves us with an inadequate characterization; for, as I have already pointed out, this negative criterion does not distinguish between someone's stepping on a bug and someone's seeing a bug. Both of these acts, if I may loosely refer to them both

[1] Although it would make it difficult for anyone else to find out whether we had seen anything; see Section 3 of this chapter.

[2] It may be that one finds the notion of a sentient being, particularly a human being, without any beliefs inconceivable. If this is so, I only wish to point out that nothing I have said conflicts with this conception of a sentient being. I have not said that S (a sentient agent) can see something without any beliefs; I have only said that no *particular* belief is essential to the seeing. He may have many beliefs, and it may be essential (especially in the case of human agents) that he have some beliefs in order to qualify for such 'mentalistic' predicates as 'sees so-and-so'. Nonetheless, of no one of these beliefs is it essential that he have it.

as 'acts' for the moment, lack positive belief content. Our criterion merely segregates one way of seeing things from other ways of seeing the same, or related, things; but it does not tell us what is involved in seeing something in this way. The following section is an attempt to supply this missing specification.

2. Seeing$_n$

If we use the subscript 'n' to indicate a way of seeing that satisfies the negative condition specified in the last section, then our task is now to provide a positive characterization of seeing$_n$. It is possible, of course, that seeing$_n$ is, depending on the nature of what is seen and the conditions under which it is seen, several different sorts of achievement. If this is the case, the subscript 'n', suggesting as it does some unique and univocal sense of the verb, would be misleading. I hope to show, however, that we are dealing with a single sort of situation.

Why do we say to people, as we sometimes do, 'But you *must* have seen it'? What is there about the situation that prompts such a remark? It is certainly not that the person already believes he saw it (whatever *it* happens to be). Quite the contrary; he does not believe he saw it, cannot remember having seen it, or is simply dubious of whether he saw anything at all of the kind in question. Generally speaking, we say such things in the face of a person's disbelief; we say it when we are convinced that, despite what the person *thought* he saw, or whether he thought he saw anything at all, the physical and physiological conditions were such that the object must have looked some way to him. 'You must have seen that cuff link; you were staring right at it.' Whatever response this allegation may prompt, it is not refuted by an appeal to ignorance: 'I did not notice it,' or 'The drawer looked empty to me'. He may have seen the cuff link without noticing it; he may have seen it without it looking to him *as though* there was something in the drawer. What would refute the allegation is something quite different. 'No, I did not look into the drawer', 'The cuff link was not there when I looked', or 'No, I had my eyes closed all the time'.

Before we go any further, we should clear aside one possible source of confusion. One of the ways we have of *finding out* whether S saw D is to ask him whether he saw it. If he does not know, or does not believe he saw D, we may introduce collateral information which, combined with what S believes himself to have seen, or combined with how he describes the way things looked to him at the time, implies that he saw D. For example, 'You must have seen Harold; he was the only other customer in the shop at the time, and you said you saw one other customer.' Sometimes it may be more difficult to lay one's hands on this collateral information, and the difficulty is increased when the percipient can provide us with little or no *accurate* information about what he did see. In the case mentioned above, when the percipient alleges that 'the drawer looked empty', the difficulties in showing, in *this* way, that he saw the cuff link become insurmountable. But we can still insist that he must have seen the cuff link, and we can attempt to establish our point by leading him back to the drawer for a second look. This may or may not decide the issue. If he exclaims, upon looking into the drawer for the second time, 'Oh, here it is; I guess I wasn't thinking last time I looked,' it is likely, although the case is by no means clear-cut, that he did see it on the previous occasion, but, as we sometimes say, it did not *register*. He may well have seen the cuff link without realizing it, without seeing that it was a cuff link or, in fact, any sort of object (and, hence, some *thing* in the drawer). In such extreme cases as this, collateral information is useless. We must resort to indirect methods, arguing by analogy that since, in all likelihood, the conditions affecting the visibility of the cuff link are the same now as when he formerly looked in the drawer, and since it is clear that he now sees the cuff link, it is plausible to suppose that he also saw it beforehand without, of course, realizing it. His lack of attentiveness on the former occasion can be held responsible for his failure to appreciate what he saw. In such cases as this one may feel that the difficulties which stand in the way of our finding out whether or not S saw D are formidable indeed; perhaps we can never establish, to anyone's complete satisfaction, that S did see the cuff link. But our inability to find out, with any degree of conclusiveness, that S saw the cuff link should not be confused with the question of whether, in fact, S saw the cuff link. He may have seen it, but we may never be able to discover this fact.

Let us return, then, to the positive characterization of seeing$_n$. If this state of affairs has no belief content, what content does it have? My examples have already suggested an answer to this question. I shall cast my answer in the form of an equivalence, and then go on to explain the manner in which the right-hand side is to be understood. The very fact that such explanations are required is enough to belie the definitional character of this equivalence; that is, I do not suppose that anyone is going to learn the meaning, or one of the meanings, of the verb 'to see' by examining this equivalence. But it is not my desire to teach anyone what this term means. It is my hope that the reader is already sufficiently familiar with the way this verb is used to tell, from the equivalence and the subsequent explanation, whether I have provided an alternative (and, hopefully, more nearly analytic) expression of the meaning of this verb.

S sees$_n$ D = D is visually differentiated from its immediate environment by S

The phrase 'visually differentiated' is meant to suggest several things, the most important of which is that S's differentiation of D is constituted by D's *looking some way* to S and, moreover, looking different than its immediate environment. Let me put the salient features serially:

(1) The term 'visual' in this equivalence is meant to signify only one thing: that S's differentiation of D is by visual means, in terms of D's looking some way to S instead of D's feeling or tasting a certain way to S.

(2) When I say that D *looks some way* to S, I do not wish this to be understood to mean that, for some character C, it looks to S *as though* (as if) D (or something) were C. The locution 'looks as though (or as if) it were' usually signifies that the percipient believes, or is inclined to believe, or is prepared to cautiously put it forward that, what he sees is a certain sort of thing or possesses a certain property. That is, it suggests or implies something about the belief attitude of the percipient, and I want the construction 'D looks some way to S' to be free of this implication. D can look some way to S without it looking to S as though it were C (for any C).

Similarly, when we say of S that D looks like so-and-so to him, the suggestion is unavoidable that S believes that something looks, in certain respects, the way so-and-so's ordinarily (or sometimes) look to him. Once again I wish my use of the term 'look' to be free of this implication. As I am using this phrase, D's looking some way to S presupposes a sentient being (S) equipped with an appropriate visual apparatus by virtue of which, to employ an expression of the psychologists, D occupies a portion of S's visual field. It presupposes or entails nothing about whether S *notices* D, whether he *takes*, or is inclined to take, D to be something in particular, or whether he *exploits* his visual experience in any way whatsoever. It is a sense of the term 'look' in which one might say of S, 'He did not notice D, but judging from the conditions he was in, and the direction he was looking, it is likely that D *looked some way* to him.' It is the sense of this term which we may use to give expression to a conviction that although S denies having seen D, although he denies having seen anything which might plausibly be identified with D, yet D must have looked some way to him.[1]

It is always difficult to avoid circularity at this stage of an explanation. I have little doubt but that the reader is more familiar with the relevant use of the verb 'to see' than he is with the use of those terms I am employing to clarify it. Nonetheless, I would like to make one more brief attempt to pinpoint my meaning. To use an example of the sort mentioned previously, suppose that S at a given time, or rapidly in succession, sees thirty-three distinct items (stars, the lights in a chandelier, the letters on a page, people in a crowd). He sees them only for a brief moment, but given S's position, and the arrangement of the elements, it is clear that he saw *all* of them. S himself will testify that he saw a 'lot' of them, but since he saw them so briefly, he is unsure of exactly how many he saw. There are now thirty-three logically distinct true statements we can make about what S saw—one for each of the thirty-three different elements. Any one of these statements could have been false and the remaining thirty-two true. Now, whatever differentiation in S's visual experience is responsible for these thirty-three different statements being true, I think we must admit that, in the conditions as described, this kind of differentiation is not a feature of his beliefs; he does not believe he saw thirty-three distinct items, nor is it plausible to suppose that he acquired thirty-three distinct beliefs, one for each of the different elements which he saw. It seems, then, that we must conclude that the differentiation in S's visual experience, the differentiation which accounts for the

[1] For a discussion of some of the distinctions just mentioned see G. E. Moore's 'Visual Sense Data' and Vesey's 'Seeing and Seeing As', both reprinted in *Perceiving, Sensing and Knowing*, Robert J. Swartz (ed.) (New York, 1965).

independent truth of these thirty-three distinct statements, must lie in some aspect of that experience other than S's associated beliefs (if any). What I am referring to as 'The first element's looking some way to S', 'The second element's looking some way to S', and so on is precisely this differentiating feature of his experience, those differing states of affairs which, independently of what S happens to believe, are the basis in S's visual experience for the mutual independence of those thirty-three true statements we can make about what he sees.

(3) One further point about the construction 'D looks some way to S'. I wish this to be taken in such a way that D *need not* be some physical object, the light from which stimulates S's visual receptors. I do not wish to restrict the range of 'D', the sorts of things which can look some way to S, by supplying some technical characterization of what it means for something to look some way to someone. Granted, when we see a tractor or a cloud, it looks some way to us. I think it is also clear, however, that an after-image, an element in a mirage, or an element in a visual hallucination looks some way, in the sense of this phrase that is now in question, to the person who is experiencing them. If we are cognizant of the nature of our visual experience, if we know, for example, that what we are experiencing is an after-image, then, of course, we are not likely to *say* that it looks purple. Rather, we would be inclined to say, if we said anything at all about its color, that it was purple. But this does not mean that it does not look some way to us. If I know that the man in front of me is Harold, I am not likely to say that he looks like Harold; and if I know that I am experiencing an after-image, I am not likely to say that it looks like an after-image. But if I believe, mistakenly, that what I am seeing is a spot on the wall, there is nothing exceptional about my saying *of* the after-image that it looks purple or like an after-image. Similarly, if I do not realize that the man in front of me is Harold, there is nothing untoward about my saying of him that he looks like Harold. What we say, or what we find it appropriate (or non-misleading) to say, about the way things look to us is partially a function of what we, or our listeners, believe about them; but what looks to us in some way, and the way they look, is not in the same way a function of what we believe.[1]

[1] H. P. Grice has an excellent discussion of the connection between saying something looks so-and-so and the kind of contexual conditions (doubt or

I shall go into the question of seeing after-images, pressure phosphenes, hallucinatory dragons, and mirages a bit later in this chapter; for the moment it is enough to say that the manner in which I am using the locution 'looks some way' is largely neutral with respect to the sort of thing which looks some way. It need not be a physical object. It need not be something which is capable of reflecting light rays into our visual receptors. It need not be something which could also look some way to another person. It could be an after-image, a shadow, or a ball-game.[1]

(4) The term 'differentiated' is meant to describe a particular way in which D must look to S in order for it to be true that S sees$_n$ D. Perhaps I can make the force of this modifier clear by several examples. Suppose that we attach a piece of beige paper to a beige wall and dim the lights until the paper appears (from where we are standing) as an undistinguished portion of the wall. Does one, under these circumstances, still *see* the piece of paper? Or take nine cubes and place them in the form of a square: (see diagram p. 24). Once again, dim the lights, or retreat to a sufficiently great distance, so that the ensemble of blocks appears to one as a uniform mass without distinguishable parts (i.e. as a square). Can one, under these conditions, see cube $\#5$? Although cube $\#5$ makes a positive contribution to the way the 'square' looks, in the

disbelief) under which it is said ('The Causal Theory of Perception', reprinted in *Perceiving, Sensing, and Knowing*). Incidentally, I am not denying that our beliefs may have an influence on the way things look to us, even in the sense which I am using this term. One may wish to cite such phenomena as size and shape constancy as examples of situations in which the percipient's beliefs play a role in the way 'things look to him'. It may even be that a person's beliefs are capable of causing an object to no longer look some way (much less a particular way) to him. Nothing I have so far said commits me to denying these facts—if, indeed, they are facts.

[1] Chisholm, (*Perceiving,* pp. 149-50) defines the non-propositional sense of 'to see', a sense which approximates my seeing$_n$, in the following way: S perceives x means that x appears in some way to S. This looks deceptively like my own characterization, at least as far as I have taken it. Chisholm, however, has a quite technical sense of 'to appear' (see pp. 143-8) in which, if I understand him correctly, one cannot perceive perfectly black shadows or after-images since no light from them stimulates one of the perceiver's visual receptors. His definition also leaves it unclear in what sense an *event* can be perceived. Does an automobile accident (in contrast to the colliding automobiles) reflect light into one's visual receptors. I shall, later in this chapter, reject any attempt to provide a causal analysis of seeing$_n$.

sense that without it the square might appear to have a hole in the center, and in the sense that the light from #5 is stimulating your visual receptors, I do not think we would go so far as to say that one could see cube #5. In some sense, yes, cube #5 looks some way to you. One might wish to say that it appears to you as an undifferentiated part (the central part) of the square which you do see. But if one allows this as a way in which something can appear to one, as a way in which a thing can look, then I do not believe that something's looking to you in some way is a sufficient condition, for your seeing it. It must, if indeed it is a distinct part of what one sees, appear to one as a more or less differentiated part.

When dealing with surfaces, and the parts of surfaces, however, a minor complication arises. Suppose S 'runs his eye' over the entire surface of a wall. After having done so, someone asks him if he saw 'this part of the wall' while indicating some appropriate section of the wall—e.g. the left-hand side, the central portion, or the triangular section over here (which he traces out). I think the answer to this question might naturally be 'Yes' even though, at the time S saw the wall, he did not visually differentiate that particular section of the wall from the remainder of the wall's surface. He failed to differentiate it, of course, because at the time he saw the wall there was nothing to differentiate. There was nothing distinctive about that triangular section of the wall, nothing which gave it an identity, nothing which set it off from the thousands of other arbitrary shapes and sections which we can subsequently trace on the surface of the wall. In such cases as this I think we can say that S saw$_n$ that (triangular) section of the wall simply on the condition that *that part of the wall* looked some way to him at the time he saw the wall. Differentiation is unnecessary when the individuality of what is seen rests *solely* on such arbitrary tracing operations or *exclusively* on its relative spatial location and configuration. Notice, this peculiar feature of a surface, and the parts of a surface, allows us to say of our 'square' (the ensemble of nine cubes mentioned above) that the percipient can see$_n$ the central portion of the square, and in so far as 'the center portion of the square' can be made to coincide with *the front surface of cube #5*, it can thereby be said that the percipient sees$_n$ the *front surface* of cube #5. Indeed, for the same reason, he can see$_n$ the front surfaces of all nine cubes. He can be said to see$_n$ the front surface of #5 because what he can see$_n$ without differentiating (the central portion of the square's surface) happens to coincide, in these circumstances, with the front surface of #5—something which, under altered circumstances, could not be seen$_n$ without some element of differentiation. None of this is to say, however, that he can see cube #5 under these conditions; for he does not visually differentiate cube #5, nor is there anything which he can see$_n$ without differentiation (e.g. various surface sections of the square) which can be identified with *the cube*.

Aside from these peculiarities, the differentiation clause is generally operative. Suppose an astronaut looks down from his orbiting satellite and the portion of the earth beneath him looks uniformly green. He knows there is a hill beneath him somewhere, but there is no pattern or differentiation in the landscape. Does he see the hill? I feel it is stretching things a bit to insist that he must see it since, after all, if the hill is down there (where he is looking) it must be appearing to him in some way—at the very least light is being reflected from the hill into his visual receptors. In this sense, yes, the hill is appearing to him in some way, but it is appearing to him in such a way that it looks the same as its surroundings. Notice, the question is *not* whether the hill appears to him sufficiently differentiated, or sufficiently unique, to allow him or anyone else to *identify* it as a hill; this would depend on how good our astronaut was at identifying such things. On the contrary, I am asking about a more primitive way of seeing the hill, a way of seeing which, even though he did not identify what he saw as a hill, it would still be true to say that he saw a hill. And I think that, under the conditions described, we must say that he could not see (see$_n$) the hill. When the sun is directly overhead and there are no shadows, one cannot see the hill; there is no contrast available, nothing marks it out as an isolable element in the landscape. One sees the earth, and the hill in question is in that portion of the earth which one sees, but one does not see the hill. From this distance, under these conditions, the familiar landmarks *are not visible*.[1]

Having said this much I must mention a limiting case. Touch your nose to a large smooth wall and stare fixedly at the area of the wall in front of you. There is not much doubt about the fact that you see the wall, or at least a portion of it. It is also fairly clear that you do not differentiate it from its immediate surroundings. In this position it has no environment, and so one could hardly be expected to differentiate it from one. I call this a *limiting case* because, normally, we see things in an environment, against a background, or surrounded by other things (which we also see). Let us understand, then, that in these limiting cases, when everything that appears to S is a part of D, when D is seen under conditions which do not provide it with an environment, then a necessary and sufficient condition for S to see D (or a portion of D) is that D (or that

---

[1] In this connection it is interesting to note that the American astronaut Maj. Leroy Gordon Cooper reported that he 'clearly saw houses and streets in the Himalaya mountains, on the plains of Tibet and in the southwest United States'. He said he sighted a vehicle moving on a road, a boat on a river, and a steam locomotive on a track (from the *Capital Times*, Madison, Wisconsin, February 6, 1964). The newspaper article continues somewhat confusingly, however, to explain (in the words of the examining psychologists) that his ability to see trains, houses, and boats from such a height was assisted by 'his utilizing aavilable clues' to identify the items. I say this is confusing because whether he utilized available clues makes absolutely no difference to whether he saw houses and trains. Whether he saw these things or not is a question which is independent of how he managed to identify what he saw. To put it in my own terminology, Cooper saw the houses if he visually differentiated them from their surrounding environment. The question of whether he successfully identified what he saw, and how he achieved this, is another matter entirely, a matter which is quite independent of whether he saw them or not.

portion of D) look some way to him. That is, the differentiation clause becomes inoperative when nothing appears to S that is not part of D. We may put it this way: when S sees$_n$ D, then *if* D is only one among several things which look some way to S (where these 'other things' also comprise D's background), then D must appear to S as a differentiated element in this aggregation or background.

How much of D must be visually differentiated? How much of D must look some way to S? Must every part of D look some way to us or just all of the facing surface? In general, I think it is clear that one need not see every part of something to see it, nor need one see all of its surfaces or even all of one surface. How much of a thing S must visually differentiate in order to see$_n$ it is a question that, in the abstract, divorced from the sort of thing he is seeing, and the circumstances under which he sees it, cannot be answered. We can say, as a necessary condition, that *some* part of D (not necessarily a *proper* sub-part) must look some way to S, but this will hardly do as a sufficient condition. For example, do we see$_n$ Harold when we only see$_n$ the tip of his finger? As he emerges from behind a wall, little finger first, when do we first see$_n$ Harold? Clearly this is not a question of when we see enough of him to identify him as Harold; if this were the case we could never see Harold when his birthmark, the only feature that allowed us to distinguish him from his twin brother, was concealed under his bathing trunks. If Harold can be seen in a bright light when naked, when does he cease being seen? When he is fully dressed? When he slips a bag over his head? When all his skin is covered? When we drape a sheet over him so that his 'outline' is no longer clearly discernible? Trying to answer such questions is a bit like trying to decide when a boy, any boy, becomes a man.

However, we think of the parts of a whole, whether we do it in terms of its 'natural' parts, such as the legs and surface of a table, the keys, ribbon, carriage, and frame of a typewriter, or the arms, legs, head, and trunk of a person, or whether we do it in more or less arbitrary spatial parts, such as the top and bottom half, the front and back side, the right and left side, the inside and the outside, the following sorts of considerations seem relevant to seeing something when only some of its parts are seen.[1] (*a*) It is clearly

---

[1] What follows is a partial adaption of Warnock's discussion in his article 'Seeing'.

not in general necessary that one should see every part (in either of the above senses of 'part') of D to see_n D. Seeing is like touching in this respect; I do not have to touch every part of a person to touch that person. (*b*) The parts of D which are most privileged, in the sense that if we see these parts we see D, are those which, in the normal situations in which D is found, provide us with the most convenient means of identification. But this is no hard and fast rule. I am less inclined to say of S that he saw Harold if he only saw his little toe (in contrast, say, to his face), but whether a person sees the front or the back of an automobile does not seem to make much difference if we are trying to decide whether he saw the automobile—even if we admit that the automobile is more readily identifiable from the front. This does not mean, of course, that a person must identify what he $sees_n$; it only means that with some things, in some circumstances, those parts which are more significant to identification are also more significantly involved in our $seeing_n$ them. (*c*) The conversational context and one's particular interests (where is it? what is it? is it a so-and-so?) will also affect the question of whether enough of D was seen to see D. If a man is trying to hide, and he asks us whether he can still be seen, seeing almost any part of him is sufficient to see him. One must be extremely careful, however, to distinguish between what is $seen_n$ and what it would be appropriate to say is $seen_n$, or what it would be misleading to say is $seen_n$. There is little *point* to saying that one saw Alice this morning, when this was from a distance of two hundred yards, if the center of interest happens to be whether she has more freckles this summer than last summer. And it would be positively misleading, although still quite *true*, to add '. . . and I did not see any freckles at all'.

I shall try to confine my examples and arguments to cases that are more or less clear-cut. I shall, in other words, concentrate on those situations in which there is an optimal visual differentiation of D. By 'optimal visual differentiation' I do not mean that D is $seen_n$ in broad daylight surrounded by a system of mirrors. I simply mean that enough of D is $seen_n$ so that, *in those conditions*, and *from that point of view*, there is no question but that D was visually differentiated and not *just* a part of D.

(5) Finally, one's ability to visually differentiate D from its immediate surroundings is a capacity which may be enhanced by the acquisition of eyeglasses, by the utilization of magnifying de-

vices, or by a corrective operation on one's eyes. The successful exercise of this ability is something that is contingent upon adequate lighting, absence of obstacles, the position of one's head, and so on. These are the sorts of things which, as a matter of well-attested fact, influence what one is able to visually differentiate and what, given this ability, one actually does differentiate. Blindfolds are effective devices for inhibiting the free exercise of this ability, and radical interference with one's nervous system or visual receptors can result in the loss of this ability. The point of these apparently aimless remarks is to emphasize, once again, the fact that visual differentiation, as I am employing this phrase, is a pre-intellectual, pre-discursive sort of capacity which a wide variety of beings possess. It is an endowment which is largely immune to the caprice of our intellectual life. Whatever judgments, interpretations, beliefs, inferences, anticipations, regrets, memories, or thoughts may be aroused by the visual differentiation of D, the visual differentiation of D is, itself, quite independent of these accompaniments. It can take place with or without them (or, better, with or without any particular one of them), although with human beings it would be extraordinary indeed if it took place without any such concomitants. This is but another way of highlighting the fact that visual differentiation is something which, when it takes place, lacks a positive belief content. We would have a much different world, of course, if no one was ever inspired to believe anything as a consequence of their seeing$_n$ things, if nothing was seen in any *other* way than the fundamental way I have just depicted; but one of the differences would not be that no one saw anything in this altered world. The following chapters have, as almost their exclusive concern, the manner in which this fundamental visual endowment is related to our ability to acquire beliefs, true beliefs, and, most significantly, knowledge about the world around us. They are concerned with the way in which this primitive visual achievement, the visual differentiation of something, can be transformed into a higher-level epistemic achievement. Until such time as we can look into this matter, however, we must keep a steady focus on the perceptual state of affairs which we have already isolated—seeing$_n$.

I have mentioned five salient features of visual differentiation. They constitute essential restrictions and qualifications on the manner in which the right side of the above equivalence is to be understood. The equivalence itself is no more exact, no more precise than the explanations embodied in these five comments. What I have tried to give here is a positive description of a perceptual state of affairs which lacks positive belief content. Having done so, the reader may interpret the subscript 'n' as signifying a way of seeing things which satisfies, in both its positive and negative aspects, the description just given. The 'n' is meant to suggest that this way of seeing things is *non-epistemic* in nature. By this I mean that the state of affairs described by saying that S sees$_n$ D is a state of affairs whose realization does not depend on S's knowing anything in particular, either about D or about anything else. This non-epistemic character of seeing is a consequence of the fact that it lacks positive belief content. For I accept as a condition of S's knowing that P (where 'P' is some sentence which may be either true or false) that he accepts the truth of P. Hence, if S need not believe anything in particular to see$_n$ D, neither need he know anything in particular to see$_n$ D.[1]

Incidentally, it may be the case that if S sees$_n$ D, there is a certain sort of belief which S may possess (e.g. that something looks so-and-so to him at the moment) about which it is difficult to suppose him mistaken. I do not wish to quarrel with this view. All I want to say is that, however indubitable are the beliefs which S in fact holds about the things which he sees, his holding these particular beliefs is not essential to his seeing these things. Hence, even if we suppose that there is an incorrigibility about a certain class of beliefs associated with seeing D, seeing D is still non-epistemic in my sense. For it is still not *necessary* that one believe that which, were one to believe it, would be believed without the possibility of mistake.[2]

The number and variety of things which we see in this way is almost unlimited. I have already given dozens of examples in the preceding pages: people, books, shadows, tables, pieces of paper, walls, spots on the wall, tigers, teapots, hills, and so on. I have also mentioned such things as after-images, pressure phosphenes, and

[1] Of course, there is something which he can *not* know when he sees$_n$ D: *viz.* that he is not seeing$_n$ anything.

[2] The incorrigibility of certain beliefs about what one was seeing would, however, suggest that this way of seeing does not lack *negative* belief content. For suppose S's belief that P was the incorrigible belief associated with his seeing D; then S's seeing$_n$ D would imply (I take it) that S does not believe that not-P.

hallucinatory dragons, and I will discuss this sort of item at greater length in later sections. I have, in addition, suggested that events can be seen in this way. When the event persists over a period of time (a ball-game, wedding ceremony, prize fight, battle, etc.), then, of course, the 'part-whole' difficulty re-emerges in a new dimension, the temporal dimension. He only saw the first ten rounds; shall we say he saw the fight (to be contrasted with 'the whole fight')? She left before the play was over; did she see the play? No matter how we decide to answer these questions, and they are the same sorts of question that can be raised about tables and people (with respect to their spatial parts), I think it is at least clear that the gentleman mentioned above saw *part* of the fight, and the lady saw *part* of the play. The sense of 'part' has changed, or at least we are talking about the parts of quite different things, but the issues remain largely the same.

There is, however, one particular feature of events which demands comment before we can consider our explanation of the above equivalence complete. An event is, so to speak, a creature of time; objects are spatial creatures. An event is a happening, an occurrence, a change of some sort. We can ask of an event 'When did it happen?' and, of those which persist for a period of time, we can ask 'When did it begin?' and 'When did it end?' Events are given dates; objects (in contrast to the things which *happen* to the objects) are not. Events do not have shape and color; they have no precisely defined spatial perimeter which segregates them from neighboring objects and events.[1] Therefore, when I speak of the visual differentiation of an event, the term 'differentiation' must be understood in the sense in which it applies to events. One sees$_n$ an event when it is visually differentiated from its immediate *temporal* environment. In order to make this clear, let me speak for the moment of a minimal sort of event, an event which is constituted by a single change in state, a change in state from S_1 to S_2. For example, something, call it A, changes position; it goes from point X to point Y. Of course, when changes like this occur we can usually speak of intermediate states corresponding to the different intermediate positions between X and Y. And many

---

[1] Although it certainly makes sense to ascribe a spatial location to most events: e.g. 'Where did the accident take place?' 'Where did the battle occur?'

events involve two or more objects (collisions, battles, fights, arguments) and a continual change of state among the participants in the events. Other events do not persist at all (scoring a goal, arriving, winning a race), but merely occur at a time. All events, however, involve some change; if nothing changes in any respect, nothing happens. So let us confine our attention to the simplest possible sort of change, a 'just noticeable movement', the change of state of an object A from the state S_1 (being in position X) to state S_2 (being in position Y). Call this change of state, this event (the movement of A), e_1. Now, when I say that this event must be visually differentiated from its immediate temporal environment, I mean that the percipient must see$_n$ A at the time it passes from state S_1 to S_2 *and* A's *being* in state S_1 must look different to him that A's *being* in state S_2. There must be some visual differentiation between the temporally successive states whose succession constitute the event. If A's being in state S_1 looks the same way to you as A's being in state S_2, then you do not see$_n$ the event e_1 even though you see$_n$ A during the time it occupies these different states. Once again, you need not believe that an event is taking place; you need not believe that a change of state is occurring. All that is necessary to seeing$_n$ the event is that it be visually differentiated from its temporal neighbors, or that the states which constitute the event are themselves visually differentiated.[1]

Normally, liquid water and frozen water look different. If one is operating in normal circumstances, one can see$_n$ water freeze. Whether one knows it is freezing is another matter entirely. On the other hand, milk may turn sour in front of my eyes without my being able to see this occur. Sweet milk and sour milk look the same to me; hence, the passage from one state to the other represents an event which I cannot visually differentiate. I can watch the milk while it is turning sour, but I cannot see that event which might be referred to as the milk's turning sour. Analog-

[1] The intent of this characterization is that S sees$_n$ the movement of A (at time t_1) if and only if S visually differentiates successive states of A (at t_1). If it sounds paradoxical to speak of visually differentiating *successive* states of A *at* a particular time, one should recall the mildly paradoxical notion this is supposed to reflect: *viz*. that although movement, any movement, *takes* time, we see it, if we see it at all, *at* a time. In other words, the time at which S sees$_n$ the movement of A (visually differentiates successive states) is not to be understood as a mathematical instant.

ously, I can watch a man *while* he is changing his mind, but this does not mean that I see him changing his mind.[1]

The last example points up an ambiguity involved in our reference to events. I would like to discuss the ambiguity now since I believe it will help us to get a little clearer on what is involved in seeing$_n$ an event. Consider the statement:

(1) S saw the man waving to his wife.

It is possible that anyone saying this might mean that S, while waving to his (S's) wife, saw the man. But let us put aside this possibility (and the various sources of ambiguity inherent in the pronoun 'his'); there are still three distinct things that such a statement might be taken to mean.

(i) S saw the man *who was* waving to his wife.

That is, the modifier 'waving to his wife' may be acting simply as a relative clause to the noun phrase 'the man', thus helping to identify which man it was that S saw. If this is the way it is to be understood, then S need not have seen the man waving, need not have been close enough, or in the right position, to see him move his arm in the way that is characteristic of 'waving'. That is, S might have seen the man who was waving without seeing him wave. In this case, then, the situation is simply one of seeing$_n$ *the man*, and S need only have visually differentiated *the man* (who happened to be waving to his wife) to see the man waving to his wife. On the other hand, (1) might be interpreted to mean something like the following:

(ii) S saw the man wave to his wife (or the man's wave to his wife).

Here it is not *enough* that S seen$_n$ the man; he must also have been in such a position to differentiate some of the movement which constitutes a wave. From a distance of four hundred yards I might be able to see the man (who is waving to his wife) but not be

---

[1] Even if he (say) raised his hand every time (and only when) he was changing his mind, this would not permit me to see$_n$ his change of mind (although I might be able to see *that* he was changing his mind by noticing the gesture; for this possibility see later chapters). For in this case the succession of states which I do visually differentiate are quite distinct from those states a succession of which constitute his change of mind.

able to see him waving to his wife. In order to see the man waving
to his wife, under the present interpretation, I must see him from
such a position, and under such conditions, that his waving looks
different to me than his not waving. There must be some visual
differentiation among the various stages of this activity, and if one
sees him against a temporal background (i.e. sees him before he
starts waving, while he is waving, and after he is finished waving),
then there must be some visual differentiation of the 'waving stage'
from the 'non-waving stages'—his waving must look different
than his not waving. Notice, and this is particularly important,
one need not see *what he is doing*. One need not believe a man is
waving in order to see him wave; nor need one believe that he is
moving his arm. The likelihood is, of course, that if one sees him
moving his arm, one will believe that he is doing something, or
that something is happening, but, once again, this belief, or any
belief, is not necessarily involved in the seeing. One might have to
be told later that what one saw was the man's wave to his wife, but
clearly one is, in this case, being told *what one saw*.

The distinction between these first two interpretations, then,
depends on the way one interprets the noun phrase 'the man
waving to his wife'. If one interprets this as a noun phrase ('the
man') plus relative clause ('waving to his wife'), then we have a
phrase which, in this context, refers to the man. If, on the other
hand, one understands the phrase as a single unit, the man's waving to his wife, then one is referring not to the man but to a particular action of his. One can see$_n$ both the man and his action,
but a more elaborate set of conditions must be satisfied in the
latter case.

There is one further sense in which (1) may be understood. It
may be taken to mean not only that S saw the event but that he
identified it as described; i.e.

(iii) S saw *that* the man was waving to his wife.

We do, frequently, read this interpretation into statements such as
(1), and I shall discuss some of the issues which this raises in the
following section. But a full discussion of this way of seeing, a
way of seeing which involves a positive belief content, must be
postponed until later chapters.

Some of the same remarks can be made about seeing$_n$ events
(occurrences, happenings) as were made about seeing objects. A

frequently used device for discovering whether someone saw something happen is simply to ask him whether he saw it happen. If he does not believe he saw anything of the kind, and we have reason to believe that he must have seen it, we can ask about the things which he believes himself to have seen. Or we can re-describe the event in terms which he might recognize as applicable to what he did see. For example, 'You must have seen the Queen ride by; didn't you see that woman waving to people from a coach?' The frequent success of this technique does not show that we *cannot* see an event without reaching some sort of accurate identification of it. Rather, it testifies to the fact that, in the vast majority of cases, we *do not* see$_n$ an event without *also* seeing, on some appropriate level of identification, *what is happening*.

The remaining sections of this chapter constitute an examination of the implications, and absence of implications, which this way of seeing involves. In a sense, my description will not be complete until the last page of this chapter. Let us turn, then, to a matter which is, perhaps, the most fertile source of confusion in the entire literature of perception: *viz*. the language we use to describe what we see, and the distinction between what we see and what we find it appropriate, fitting, or non-misleading to *say* we see.

3. *Seeing and Saying We See*

If S asserts that so-and-so is the case, we may distinguish two sorts of implication. There is, first, what we might call the truth implications: Q is a truth implication of S's statement if S's statement would not be true unless Q were true. Secondly, there are the utterance implications: Q is an utterance implication of S's statement if S would not, normally, have made the statement unless Q were true. This distinction is simply an expression of the difference we feel between 'what he said implies' and 'his saying that implies'. For example, if S asserts (says in an assertive tone) that it is raining, then an utterance implication, but not a truth implication, is that S believes it is raining; for his saying (in that way) that it is raining implies that he believes it is raining, although what he said ('it is raining') does not by itself imply that he believes it is raining. If S did not believe that it was raining, this would not show that his statement was false; it would tend to show, however, that his statement went wrong in other ways (deceitful?).

Generally speaking, the failure of an utterance implication to be satisfied earns for the statement such epithets as 'misleading', 'inappropriate', 'beside the point', 'ironic', and 'deceitful'.

This is a rough-and-ready distinction,[1] but I believe it will do the job I have in mind for it. Many reports about what is seen are in the first person, singular, present indicative, active: I see the camels, I see the bus approaching, etc. Such reports imply that the speaker has identified (or believes himself to have identified) what he claims to see. Normally, people do not *say* they see a bus approaching unless they have identified, in some way, the approaching vehicle *as* a bus. But, clearly, this is an utterance implication, not a truth implication. It is his *saying* he sees a bus, not his *seeing* a bus, which implies that he believes the approaching vehicle to be a bus. *S*'s statement 'I see a bus approaching' can be quite true without its being true that *S* believes he sees a bus approaching; he may have said this (without believing it) for the purpose of distracting the attention of his companions at the bus stop.

If one confuses truth implications with utterance implications one will also tend to suppose that seeing a bus involves, in some essential way, the belief that a bus is seen. That is, one will take the utterance implication 'I believe that that is a bus' to be a truth implication of 'I see a bus approaching' and, thereby, commit the mistake of supposing that if I do not believe that that is a bus, then I do not see a bus approaching. The same mistake would be committed by supposing that we must identify the sleeping dog in the dark hallway before we trip over it; for certainly I would never *say* of myself that I tripped over a sleeping dog unless I had identified what I tripped over as a sleeping dog.

As soon as the tense, or the person, of the report is shifted, the

---

[1] A word or two about these definitions. My definition of 'truth implication' does not, of course, distinguish between *P*'s logically implying *Q* and the situation in which *P* would not be true unless *Q* were true by virtue of some empirical regularity. For example, one might wish to say that *S*'s statement that there was a lightning flash at 1.15 p.m. would not be true unless there was an electrical discharge at that time, and yet deny that this was logically implied by what he said. I am quite happy about calling this a truth implication since, for my purposes, this further distinction within the class of truth implications will not be necessary.

Also, it should be noticed that utterance implications may also be truth implications. For example, if *S* says 'I am cold', we might wish to say that the truth implication '*S* is cold' is also an utterance implication since, normally, *S* would not have said what he did unless he was cold.

possibilities for this type of confusion diminish considerably (but not altogether). Whereas it is paradoxical to say, 'I see a bus approaching, but I do not believe a bus is approaching' (except as a way of saying that, although I know better, it looks just like a bus is approaching),[1] it is quite routine to say, 'I *saw* a bus, but, at the time, did not know what it was', or '*He* sees the bus but cannot make out what it is'. This is made possible in the past tense (first person) because sufficient time has elapsed to allow the speaker to identify something that, at the time he saw it, he failed to identify. The paradoxical air is lacking in the third-person reports because the speaker may identify something which the person about whom he speaks (the percipient) does not. In other words, neither statement involves a conflict between truth and utterance implications as does 'I see a bus, but do not believe I see a bus'.

A failure to distinguish between what we see, in this way, and the things we are prepared to say we see, between truth implications and utterance implications, can lead to the following type of confusion:

> How should we regard a man's report that he sees x if we know him to be ignorant of all x-ish things? Precisely as we would regard a four-year-old's report that he sees a meson shower. 'Smith sees x' suggests that Smith could specify some things pertinent to x. To see an X-ray tube is at least to see that, were it dropped on stone, it would smash.[2]

Hanson begins this passage in an unobjectionable way. We would, no doubt, be puzzled over the man's report. Does this mean, however, as Hanson seems to suggest, that he does not see that which it would be puzzling for him to *say* he sees? It would also be puzzling, in the same way, if this man said he was standing next to an x. Does this mean the man is not standing next to an x? If a man cannot see an x because he is ignorant of x-ish things, how could such unfortunate people relieve their ignorance? Certainly X-ray tubes can be seen by four-year-olds, and not just well-informed four-year-olds.[3] Why should they not see them? Are they invisible?

[1] For a discussion of this use of the verb 'to see' see Section 4 of this chapter.
[2] N. R. Hanson, *Patterns of Discovery* (Cambridge, 1958), p. 21.
[3] I leave aside, here, the question of meson showers. I take up in a later chapter (Chapter VI, Section 5) the question of seeing collections, showers, herds, systems, aggregates, crowds, swarms, etc. I believe that such things can be seen (even by four-year-olds), but there are complications into which I cannot now enter.

Does the four-year-old see through them? The fact that a four-year-old does not see that it is an X-ray tube, does not know what X-ray tubes are, does not even know whether it will break when dropped on stone, are things which can, with equal truth, be said about his baby rattle the first time he saw it.

There is, however, a way in which third-person reports can be as misleading as first-person reports. There is a certain linguistic economy achieved by couching one's reports of what is seen in terms commensurate with the level of identification attained by the person who does the seeing. This serves a double purpose; it not only tells us *what* is seen, but it also tells us *how*, at what level of specificity, the observer identified what he saw. For example, one might say of a child returning from a visit to the zoo: 'He saw the animals' or 'He saw three camels'. One might be less inclined, however, to say that he saw two dromedaries and a bactrian even though *this is precisely what he did see*. The disinclination stems from the fact that this choice of words, when used without any qualification at all, suggests a level of identification which surpasses that of the percipient (the boy). Commonly, we select words to describe what is seen that approximate the level of identification which it is thought the observer himself achieved; we choose words that the observer himself, were he able to describe what he saw, would have chosen. This is convenient because, for one thing, it allows the percipient himself to corroborate our statements about what he saw. I think this is a discernible tendency in the way we describe what other people have seen, and it is this tendency which gives to such a report as 'He saw three camels' the suggestion that he identified them as camels. But this 'suggestion' should not be confused with what is necessarily involved in someone's seeing three camels. For we always have available the qualifying device ' . . . but, of course, he did not realize they were camels'. The fact that this qualifying device is available, and can be used without any hint of paradox, shows that 'S saw three camels', although it might 'suggest' that S identified what he saw as a trio of camels does not imply, as either a truth implication or an utterance implication, that S must have so identified them.

The reader may be surprised at my last statement; for it may be supposed that S's identification of the camels, although it is not a truth implication of the statement that he saw three camels, is at least an utterance implication. This is not so. Suppose Little

Jimmy, on the way to the zoo with his father, sees his uncle wave to him from a passing automobile, but, in his excitement to get to the zoo, fails to recognize him. He does not even realize that the man was waving to him. Furthermore, suppose that upon returning home Jimmy's father reports to his wife that Jimmy saw his uncle today. He mentions this in passing, and he does so without qualifying it in any manner (e.g. 'but he did not recognize him'). Is there anything wrong with this unqualified report? In the first place, I think we must say that, in so far as truth and falsity are concerned, there is nothing wrong with the father's report: Jimmy *did* see his uncle. Secondly, even if Jimmy did not recognize him, there is still nothing improper with his father saying of Jimmy, with *no* qualification whatsoever, that he saw his uncle. There would be nothing improper about this *if* his father believed that Jimmy *did* recognize his uncle. We only believe that there is something perverse about his father saying, in a totally unqualified manner, that Jimmy saw his uncle when the father does not believe that Jimmy recognized his uncle. For if his father knew that Jimmy did not recognize his uncle, he should have mentioned this fact in order to forestall such questions as 'Why didn't Jimmy mention this to me when he came home?' or 'Why didn't Jimmy wave to him?' What this shows is that, generally speaking, the statement '*S* saw his uncle', when this is said without any qualification at all, either explicit or implicit, has as one of its utterance implications the fact that *the speaker* (not *S*) believes that *S* identified what he saw as his uncle. That is, we can say that his father would not (normally) have said this of Jimmy, without qualifying it in some respect, unless he (the father) believed that Jimmy recognized his uncle. But the father may have quite naturally said of Jimmy that he saw his uncle without Jimmy having identified his uncle. Hence, we cannot say that the father's statement has as one of its utterance implications that Jimmy recognized his uncle. The *most* that we can say is that his statement has as one of its utterance implications that the father believes that Jimmy recognized his uncle.

These distinctions are mentioned in order to highlight only one fact. There is a tenuous connection between saying of some person, *S*, that he saw a table and *S*'s believing that it was a table which he saw. But one should not misinterpret this connection for either a truth implication or an utterance implication. Generally speaking, I will not say of *S* that he saw a table unless I either believe that *S* took what he saw to be a table or I am able to make clear, by an explicit qualification or by what I go on to say, that S did not know it was a table. For what would be the *point* of saying this without qualification? In many instances I would simply be misleading my listeners. Therefore, if I say of S (in this unqualified manner) that he saw a table, this has the utterance implication that I believe S identified the table as a table. And, given the fact that I do not believe things without some justification, it follows that my listeners have some reason to believe that S *did* identify the table as a table. In this sense, my saying of S that he saw a table 'suggests' that S believed that it was a table which he saw. But this 'suggestion' is tenuous indeed; for the truth of what I say does not depend on this suggestion's being true, nor does the sincerity or propriety of my saying it depend on its being true. These features of what we say, and what we find it fitting to say, should not be mistaken for the features of what we are describing when we say things. S's seeing D does not have as a necessary condition of its truth that S identifies D, although in some contexts it may be inferred that if I say of S that he saw D, and I say no more, then it is likely that S identified D.

There is one further point, perhaps the most significant of all, when we look at the relation between what we say we see and what we see$_n$. Despite the fact that seeing$_n$ something lacks positive belief content, despite the fact that this visual achievement is totally non-epistemic in character, the fact remains that everyone, or almost everyone, acquires a considerable number of beliefs about many of the things which they see$_n$. Adult human beings not *only* see$_n$ things, they also identify them, see what they are, recognize them, and learn something about them. And, no doubt, most of us feel that this is largely inevitable. How can one see$_n$ an old friend at three paces in bright light without arriving at *some* beliefs, without achieving some sort of identification, without at least believing that here is someone (or something)? It borders on the incredible to suppose that a conscious human being should be in possession of a properly functioning nervous system and visual apparatus and not learn something about what he sees$_n$. I fully share this feeling. But I also happen to think it would be most extraordinary for a conscious human being, with a properly functioning nervous system, to be eaten by an angry tiger without acquiring some pertinent beliefs about what was happening. The rarity, let us even say the non-existence, of such phenomena has nothing to do with whether seeing an angry tiger, or being eaten by an angry tiger, have, as an essential ingredient, the possession on the part of the agent of a particular belief or set of beliefs. Nevertheless, the pervasive association between seeing something and having some beliefs, however rudimentary they might be, about that which we see effects, to a greater or less extent, the way we talk about what is seen. When A is frequently accompanied by B, and in most conversational contexts B is the most significant aspect of the situation, then the simple statement at A has occurred frequently connotes, unless explicit qualifications are made to the reverse, that B is also present. When 'seeing$_n$ a man' is, for most of us, in a huge variety of common situations, invariably accompanied by 'seeing that he is a man' or, at least, 'seeing that he is a person', then since the latter achievement is, in most conversational contexts, the achievement of most immediate concern, the report that someone has seen a man carries with it the suggestion, unless some qualification is made to the reverse, that he identified him as a man—that he saw that he (or it) was a man. This kind of suggestion is even more pronounced, even more forceful, the more easily identifiable is the thing which is seen; for we assume, without much question, that if a thing is easily identifiable by the average adult, then if an adult sees$_n$ it, he also identifies it.

This association grows even more pronounced when we speak of seeing$_n$ events. For events are precisely the kind of thing which attract our attention and which we are apt to identify if they happen at close range. To say that Tony saw a boy crash through the picture window on a motor scooter is almost (but *only* 'almost') as good as saying that this is how Tony would have described it— this is what Tony believed was happening. For how could he have witnessed such an event and remained ignorant? Well, as a matter of simple fact, Tony could have seen such a thing occur without believing that something was happening in front of him. If one doubts this, I suggest that the reason is not that one considers 'seeing' inextricably connected with 'believing', but, rather, because one is unconsciously importing into the name 'Tony' the idea of an adult human being with some skill in identification. If I went on to say that Tony happened to be my pet lizard, the connection between 'Tony saw a motor scooter crash through the picture window' and 'Tony believes that something is happening in front of him' begins to dissolve. And with it should dissolve the notion that *seeing* something entails that the agent which does the seeing believes something in particular about what he sees.

I think, then, that when we report on a person's seeing an event, our reports are particularly subject to variable interpretation. For the reports frequently fail to make explicit the fact that the percipient not only saw$_n$ the event in question but also identified it in some appropriate way. They fail to make this explicit because the suggestion is ever present (when there is no qualification to the reverse) that this is what they did do. I can say 'Harold saw the *Queen Mary* arriving in New York' without adding ' . . . and he took it to be the *Queen Mary* arriving in New York' because it is assumed that Harold, being a reasonably intelligent and experienced fellow, knew that this is what he was seeing. Either that or my subsequent remarks about Harold will make it clear that he did identify the event in the way described; e.g. ' . . . and he said he never realized the *Queen Mary* was so huge'. But my actual report, taken in isolation, is consistent with his not believing that it was the *Queen Mary* or even with his not believing that a ship was arriving. This is evident from the fact that I could, if I wished, qualify my report: e.g. ' . . . but he thought it was the *Queen Elizabeth* departing' or ' . . . but the poor fellow, having just regained his eyesight, was totally baffled by everything he saw'.

The fact that we are generally more interested in what S found out about what he saw than in the fact that he saw it, more interested in whether he saw that it was D than in the fact that he saw D, helps to explain some otherwise puzzling features of our discourse. For example, the statement 'I did not see D' clearly tells us (as an utterance implication) that the speaker does not believe that he saw D and, hence, that the speaker did not identify anything as D among the things which he saw. Now, generally speaking, it is this implied information which is of greatest interest, and if *it* is accurate we tend to accept the vehicle of this information (the actual statement made) without raising questions about its literal truth or falsity. We proceed in the same fashion in a number of different cases. I can deny that I overheard *anything of significance*, anything which you might not have wanted me to hear, in your conversation with the protest 'I did not hear a word you said'—a statement which, if taken quite literally, may be false. But the statement itself is not the focus of interest; it is what this statement implies that concerns my listeners (if I did not hear a word they said, then I did not hear what they said about me). To quibble over the question of whether I heard one word or not is to miss the point of what I was doing—*viz.* reassuring them. Likewise, when our harried husband returns from the drawer and insists that he did not see the cuff link, it would (normally) be missing the point to insist that he must have seen it because it was lying right there, etc. etc. For the *point* of his statement was that he did not find it even though he looked in the drawer where it was alleged to be. But an appropriate shift of interest may lead us to question the literal truth or falsity of the statement he actually made. For instance, if we happen to be interested in demonstrating to the poor fellow how preoccupied he is, or how inattentive he happens to be, we can quite rightly insist that he must have seen it without realizing it and lead him back to the drawer for another look. An appreciation of what is being done in these linguistic situations will, I believe, help one to understand why the man may assert, in an informative and completely unobjectionable way, that he did *not* see the cuff link when, in fact, he *did* see it and we have grounds for so believing.

So much for a few (but only a few) of the confusions which must be avoided when we are talking about what we see. There are other sources of confusion, and some of them can be traced directly to the way we describe what we have seen, but I shall not take them up at this time. The reader will find a discussion of them in later chapters where the examination can be more profitably pursued, 'more profitably' because the contrast between the different ways of seeing will then be clear.

4. *Existence and Causal Conditions*

The manner in which I have characterized this first way of seeing provides us with an existential implication: if S sees$_n$ D, then there must be something satisfying the description, or having the name, 'D', which S sees$_n$. One cannot see a unicorn if there are no unicorns. For if there are no unicorns, it is false that S visually differentiates a unicorn from its immediate environment, false that a unicorn looks some way to him, and, therefore, false that he sees$_n$ a unicorn. Once again, we may compare seeing$_n$ D with stepping on D; both of these relationships require that D exist. Unlike such verbs as 'to desire', where it is possible to desire a speckled poodle without their being any speckled poodles, one cannot see a speckled poodle, or step on a speckled poodle, without there being one.

The existence condition has generated some dispute. Pointing to situations in which we use, or are said to use, the verb to report seeing things which do not exist, some writers have thought to establish that there is no existence condition governing the use of this verb, or, if there is, there is another equally legitimate sense of this verb which is not regulated by such a condition. J. R. Smythies, for example, maintains:

> . . . in actual English usage, the words, 'see', 'look', 'hear', etc. are used to describe hallucinatory sense-experiences as well as veridical ones. I am not referring here to people whose wits are bemused by drink or delirium who, it might be claimed, were no longer in a state to observe properly or to adhere to correct English usage. I am referring to the extensive factual evidence available in the reports of those experimental subjects who have taken mescaline. . . . The only criterion for correct usage in English is to find out what most people in the circumstances under consideration in fact say. Since people describing their hallucinations almost invariably say 'I see' and not 'I seem to see' or 'I have', it as is much correct English usage to say 'I saw a flower' when the flower was hallucinated as when it was a botanical flower.[1]

G. E. Moore, A. J. Ayer, and others have also tried to distinguish uses of this verb which are consistent with the non-existence of what is seen.[2] Since this is a matter of some importance, let me sort out a few of the issues which must be kept clear in trying to arrive at a final judgment on this matter.[3]

First, anyone interested in establishing that there is a sense of the verb to see' which is not regulated by the existence condition must be careful in how they appeal to what people *say* they see. For it is quite possible, and, indeed, this often seems to be the case, that people only say they see D *when they believe* that there is a D, a real D, which they see. This is a trivial point, but let me take a moment to amplify it. One cannot argue (plausibly) that there is

---

[1] *Analysis of Perception* (London, 1956), p. 32.
[2] See Moore's 'The Nature and Reality of Objects of Perception', in *Philosophical Studies* (London, 1958), p. 64; and Ayer's *Foundations of Knowledge* (London, 1962), p. 21.
[3] In a later section I shall take up the question of *when* D must exist to be seen. That is, can we see stars that *no longer* exist?

a sense of the verb 'to see' which is not regulated by the existence condition because people frequently say they see *D* when there is nothing answering to the description '*D*' for them to see. For their *saying* this can often be attributed to a mistaken belief that the existence condition *is* satisfied. One can argue that they would not have said they saw rats scurrying around the room unless they believed that there were rats, *real* rats, scurrying around the room. Hence, this appeal to 'what people ordinarily say' may show nothing more than that people are sometimes mistaken about what it is they see. It certainly does not show, by itself, that there is a sense of the verb 'to see' which is not governed by the existence condition. It should be noticed, however, that in the above passage Smythies does *not* commit this mistake; here, and in other passages throughout the book, he makes it quite clear that he is speaking about individuals who *know* that what they are describing is hallucinatory, who know that there is no real flower which they see, and yet continue to use the verb 'to see' and continue to describe what they see as a flower.

Secondly, it is extremely important to observe the language used in attempts to exhibit examples of a non-existence sense of the verb 'to see'. I do not think it will do to speak of people seeing, or saying they see, dark patches, flashing colors, blurs, blobs, spots before their eyes, and so on. For in these cases it is not at all clear what must exist in order for these uses to fulfil the existence condition. Must there be some *publically observable* dark patch, gray blur, or array of spots for one to see, *in the existence sense of the verb*, a dark patch, a gray blur, or an array of spots before one's eyes? Why? The fact is that these words are characteristically used to describe what is not public, or, at least, something which need not be public. Hence, the fact that no one else sees the gray blur which I see, the fact that there is no *objective* gray blur for others to see, does not show that I do not see a gray blur in the sense of this term which implies that there must *be* a gray blur for me to see it. Likewise, the failure of other people to see the after-image which I see does not entail that I do not see it, or that I see it in a sense in which there need not be an after-image for me to see it. It simply means that after-images, spots, and blurs are the sorts of things which one can see when others cannot (not because they are not appropritaely positioned to do so, but because it would not make much sense for them to see *my* after-images or the spots in front of *my* eyes). Nothing I have said about seeing$_n$ in the preceding pages rules out the possibility of seeing$_n$ after-images, spots before one's eyes, and hallucinatory rats. In each of these cases there is an element or set of elements which are visually differentiated from their immediate environment, and in each case these elements *must exist* in order to be seen.[1]

Even if we keep these points in mind, there are still difficulties with the view that S cannot see a D unless there exists a D which S sees. For we still have not adequately countered Smythies contention that there are situations (hallucinatory) where the percipient, in full cognizance of the fact that there are no real flowers (which he sees), persists in saying that he sees some flowers. And if we let this stand, it seems as though we must admit that there is a use of the verb 'to see' which is not governed by our existence condition, a use of the verb 'to see' in which one can truly, and in all propriety, say that one sees some flowers when there are no real flowers to be seen. I do not think we can quarrel with Smythies' claim that people do say such things in the circumstances he describes.[2] Let us even grant that they are not false; at least let us suppose that they are said in circumstances in which no one who understands the speaker feels inclined to correct him—either on matters of fact or matters of linguistic usage. One need not look far for illustrations of this, but do such examples show that there is a use of the verb 'to see' which is not governed by the existence condition? Does the utterance 'Last night I dreamed that I met

---

[1] I do not include in the class of things one can see 'dream dragons' or 'imaginary rats'; for I think such statements as 'He imagined he saw a rat' or 'He dreamed he saw a dragon' must be understood, not as saying that he visually differentiated an imaginary rat or that he visually differentiated a dream dragon but, rather, that he imagined he saw (visually differentiated) a rat or dreamed he saw a dragon (in which case no visual differentiation occurs; hence, the existence condition is not appropriately invoked). To dream (or imagine) that one is flying to the moon is not to fly to a dream (or an imaginary) moon. I am unsure about hallucinations and mirages. In one respect I believe they are closer to dreaming and imagining; if this is so, we must not say (as I have in the text) that S sees an hallucinatory dagger (where the existence condition must be satisfied in the sense that there must be an *hallucinatory* dagger); rather, we must say that S hallucinates that he sees a dagger.

[2] Smythies provides a full documentation of his claim on pp. 87-98, *op. cit.* It should be pointed out here that Smythies is arguing for a slightly different point: *viz.* that we can *see* things (hallucinatory flowers) which are not physical in nature.

46

the President . . . ', because it is perfectly unexceptional, in both meaning and (let us say) truth, imply that there is a sense of 'meeting someone' which does not imply that you have really met him. One might, of course, wish to claim this; if so, thousands of words would suddenly acquire two (or more) senses. There seems to be a more plausible and economical alternative, however, an alternative which minimizes the number of different senses of a word but acknowledges the various devices available for modifying some of its normal implications.

When we preface a narrative with the words 'Last night I dreamed' there is an automatic suspension of certain standard implications. We can ride horses that do not exist, know things that are not so, and see events which never happened. At least we can say these things without fear of rebuke about either our veracity or our command of the language. We can, in the proper setting, achieve the same effect with the preface 'Once upon a time'. There is nothing especially mysterious about this, nor should it suggest that every word or phrase which can appear in such a context has a double sense. I think this much would be generally acknowledged. What is not generally recognized, however, is that there are literally scores of different devices, some of them linguistic, others not, which operate in precisely the same way; they suspend one or more of the standard implications of what we say in order that we may utilize the 'residue of meaning' to describe what we are attempting to describe. Especially prevalent are the devices, the signals, cues, and special settings which operate to suspend the existence implication on our use of the verb 'to see'. The question 'Look at that cloud and tell me what you see' is not designed to elicit the response 'A cloud, of course'. A question such as this is a signal, an open invitation, to ignore the normally operative existence condition in order to describe how the cloud appears to one, in what suggestive shape or form. This is why we can respond to such a question with the words, 'Well, I see the head of an old man.'

It is not always necessary to be as explicit as: 'I thought I saw . . .', 'It seemed to me I was seeing . . .', or 'It looked as though . . .' We can often achieve the same effect with quite different devices. Occasionally a pointedly fantastic description of what we have seen will do the trick. For example, if someone says in the course of describing his disoriented state, 'I kept seeing the statue wink at me,' it would be perverse to correct him by

47

pointing out that he could have seen no such thing since the statue's eyes, being solid stone, never moved. But this should not be taken to mean that there is a sense of the verb 'to see' in which we can see a statue wink at us without the statue winking at us. This would be almost as heavy-handed a treatment of a conversational context as to conclude that we can see people who are not there because the statement '*S* thought he saw his son' can be quite true without his son being there for him to see. Yes, the *words* 'he saw his son' are uttered, but one simply cannot ignore what comes before, what goes on during, and what comes after those words. No one, perhaps, would think of ignoring the crucial words '*S* thought' in this situation, but they seem more inclined to ignore every other device in a conversational context which operates in precisely the same way. Some philosophers become very puzzled when other people poke their fingers in their eyes and 'see two pencils instead of one'. The conclusion they draw from this is that there is a sense of the verb 'to see' in which one can see two pencils when there is only one (real) pencil, hence, a sense of the verb which is not governed by the existence condition. Somehow it never occurs to them that a person behaving in this unusual fashion is as significant for what he is saying as is the fact that the person uttered the words 'It seems as though' before his perceptual claim. But both pieces of behavior, the one linguistic, the other nonlinguistic, function in precisely the same way with respect to the words 'I see two pencils': they suspend the existence condition on the verb 'to see' in order to exploit the residual meaning of this verb to describe their visual experience.

In general, one can use the verb 'to see' without satisfying the existence condition as long as, and only so long as, one makes it clear to one's listeners, by some conventional device, linguistic or otherwise, that you, the speaker, acknowledge its suspension. A miner, trapped for weeks in a dark mine-shaft, can report having seen the most fabulous cuisine set before him. He does not have to preface his report with the words 'I thought' or 'It seemed to me'. His being down in the shaft for two weeks in the dark, and his voracious appetite, are already ample testimony to his conscious suspension of the existence condition which governs the use of the verb 'to see'. This kind of report is greeted with knowing smiles *as long as* the listener is convinced that the reporter believes these experiences to be unrelated to the food facilities at the bottom of the mine shaft. And there is no question, in this sort of case, that the fellow is being taken in. Why correct someone who calmly reports seeing wild lions in the street? He must, judging from his behavior, *already* know there are no wild lions in the street. Obviously his statement is his way of describing a particular experience he is having—an experience which is, in certain respects, just like seeing wild lions in the street except, of course, for the fact that there are no animals in the street. But he has signaled his suspension of this existence condition by the *manner* in which he reports. Why deprive him of this way of describing his experience when it is perfectly clear to everyone involved, including him, that not all the conditions are satisfied which ordinarily must be satisfied for truly saying 'I see wild lions in the street'? If we can suspend this condition with the preface 'It is just as though', why can we not suspend it by our *manner of saying* 'I see wild lions in the street'?

In the cases that Smythies mentions it is clear that the persons who are describing their hallucinations are fully apprised of their hallucinatory character.[1] Why *should* they preface everything they say with 'I seem to see'? Obviously the context in which the report is being made already functions to make this qualification apparent to everyone. There are already adequate cues in the setting which signal the suspension of the existence condition. If there were not, if it is suspected that the speaker does not know that what he is describing is hallucinatory, then it seems quite appropriate to point out to the speaker that he could not be seeing any flowers. Why? There are none.

I should want to say, then, that *unless* the existence condition is suspended by some signal, linguistic or non-linguistic, one cannot truly say of S (whether this be some other person or yourself) that S sees a D unless there exists a D, a real D, which S sees. The fact that there is only *one* sense of the verb in question here (in relation to the existence condition) is supported by the fact that unless we signal our suspension of the existence condition by some manner or means, our listener can object to our claim to have seen a D on the grounds that there are no D's (or no D's in the vicinity). If there were two senses of the verb, one of which was not governed by an existence condition, this type of objection

---

[1] On p. 32 Smythies states: 'These subjects can of course distinguish between their hallucinations and their veridical perceptions...' (*op. cit.*).

would not be generally available. For, then, it would be possible, with a straight face and in all sincerity, to *truly* say one saw Harold at the scene of the crime without even believing he was there, and indeed without his having been there.

There is another condition governing our use of the verb 'to see' although it has a different character than the one just discussed. Roughly, one may say that for any D which has a position in space, one must, in order to see$_n$ it, be within its general vicinity and be looking in the appropriate direction. The 'general vicinity' and the 'appropriate direction' will, in turn, be specified by means of the available avenues and distance in which light can be transmitted from the object seen to the viewer. This is simply to say that we do not believe that S can see$_n$ D if there is no 'causal linkage' (involving light rays) between D and S. I say 'we do not believe' because I wish to emphasize that this is not, as with the existence condition, a defining characteristic of seeing$_n$ something. Rather, it is simply something that happens to be true of an enormous number of things which we see.[1] No one, perhaps, believes that a person could leap twelve feet straight in the air. Nonetheless, it is not part of what it means to 'leap into the air' that one leaps less than twelve feet. Similarly, no one (perhaps) believes that S can see a table from a position which prevents the transmission of some light, via some natural or artificial means, from the table to S. Yet, despite what certain causal theorists would like to maintain, this condition is not constitutive of seeing; its failure does not entail that S does not see D or could not see D.

Consider the following case. A person, standing behind a massive wall, claims to be able to see everything on the far side. He dutifully recites the appearance and behavior of every item; he never fails (or fails only on those occasions when he could be expected to fail on other grounds) despite our manipulation and alteration of the objects which he purports to see. He does not detect anything which depends on his ability to hear, feel, or smell.

[1] An 'enormous number' but not 'all' of the things which we see. Aside from the difficulties which might be mentioned with respect to shadows and events, I have already pointed out that, in the way of seeing now under consideration (seeing$_n$), one can see after-images and spots before one's eyes (of the sort that occur when one is hit on the head). I do not think it plausible to talk about causal connections between the percipient and what he sees in all of these cases—especially not if this is formulated in terms of the transmission of light rays.

When he turns away, or closes his eyes, he ceases to 'see'. Elaborate checks reveal no transmission of light from the objects to him. Does he see what he claims to see? How could one deny it? By insisting that he is imagining or somehow being supplied with images which accurately represent the appearance and behavior of the objects on the other side of the wall? But why does this cease when he turns away or closes his eyes? Is it some miraculous sixth sense? But he only detects those things whose detectability is associated with our sense of sight. He cannot 'read other people's minds' or 'see into the future'. It may be somewhat difficult to imagine what we would say in such a situation. It is certainly extraordinary, and perhaps most of us, despite our familiarity with such science fiction notions as 'the man with the X-ray eyes', are convinced that something of this sort could never happen. We are confronted with a situation in which there would be no known causal explanation for the man's phenomenal powers of detection. But I find nothing logically incoherent about saying that the man somehow sees the objects on the far side of the wall, but that our investigations have so far not revealed *how* he sees them. That is, the fact that we cannot (at a certain moment in time) explain how a person sees does not entail that he does not see; there may be causal linkages between the objects and our percipient which have yet to be discovered (or which will never be discovered).

I do not, of course, wish to deny the well-established facts of physics, physiology, and neurophysiology. We have learned from these disciplines what, in point of fact, takes place in the intervening medium, the percipient's eyes, his nervous system, and (to an extent) his brain when, as we ordinarily say, he sees various objects around him. I see no reason to question these accounts. What I do wish to deny is that these accounts of the mechanics of perception are in any way part of *what we mean* when we say of someone that he sees a particular object, that these accounts, or something like them, are entailed by our saying of someone that he sees a chair. Neither am I quarreling with those causal theories of perception which limit themselves to giving an account, in causal terms, of what gives rise to those experiences which prompt us to say that we see teapots and tigers.[1] I am, however, rejecting

---

[1] In Section 6 of this chapter I examine, and reject, some of the conclusions that are often drawn from a causal analysis of perception. In particular I shall reject the view that a causal analysis of perception shows us that we do

the 'Causal Theory of Perception' if this is put forward as an analysis of what we *mean* when we say of S that he saw a teapot. If one supposes that part of what we mean when we say that S saw a teapot is that there is a particular causal sequence of events, call it C, between D and S, the first question that must be asked is whether the meaning is to include a specification of *what* particular causal sequence C might be. If we are told that C is the sequence which is now fairly well understood, involving the transmission of light rays, stimulation of visual receptors, etc., then it follows that prior to the discovery of these matters, no one knew what the verb 'to see' meant and that a great many people *now* do not know what the word means. Chisholm advances a view similar to this.[1] That is, he defines his 'non-propositional' sense of seeing (similar in other respects to seeing$_n$) in terms of physical processes (light rays, etc.), which, as a well-established fact, accompany our visual experiences. This has the expected effect. People can see things (in Chisholm's sense) without knowing they are seeing anything because they perceive things 'without knowing anything about the physical processes in terms of which we have defined the non-propositional senses of perception words'.[2] I would agree with Chisholm that people may see things without knowing they are seeing something, but *not* because they are ignorant of physics, physiology, or neurophysiology. This strange consequence of his view, strange at least if we interpret it as an analysis of what we mean when we say of each other that we see something, is evaded by the admission that he (Chisholm) is not attempting to say what is ordinarily meant by this verb; rather, his non-propositional sense of 'to see' is a special, highly technical (and, I would add, never used) sense of the verb.

If, on the other hand, a proponent of a causal theory of perception insists that part of what we mean when we say that S saw D is that *some* (unspecified) causal chain links D with S, then I do not see that there is much left to quibble about. We may or may not mean this, and whether we mean it or not will most likely depend on how loosely one is allowed to interpret the notion of a 'causal chain linking D and S'. But there is nothing here that is incompatible with the man described above seeing the objects on the far

not see objects *directly*—only certain 'images' that are aroused in us as a result of a sequence of events originating with the object.

[1] *Perceiving*, Chapter X.   [2] *Ibid.*, p. 150.

side of the wall. For we can continue to maintain that the objects on the other side of the wall are responsible, causally responsible, in part at least, for his phenomenal accuracy in describing them. We might even support this claim by pointing out that without this connection between D and S, S's phenomenal powers would be inexplicable. Hence, he *does* see them; he *must* see them; we simply have not yet discovered how he sees them—what, specifically, the causal connection happens to be.

The key to whether a person can see D is whether he can visually differentiate D from its immediate environment. One of our surest guides to whether *it is* D which is being differentiated is whether the percipient is appropriately placed to receive the reflected (or emitted) light from D. Is he looking in the right direction? Is it too far away to see? But this guide, although it operates as an effective, indeed, sometimes decisive, criterion for deciding whether S sees D or not, operates as a criterion only because of what is already known about what men can and cannot differentiate under various conditions. The guide is by no means a logically decisive criterion. To dispense with it would necessitate some rather radical revisions in what had been taken, up to this time, as well-established scientific fact, but it would not necessitate a revision in what we meant by saying of someone that he saw something. It has been found that men cannot see such things as trees unless there is a ray of light with sufficient intensity between them and the object seen, but this fact about what we can see should not be mistaken for what it means to see. This would be to collapse the explanation with what is explained. It makes a skeletal theory of how we see into a logical consequence of our seeing anything at all.

This second feature of the verb, then, is not, as in the case of the existence condition, a logical feature of its use. We consistently rely on it, of course, in conjunction with other data, to determine whether someone *could* have seen the thing they claimed to see. But this 'could' should not be mistaken for the 'could' in 'You could not have seen a centaur; no such beast exists.' It is, rather, the 'could' of 'You could not have jumped that wall; it is over twelve feet high.' That is, as a matter of well-attested fact people *cannot* jump twelve feet high; and as a matter of well-attested fact people cannot see things behind opaque walls or in the dark. If some fellow insisted that, in total darkness, and from behind a thick wall, he could see the objects on the other side, I should think the course of action (given that he was trustworthy and sincere in every respect) would be to find out, and there *are* ways of finding out,[1] whether this was so or not. He may be factually mistaken, and the odds are overwhelmingly great that he is, but I see no reason to suppose, from his statement alone, that he does not know how to use the English language or that his logic is seriously deficient.

5. *The Principle of Substitutivity*

Implicit in the preceding discussion is a principle which has yet to be given full expression. Let us call 'D_i' an associated description of D if and only if 'D_i' and 'D' are either proper names or noun phrases and the statement 'D is D_i' is true. For example, 'my wallet' is an associated description of that object on the floor if and only if that object on the floor is my wallet. The principle to which I have referred can now be stated as: if S sees$_n$ D, and 'D_i' is an associated description of D such that S can see$_n$ D_i, then S sees$_n$ D_i. If S sees the teapot, then it follows, according to this principle, that S sees a rare antique if, indeed, the teapot is a rare antique. On the other hand, if the teapot happens to be what I was thinking about, it does not follow that S can see what I was thinking about simply because he can see the teapot. For, under one interpretation of the phrase 'what I was thinking about' (as an interrogative nominal), S cannot see what I was thinking about without believing, minimally, that I was thinking about something. That is, although the description 'what I was thinking about' does qualify as an associated description of the teapot, it is not an associated description which (under this interpretation) satisfies the further condition that S must be able to see$_n$ D_i; for, on this interpretation of this phrase, S cannot see what I am thinking about in a way that lacks positive belief content. Interpreted as a relative clause nominal (the x which I was thinking about), however, there is nothing wrong with concluding that S sees what I was thinking about.

Philosophers have coined other labels for the generalized version of this principle of substitutivity. W. V. Quine, for example,

[1] That is, we could manipulate the objects, rearrange them, substitute other objects, and determine whether there was a corresponding shift in what the person described himself as seeing.

speaks of a name or a phrase occurring in a *purely designative fashion* if, within the context in which it occurs, associated descriptions can be substituted for it without changing the truth value of the containing statement.[1] Some also speak of *extensional* contexts in contrast to *intensional* contexts, a context being extensional (with respect to a name or noun phrase) if that name or noun phrase is purely designative within that context. An example of an intensional context is 'S knows that —— is C'; S might know that A is C, and it may be true that A is B, but it does not follow that S knows that B is C (for he might not know that A is B). The principle of substitutivity, as I have formulated it, is an application of these more general notions, an application with a particular added reservation: *viz.* the substituends, 'A' and 'B' (or 'D' and 'D_i'), must both be descriptions that can be used in the context 'S sees$_n$ —— ' in a way that is consistent with my characterization of seeing$_n$.

This 'principle of inference', if I may refer to it as such, is a familiar one, and we often appeal to it in a variety of situations. It is at work in such statements as: 'You must have seen me; you saw the man who announced the next act didn't you? Well, that was me.' Or: 'Yes, you saw my wife; she was the blonde woman you said you saw.' Something very close to this principle is also exploited in philosophical discussions.

> Similarly, I may say 'I see a silvery speck' or 'I see a huge star'; what I see—in the single, ordinary 'sense' this word has—can be described as a silvery speck, or identified as a very large star; for the speck in question *is* a very large star.[2]

R. J. Hirst, in reply to an argument by Blanshard which purports to show that we do not perceive a distant aeroplane, points out that:

> Sometimes we do and may say. 'You see that speck over the church tower moving to the right? That's the Edinburgh plane!' or 'That patch of red down there is Jones's cottage roof.' But then we are apparently doing just the thing that he (Blanshard) says is absurd, namely saying that the speck *is* an aeroplane.[3]

[1] 'Notes on Existence and Necessity', reprinted in *Semantics and the Philosophy of Language,* Leonard Linsky (ed.) (Urbana, Ill, 1952), p. 78.
[2] John Austin, *Sense and Sensibilia* (London, 1962), p. 98. Later in this section I shall express reservations about this, and the following, example.
[3] *The Problems of Perception* (New York, 1959), p. 237.

The implication here is, of course, that we see the aeroplane since the speck which we do see *is* the aeroplane.

There are, nevertheless, difficulties with this pattern of inference—both apparent and real.[1] To begin with the former, consider the argument:

> (A-1) S saw Bobby Baker.
>
> <u>Bobby Baker</u> is the man being investigated by the committee.
>
> S saw the man being investigated by the committee.

The conclusion suggests, or might easily be interpreted to mean, that S saw the man *while* he was being investigated, or the investigation itself, and this may not be true at all. The conclusion is, of course, syntactically ambiguous in some of the ways that were discussed in Section 2. The words 'being investigated' may be understood as either a relative clause ('who was being investigated') or as an inseparable part of a noun phrase referring to something other than the man—i.e. the *investigation* of the man. Such an argument constitutes a counter-example to our principle of inference only if we exploit this latent ambiguity in 'the man being investigated'. If the second premise is to be true, however, this phrase must be understood as 'the man who is now being investigated by the committee', and if we also interpret it in this fashion in the conclusion, as we must do if we are to avoid the fallacy of equivocation, the conclusion will be true if the two premises are true.

There are also other ambiguities which can appear in this type of argument.

> (A-2) S saw the movie 'Birth of a Nation'.
>
> The movie 'Birth of a Nation' was the last movie to be shown at the Strand Theatre.
>
> S saw the last movie to be shown at the Strand Theatre.[2]

S may never have been at the Strand Theatre for the two premises to be true; yet, on a perfectly natural reading of the conclusion,

---

[1] Several of the examples which follow were suggested to me by Professor Paul Ziff. His criticisms of earlier versions of this section were extremely helpful.

[2] This example, and others like it, were suggested to me by Mr. Jack Barense.

the conclusion could only be true if S had attended the Strand Theatre. Once again, the sort of ambiguity which this argument embodies is clear enough: a type-token ambiguity between movies and performances of movies. One could construct other examples by exploiting the difference between books and copies of books, offices and occupants of offices, and so on.[1]

Other examples embody a more subtle feature, namely the feature which some phrases have of suggesting an adverbial modification on the principle verb 'to see'—a modification of when, where, or how the item was seen.

(A-3) S saw the Morning Star.
  The Morning Star is the Evening Star (Venus).
  S saw the Evening Star.

We can, of course, insist that the second premise of this argument is false; or we can maintain that, in the sense of the terms which makes the second premise true, the conclusion is also true. This despite the fact that S never saw a star in the evening. The fact remains, however, that on a natural reading of these statements, the premises might well be true but the conclusion false.

I do not know of any generally satisfactory way to avoid such counter-examples. They can be dealt with individually by isolating the particular sort of ambiguity operating in each case, but this falls short of the *formal* characterization which valid argument forms are supposed to receive. Despite this I do not believe the present pattern of argument differs much from other accepted patterns of argument, those which are allegedly formal in nature and codified in various symbolic systems. Counter-examples, in these latter cases, are simply ruled out as unacceptable instances of the relevant argument form. Indeed, fallacies, equivocations, and ambiguities are often identified by their satisfaction of an argument form's formal requirements but failure to satisfy the validity conditions (i.e. true premises necessitating a true conclusion). Logicians are not tempted to abandon the rule of double negation (P is logically equivalent to not-not-P) because we refuse to treat 'He is friendly' as equivalent to 'He is not unfriendly', nor does the logical equivalence which goes under the name of simplification (P is logically equivalent to P and P) seem to suffer much from

[1] Compare Leonard Linsky's discussion of 'substitutivity' in *The Journal of Philosophy*, Vol. LXII, No. 6, pp. 139-45.

the fact that I can *disagree* with your contention that there are girls by pointing out that there are girls and there are girls. Counter instances such as this are merely tolerated with, perhaps, some invective about the imprecision and vagueness of ordinary language.

If there is any merit to the claim that 'S sees a man; the man is a doctor; therefore, S sees a doctor' is a valid argument, and if validity is a formal feature of inference, the conviction remains that the pattern—S sees X; X is Y; hence, S sees Y—*properly qualified*, is a valid pattern of inference. How it is to be properly qualified is the moot question—especially if *formal* restrictions are required to handle every instance that might appear in ordinary discourse. If, however, exceptions are always found to depend on some identifiable ambiguity or fallacy, then we can treat it, along with a host of other accepted patterns of inference, as a valid argument form. One must simply exercise extreme caution in its application, something I am prepared to do in what follows. I shall appeal to this 'principle of inference' only when the inference is, quite clearly, trouble-free, only when it is apparent that no ambiguity, equivocation, or contextual restriction interferes with the conclusion's valid derivation.

There is one other point to be mentioned in connection with this principle. I have said that an associated description of D is any proper name or noun phrase 'D_i' which makes 'D is D_i' true. Such a characterization is exposed to the difficulties associated with the word 'is'. Normally, we encounter no special trouble, at least none of a philosophical nature, when we make such identifications: this chair is the one my brother loaned me, that bright star is Venus, and the man in the grey suit is the Governor. But there are more problematic cases.

(*a*) That dark, semicircular, mass on the lake is a flock of geese.
(*b*) That dark cloud just above the horizon is a swarm of locusts.
(*c*) Blood is a collection of cells, some white, some red, suspended in a plasma.
(*d*) A cloud is a collection of suspended water droplets.
(*e*) This table is a complex system of molecules.
(*f*) The spark (lightning flash) is a stream of electrons.

Are we to sanction these as acceptable forms of 'D is D_i'? Can we, that is, apply our principle to them and conclude that we see a flock of geese (which is *not* to say, of course, that we see the individual geese in the flock) *because* what we do see (that dark, semicircular mass on the lake) *is* a flock of geese? If so, it would appear that we also see systems of molecules and streams of electrons if we see tables and sparks.

No doubt some philosophers would be eager to embrace this conclusion, but I think we must be careful lest we embrace it for the wrong reasons. Our principle of substitutivity gathers what force it has from the more generalized principle that if X is the same thing as Y, then whatever is true of X is true of Y. This generalized principle cannot be applied without severe restrictions, but something similar to it is at work in such inferences as: if this chair is, indeed, the chair my brother loaned me, then if this chair is made of oak (has four legs, has a broken back, is now in the kitchen), then the chair my brother loaned me is made of oak (has four legs, has a broken back, is now in the kitchen). The identifications we find in (a)–(f), however, do not easily lend themselves to similar substitutions. If what I see is a dark, semicircular mass on the lake, does it follow that the flock of geese is dark and semicircular. If this dark mass becomes gradually larger (as I walk toward it), does the flock of geese also become gradually larger? If blood is red, is the collection of cells suspended in plasma also red? If the table is smooth and solid, and possesses very sharp edges, is the system of molecules smooth and solid, and does it possess sharp edges? If I touch the table, do I touch the system of molecules? If the spark is blue, is the stream of electrons blue?

One could answer all of these questions, and dozens more like them, in the affirmative, secure in one's faith that the corresponding identifications listed in (a)–(f) justified such answers; but I believe this comes close to begging the question. Yes, in *some* sense, the table is a system of molecules; yes, in *some* sense, that dark cloud on the horizon is a swarm of locusts; but is this sense the sense in which whatever is true of the one is thereby true of the other? In the case of (a)–(f) this is not at all obvious, and, therefore, it is not at all obvious that we can validly infer that we *see* the one because we see the other.

I shall argue, in the last chapter of this book, that we do see collections of molecules and streams of electrons, but the considerations which I advance in support of this conclusion do not depend on the principle of substitutivity. For I have said that I would use this principle only when the inference was quite clearly trouble-free, and I do not think that in the case of (a)–(f) the infer ence is *quite clearly* trouble-free. I do not believe that the kind of identity represented by (a)–(f) is the kind of identity presupposed by our principle. The sense of the word 'is' on which this principle relies approximates the sense of identity with which Paul Benacerraf is concerned in the following quotation:

> If an expression of the form '$x = y$' is to have a sense, it can be only in contexts where it is clear that both x and y are of some kind or category C, and that it is the conditions which individuate things *as the same C* which are operative and determine its truth value. .... I am arguing that questions of the identity of a particular 'entity' do not make sense. 'Entity' is too broad. For such questions to make sense, there must be a well-entrenched predicate C, in terms of which one then asks about the identity of a *particular C*, and the conditions associated with identifying C's as *the same C* will be the deciding ones.[1]

In Benacerraf's terms there is, generally speaking, no well-entrenched predicate C which will mediate the identification of *an X* with a collection (swarm, flock, assembly, arrangement, etc.) of Y's. As a rule, collections do not have the same criteria of identity as the objects with which they are identified. For instance, we can say that collection A is not one and the same collection as collection B if c_i, say, is a part (or member) of collection A but not of B. Yet, we can say that this is one and the same chair that was here yesterday, despite the fact that there is one molecule missing. The considerations relevant to whether this is one and the same chair are different than the considerations which are relevant to whether this is one and the same collection of molecules. And, as a rule, this is the case whenever we say that one thing *is* a collection (group, bunch, arrangement, etc.) of other things.[2] Hence, there is no legitimate candidate for Benacerraf's well-entrenched predicate 'C' to mediate the identifications represented by (a)–(f). To suppose there was would be to suppose that there was a category of

[1] 'What Numbers Could Not Be', *The Philosophical Review*, vol. LXXIV, No. 1, p. 64-5.

[2] In Section 5 of the last chapter I discuss an exception to this rule which is particularly relevant to the present topic, but since it involves special issues in the philosophy of science, I leave it for later consideration.

things, C, which participated in two *divergent* sets of identity criteria, an open invitation to contradiction.

I should like, therefore, to restrict the principle of substitutivity to cases where D is the same C (object, table, person, event, etc.) as D_i. I am not denying the legitimacy of statements (a)–(f). I think they are all quite meaningful and may all be true. I only wish to deny that the identifications they represent are suitable for applying our principle. As far as I have gone, then, the question of whether one can see collections of molecules or streams of electrons is still an open question; the principle of substitutivity cannot be utilized to close it.

One final remark. Several of the examples with which I introduced the present discussion have become, in the light of our additional restrictions, somewhat more problematic. It was originally suggested that we could see the distant aeroplane (or huge star) because the speck (which we admittedly do see) *is* an aeroplane (or huge star). If we cast around, however, for a well-entrenched predicate 'C' to mediate the identification between the speck and the aeroplane, the suspicion arises that there are none—at least none that approximate what Benacerraf had in mind by 'well-entrenched'. What familiar category of things is it to which both the speck and the aeroplane belong? There does not seem to be any. For it seems reasonable to say that (as the aeroplane draws closer) the speck grows larger but the aeroplane does not. And if there was a category, C, to which both the aeroplane and the speck belonged, then we should be forced to conclude that one of these C's is both growing larger and not growing larger at the same time. Hence, statements such as 'That speck over the rooftops is an aeroplane' seem to be, in this respect, in the same class as statements (a)–(f); we *cannot* appeal to our principle of substitutivity to conclude that because we see the speck we see the aeroplane. This does not mean, of course, that when we see the speck we do *not* see the aeroplane. On the contrary, I shall argue that the inference is fully justified, but its justification does not reside in an appeal to the principle discussed in this section. Its justification is, in essential respects, similar to that which can be given for concluding that one sees a collection of molecules because the chair which one does see is such a collection (in whatever sense of 'is' is appropriate here). But this justification is quite independent of the principle of substitutivity.

6. *Direct Versus Indirect Perception*

Some philosophers have tried to distinguish between a direct and an indirect mode of seeing things. Such a distinction is usually inspired by epistemological considerations, although, on occasion, it is introduced on the supposition that it depicts what science has to tell us about the causal mechanism of perception. As a general rule, it turns out that we do not directly see the chair or the chessboard; we are told, instead, that the objects and events which compose our commonsense world are seen only indirectly. Direct perception is reserved for a very special class of elements.

There are a variety of ways of introducing the distinction between direct and indirect perception, and I do not have time to examine all of them. There are, however, three 'standard' approaches to this distinction which enjoy great popularity, and most attempts to distinguish a sense of 'direct perception', especially those which are epistemologically motivated, seem to depend on one or more of these standard or traditional methods. For this reason I have chosen to concentrate on these three methods. What I hope to show is that none of them achieve what they set out to achieve.

(1) One *directly sees* (or *senses*) D only if one cannot be mistaken about D, about the fact that one is seeing (or sensing) D, or about the properties, or some of the properties, of D.[1] For the purposes of this discussion I think we may select just one of these alternative characterizations for examination. Let us say, then, that S sees D directly if and only if there are some properties of D about which S cannot be mistaken.

I have said that there are *some* properties of D about which S cannot be mistaken because it seems clear that those who propose such definitions do not wish to commit themselves to the view that when we see something directly, we cannot be mistaken about *any* of the properties of the item or about *any* of the relationships into which it enters with other things. For example, when I see D directly, it may be that D is the four hundred and eighty-fourth item of this sort that I have (directly) seen in the last two days. I do

---

[1] Norman Malcolm, following G. E. Moore, adopts this as the main feature of the standard philosophical conception of 'direct perception' (see his 'Direct Perception', reprinted in *Knowledge and Certainty* (Englewood Cliffs, New Jersey, 1963).

not think it is the intent of those who propose such definitions as this that I cannot see D directly if I believe (mistakenly) that it is the four hundred and eighty-third such item. Nor am I precluded from seeing D directly if I mistakenly believe that it is an omen from God. Rather, the intent seems to be that there is a certain class of properties, call them *visual* properties, about which I cannot be mistaken.

Notice also that to see D directly I *need not* believe something about the character or properties of D. The point is rather that *if* I do believe that D has (or lacks) one of these 'visual' properties, then I cannot be mistaken in this belief. One need not *truly believe* something about D in order for it to be the case that one cannot be mistaken in one's beliefs about D.

The 'cannot' is, of course, the key word in this definition. One may see a book and (as a matter of fact) not be mistaken about its being a book, nor about its color, shape, and relative size. But this does not mean that one sees the book directly (according to the above definition) since one *could* be mistaken about these matters. That is to say, direct perception, as defined above, is supposed to be *stronger* than what we might call a mistake-free way of seeing D defined as: S sees D in a mistake-free way if and only if S sees D and is not mistaken about any of the visual properties which D has. This latter way of seeing does allow us to say that if someone sees D (in this mistake-free way), then he *cannot* (by definition) be mistaken about the visual properties of D. But this is completely trivial; he cannot be mistaken because, by hypothesis, he is not mistaken. Presumably the 'cannot' in our original definition of direct perception is not meant to be understood in such a trivial fashion. For if it were taken in this way, there would be nothing preventing us from seeing books, tables, chessboards, and people *directly*.

With these preliminaries out of the way, let us ask whether there is anything which we see directly. Does anything qualify? Familiar objects and events are quickly ruled ineligible; in some sufficiently strong sense of 'could' it would seem that we *could* be mistaken in supposing they had the properties we believed them to have. Although I am quite certain that the coffee cup before me is brown, I could (I suppose) be mistaken about this. My seeing the coffee cup and being certain that it is brown do not imply that *it is brown*. Well, then, what about such things as after-images, hallucinatory mice, mirages, and spots before your eyes? These do not seem to qualify either; for it seems clear enough that I *could* mistake one of my after-images for a smudge on the wall, and if I can make this mistake I can also (mistakenly) believe that it *only looks purple* but is *really* some other color.[1] Of course, if I know it is an after-image I will not make such a mistake, but this, again, is completely trivial. If I know that what I am seeing is a coffee cup, there are certain mistakes I will not make either. Similar remarks can be made about hallucinatory daggers, eidetic imagery, mirages, and so on. We *can* mis-classify these things, and if a mis-classification is possible, we can also mistakenly suppose that these things have properties (even *visual* properties—however one cares to specify these) which they do not have.

It would seem, then, that the dichotomy between direct and indirect perception, as defined above, does not correspond to any distinction one might wish to draw between the 'physical' and the 'mental' or between the 'objective' and the 'subjective'. True enough, I cannot see my coffee cup directly; but neither can I see my own visual imagery *directly*. What is left? At this point one is inclined to say that the above definition introduces a vacuous concept; everything that we see, everything of which we are visually aware, is seen *indirectly*. I would prefer to leave the matter here, but, unfortunately, some people have expended considerable effort inventing things to satisfy this otherwise empty notion. And I feel obliged, if only for the sake of completeness, to mention briefly the lines along which such thinking has developed.

When I see an object, my coffee cup, for example, the cup looks a certain way to me. Although I can be mistaken about what properties my coffee cup possess, I can hardly be mistaken (so it is said) about what properties *it appears to me to have at the moment*. This has been disputed, but let it pass for the sake of the argument. If we now speak of the 'look of the coffee cup' or the 'appearance of the coffee cup' as something we (visually) *sense*, then it would seem that the sensing of these 'looks' or 'appearances' qualifies as a form of direct perception (as defined above). For I cannot be

[1] Malcolm, *op. cit.*, maintains that our awareness of after-images is a case of direct preception; after-image descriptions are incorrigible (p. 83). I do not know why he supposes this. I would agree with him that it is a fairly simple matter to identify after-images (e.g. by moving one's head), but I do not think it any easier than identifying, say, the coffee cup in front of me.

mistaken in supposing that 'the look of my coffee cup' is brown since this is tantamount to being mistaken about how my coffee cup looks to me at the moment. Hence, if we call these 'looks' or 'appearances' of things *percepts*, *sensa*, or *sense-data*, then we can say that the sensing of percepts (or what have you) is a form of direct perception; there are certain properties of these percepts about which we cannot be mistaken.

A brief look at the philosophical literature will show that this theme has numberless variations, rebuttals, counter-rebuttals, refutations, reformulations, and so on. Nothing I can say in a page or two is going to be decisive. Nonetheless, I feel compelled to make one or two remarks if only to indicate some of the reasons I have for rejecting this maneuver.

First, in many situations it is totally implausible to say that *anything* (of which I am aware) has those properties which some things look to have. For example, something (a stone, say) may look edible; does this mean that I sense something which is edible? I shall be told that 'edibility' is not a visual characteristic, but I know of no non-circular way to specify what is to count as a visual characteristic. Suppose something looks rough, hard, hot, far away, and larger than the moon. Is there any sense of being visually aware of something in which if something looks that way to me I must be visually aware of something which *is* rough, hard, hot, far away, and larger than the moon?

Secondly, if we grant (for the sake of argument) that one cannot be mistaken about how something looks to one (at the moment), then why not take this fact as a sufficient indication that we directly see *the object* which looks that way to us; for there are certain things about the object (how it looks to us at the moment) about which we cannot be mistaken. That is, I see my coffee cup directly (according to the above definition) because I cannot be mistaken about the way it looks to me at the moment. That which looks brown to me may not be a coffee cup, but whatever it is, I cannot be mistaken in believing of it that it looks brown to me. Hence, I directly see whatever it is that looks brown to me, and this, it should be noticed, might very easily turn out to be the coffee cup itself. I expect to be told that 'looks brown to me' is not a *legitimate* property of things, and so even if one cannot be mistaken in supposing that something has this pseudo-property, it does not count toward satisfying the definition of directly perceiving the thing (whatever it turns out to be) that looks this way. The total arbitrariness of this reply should be apparent; 'looks brown to me' is not (it is said) a legitimate property of things, but 'the look (or appearance) to me of the coffee cup (or whatever)' is a legitimate subject for such properties as 'brown' and 'coffee-cup-shaped'. If such an obsession can still be said to represent a philosophical view, it is a view which I do not intend to discuss in any greater detail.

I conclude that in so far as we are talking about items which we commonly say we see (and I include in this category mirages and after-images), *nothing* is seen directly according to the above definition. And in so far as we are allowed to bring into consideration 'the look of a thing', and in so far as we cannot be mistaken about how a thing looks to us, we can, with as much plausibility as any alternative description, say that we directly see anything which looks some way to us. This, though, takes in everything that was to be excluded.

(2) A second way one might try to press epistemological considerations into service is by defining a certain special class of objects. These objects (by definition) *are* the way they appear. If one of these objects looks elliptical, then (by definition) it *is* elliptical. Only objects of this special class are perceived directly. Once again, teapots and tigers are quickly disqualified; there is nothing about such things which implies that they are the way they appear. The tiger may look grey without being grey.

Presumably, once we have such a definition, it is an empirical question whether there are any objects which satisfy the definition. Casting around for plausible candidates, we might decide that, surely in this case, after-images qualify. What sense would it make to say that an after-image was really red although it looked blue or that it was really round although it looked elliptical. It seems that after-images are the way they appear; if they look elliptical, they *are* elliptical. The same might be said for hallucinatory daggers, eidetic imagery, and spots before one's eyes. Therefore, we perceive such things directly.

As a philosophical pastime I see nothing objectionable in this procedure. I do consider it somewhat pointless since the modifier 'direct' tells us nothing more than what we already know when we are told that it is an after-image which is seen. Why not just say that we sometimes see after-images or eidetic images, and, incidentally, they have this special feature of being the way they appear to be? We also see optical illusions and, incidentally, they have the special feature of not being the way they appear. Why add the word 'direct' to our statements about the former? This last question raises the crucial point. For philosophers, I believe, are inclined to use this word because they mistakenly suppose that if we do see objects which are (necessarily) the way they appear, then our way of seeing them must, in some way, be *epistemically* superior to our way of seeing objects which need not be the way they appear. That is, our perception of these special objects puts us in a very privileged position with respect to finding out what properties these objects have. Hence, one is led to emphasize this alleged epistemic superiority by using the word 'direct' in connection with our seeing such objects.

The confusion underlying this move is apparent. We do not put ourselves into an epistemologically superior position by defining a class of people, call them Open-People, who always talk and behave in precisely the way they feel, who never conceal their 'true feelings' so to speak. Such a definition does not solve an epistemological problem; it merely shifts its locus. For the difficulty, if indeed there is an epistemological difficulty in this area, now shifts to how we are to identify Open-People. *This* person, the one who talks and acts as though he were jealous, is he an Open-Person or not? If so, and we *know* that he is, then we can easily and reliably conclude that he is jealous. But how can we tell whether he is a member of our specially defined class? We are in no better position for finding out whether this fellow is jealous or not than we were without our definition. Similarly in the case of direct perception as defined above. We can, if we are so inclined, define a special class of elements and say that we are directly perceiving when, and only when, we are perceiving one of these elements. The resultant difference between seeing something directly and seeing something indirectly is *not*, however, an epistemological difference. There is nothing about direct perception which makes it any easier to discover what properties a thing has when one is directly perceiving it. For it is quite possible to directly perceive one of these special objects and mistakenly believe that it is quite different than it appears to be. For instance, to repeat the examples of an earlier page, I can see an after-image or an hallucinatory pink rat and mistake these items for a textured area on the sofa (which only looks purple from this distance) and a real gray rat (which *only looks* pink in this strange light). And if someone wants to insist that in these cases we see the after-image and the pink rat *directly*, then I think it must be conceded that for the purpose of avoiding mistakes, direct perception, as currently defined, provides us with no infallible insurance.

Direct perception, as defined in this second way, is simply a rather misleading way of commenting on the different sorts of things we can see. It does *not* show us that there are two distinguishable ways of seeing things. If there were any Open-People, this would not show that we see these individuals in a different way than the rest of mankind. We would see Open-People, Closed-People, after-images, and artifacts in the same way. But to say this is not to say that there are not significant differences between all of these things.

I shall discuss one more attempt to establish an epistemologically significant distinction between direct and indirect perception. By 'epistemologically significant' I mean, of course, a distinction other than that reflected in such contrasts as: seeing him directly *vs.* seeing him in a mirror. I do not wish to deny that we can meaningfully talk about seeing something directly, nor that it is quite good common sense to talk this way on occasion. What I am concerned to deny is that this distinction can be drawn in the way that philosophers have traditionally tried to draw it: *viz.* at the expense, the very considerable expense, of common sense. This last method of introducing the distinction does not rely on epistemological considerations, but the perceptual distinction, once made, is usually pressed immediately into epistemological service.

(3) Most of us are familiar with the outlines of a causal description of the normal perceptual process. If the statement 'S sees a coffee pot' is true, then, as a matter of well-established fact, light is being reflected from the coffee pot into S's eyes, the light is stimulating certain sensitive cells which, in turn, are transmitting electrical impulses via the cortical nerve to the cerebral cortex where a pattern of excitation occurs. As a consequence of this chain of events, S undergones an experience, an experience which we might ordinarily describe by saying that S (first) sees the coffee pot. Let us refer to this typical or standard sequence of events with the notation $e_1, e_2, e_3, \ldots$; the terminal event or stage, e_n, will be

that last event or state of affairs which, until it happens, S has not *yet* seen the coffee pot.

There is some dispute about the last member of the causal sequence. Some dualists wish to treat it as a distinctively mental event caused by, or at least following upon, the excitation which occurs in the cerebral cortex. In this case we should think of event e_{n-1} as the last physiological event in the sequence (i.e. the appropriate excitation of the cerebral cortex). Others have wished to treat the final event, e_n, as itself a happening in the brain, a physical occurrence of some sort, which was, so to speak, possessed of a double aspect—the physical aspect being the physiological event, the mental aspect being our consciousness of something. Others might wish to deny that there was anything 'mentalistic' involved at all. Since I do not want to become embroiled in this sort of dispute, I shall simply refer to e_n as the *terminal stage* in the standard causal sequence associated with 'seeing a coffee pot'.

If the sequence e_1, e_2, . . . e_n is interrupted at any stage, by inserting a barrier between S and the coffee pot, by S's closing his eyes, or by some severe damage to S's nervous system, then the latter members of this sequence will not occur and S will not (as we commonly say) see the coffee pot. Nonetheless, the terminal stage in this sequence of events, or something very much like the standard terminal stage, that which does not normally occur until e_1 through e_{n-1} have occurred, can occur without these particular causal antecedents. We might, theoretically at least, stimulate S's cerebral cortex by a set of electrodes and thereby create for S a visual experience which was, from its subjective side, indistinguishable from the one that was initiated by light from the coffee pot in the standard or normal case. Or, if S is suffering from some kind of hallucination, the last member (or something very much like the last member) of our standard sequence may occur, or the latter members of it may occur, without the usual antecedents; S might (if he makes a mistake) describe himself as seeing a coffee pot when there is no coffee pot which is reflecting light into his eyes.

Finally, to finish the account of the facts which are, I hope, scientifically sound (albeit sketchy) and philosophically neutral, there is a brief temporal interval, measurable perhaps only in microseconds, between the time when the light leaves the coffee pot and the occurrence of the terminal stage (i.e. between e_1 and e_n). When we speak of seeing the moon, the sun, or the stars, the temporal interval becomes appreciable. In some of these cases one can legitimately speak of the causal sequence as beginning many years prior to the occurrence of the terminal event itself. This is sometimes expressed by saying that when we see a star we see it *as* it was many years ago, light requiring that long to reach us from the star.

So much for what I take to be the facts of the case. How do they lend themselves to philosophical exploitation? Well, if the above description is reasonably accurate, it seems to follow that the terminal stage itself is the most significant stage of the causal sequence; if it occurs, whatever its causal antecedents, then the percipient will undergo an experience which, in its subjective aspect, is indistinguishable from what he experiences when he (as we ordinarily say) really sees a coffee pot. But when he really sees a coffee pot, we want to say that the coffee pot looks some way to him. And this seems to suggest that within the terminal state itself there is something describable as a coffee-pot-looking-something, an element which he takes to be the coffee pot in the standard case and which he might mistakenly take to be a real coffee pot in the non-standard case. When this terminal event has the standard causal antecedents we ordinarily say that S sees a coffee pot (*the coffee pot* looks some way to S); when it does not have the standard causal antecedents, we say he is hallucinating or whatever—in this case it definitely is not a coffee pot which he might mistakenly take to be a coffee pot. But there is no significant difference between these two events aside from their causal antecedents. We seem forced to the view that in both the standard and the non-standard case an event occurs which may be described by saying that S is visually aware of something which he may or may not take to be a (real) coffee pot. In the non-standard case it is certainly not a coffee pot. But even in the standard case it cannot be said to be the coffee pot itself since, if for no other reason, the coffee pot may no longer exist when this terminal event occurs. Hence, we may say that a percipient is *directly* aware of the element which is cotemporaneous with the terminal event; when this terminal event has the standard causal antecedents we say that S sees the coffee pot, but this should now be understood to mean that S sees the coffee pot *indirectly* since it is not the coffee pot which looks some way to him. The coffee pot itself is merely associated with that causal sequence which terminates in an event (e_n) which, whether it has these antecedents or not, may be described by saying that *something* looks to him as we would ordinarily say the coffee pot looks to him. It is this something which he sees directly.

Something like this is behind every attempt to introduce a direct *vs.* an indirect way of seeing things by analyzing the causal processes of perception. The idea is that we are always, even in cases that are normally described by saying that we see an object of some sort, directly aware of an 'impression', 'percept', or 'sensation' which is aroused *in* us by the causal action of light. This is an extremely seductive argument, and I do not wish to belittle its persuasiveness. Nonetheless, there is one, perhaps two, mistakes in it. I think one of the confusions may be put this way. In hallucination (or artificial stimulation of the brain) we may have a visual experience, call it e_n', which is indistinguishable from the experience we have when we are said to see a real coffee pot—call this e_n. Now, since e_n and e_n' are (or may be) indistinguishable and in the case of e_n' it is clear that we are aware of something which is not a coffee pot (although we may take it to be a real coffee pot), then also in e_n, the so-called veridical case, we must be aware of something which is not a real coffee pot. The pattern of this argument is obviously fallacious. I may not be able to distinguish between S's handing me a genuine one-dollar bill (e_n) and S's handing me a counterfeit one-dollar bill (e_n'). If the counterfeit is good, these two events may be indistinguishable. Surely, however, we cannot conclude that because I am being handed a counterfeit bill in the one case, I must therefore be receiving a counterfeit bill in the other case. It may well be that in what we commonly refer to as the experience of seeing a coffee pot, there are other (hallucinatory) experiences which are indistinguishable from it. But this does not imply that the two sorts of experience involve an awareness of the same sorts of things. We can quite consistently maintain that in the standard case we are visually aware of the coffee pot, it is the coffee pot itself which looks some way to us, although this experience is indistinguishable (subjectively) from other experiences in which we are not aware of a coffee pot.

But I have not presented this argument in its strongest form. It is usually supplemented with what has been called the 'time-lag argument'. It goes something like this. When we see the coffee pot, the terminal stage in the causal sequence *could* occur at a time when the coffee pot no longer exists. This is easier to appreciate in the case of distant objects (stars), but even in routine cases the same feature is present although the temporal interval which makes this possible becomes extremely small. Let us consider, then, a standard causal sequence with this minor alteration: when the terminal event, e_n, occurs, the object which initiated the sequence the object which we ordinarily say we see, has ceased to exist. Certainly this catastrophic incident will not affect the character of e_n since the object has already (before it ceases to exist) exercised all the causal influence on e_n of which it is capable. Now, when e_n occurs the percipient has the experience which is ordinarily described by saying that he sees the object. Yet, in this case, the object no longer exists. The percipient is aware of something which looks like a coffee pot, but this something *cannot* be the coffee pot itself. And if this is so, it indicates that the percipient is *always* directly aware of something other than the coffee pot; for whether or not the coffee pot ceases to exist makes no difference to the character of the terminal event, and we have just shown that this terminal event may be described by saying that something other than a coffee pot looks some way (e.g. like a coffee pot) to the percipient. Being *directly aware* of something is a state of affairs which implies that the element of which one is directly aware *must* exist at the time one is directly aware of it. Since science has shown us that coffee pots need not exist at the time when, as we ordinarily say, we see them, we must conclude that we are never directly aware of coffee pots—nor anything else the perception of which involves a causal sequence involving a temporal interval.

Some philosophers have resorted to heroic methods to avoid this conclusion. They have suggested, for instance, that 'seeing D' is an activity which *begins* at the moment when the light rays (which eventually enter our eyes) are reflected from D.[1] That is, the concept of 'seeing' is stretched far enough backward in time to ensure the existence of the objects which we see—at least they must exist when we 'begin' to see them. I call this method 'heroic' because it seems to be an outright sacrifice of common sense in order to save common sense. For if we adopt this alternative, we must say that we begin to see the star many years before we (as we ordinarily say) see it. In fact, we may begin to see the stars before we are born (or even conceived) and finish seeing them when we

[1] See, for instance, R. J. Hirst, *The Problems of Perception*, p. 308.

are four years old.[1] There is nothing preventing one from talking this way, I suppose, but I do not think one will be talking about 'seeing something' as this is ordinarily understood. For I think it is part of what we mean when we say of S that he saw D that he began to see D, or he first saw D, when and only when D began to look some way to S or, to put it in terms of the causal analysis, only when the causal sequence first reached a terminal stage, e_n.

I think we must conclude, then, that if someone builds into the notion of 'direct awareness' the idea that the object of which we are directly aware must (logically must) exist at the time we are directly aware of it, then (given the finite velocity of light and the transmission of electrical impulses) we are not directly aware of such things as coffee pots when, as we ordinarily say, we see them. I do not see how this conclusion can be avoided. But proponents of this view have gone on to draw a much stronger conclusion than the one I have just conceded, a conclusion that is totally unsupported by anything that has already been admitted. They have gone on to draw the conclusion that we *are* directly aware of *something* when we see a coffee pot. Where does this conclusion come from? Consider an analogy. We all know what is involved in receiving a message from D. D may signal us with a flag, send us a letter, call us on the telephone, or speak to us on the radio. Suppose, now, that I define a new notion, 'directly receiving a message from D', such that this is only possible on the condition that D must (logically must) exist at the time I directly receive his message. It follows immediately that I do not directly receive messages, either by radio, telephone, or letter, from distant friends. In each case my friend could have ceased to exist before I received his message.[2] Of course, if someone hands me his message in person, we might say that I received his message directly. But in cases where I did not receive D's message directly, does it follow that there is someone or something from whom I did receive a message directly? Is there anything to which I must be related by this newly defined relation? I do not see why there should be. When the

---

[1] Hirst concedes the oddity of these consequences but shrugs them off with the observation that our ordinary ways of speaking are 'theoretically very unsatisfactory', (*ibid.*, p. 308).

[2] Although in the case of the telephone and radio, his message would have to be very brief indeed if we suppose that he ceased to exist before I *started* to receive his message.

postman hands me the letter from my distant cousin, I am not directly receiving a message from my cousin. From whom am I directly receiving a message? The postman? But if we say this, then we are completely altering the original *meaning* of 'receiving a message from'. Originally this meant that the person from whom I received the message *composed it*; it is now being taken to mean 'the person *who hands me* the composed message'. Or suppose Martians signal us by radio. We are not directly receiving a message from them. From whom or what are we directly receiving a message? From the radio waves which eventually reach us? If so, and I do not know of any other suitable candidate for 'the thing which *must* exist at the time we receive the message', then we are interpreting the phrase 'receiving a message from' in such an eccentric way that it is positively misleading to continue using it in the phrase '*directly* receiving a message from'. For we are now interpreting the latter phrase in such a way that we can be related by it to such things as electromagnetic waves. In short, we can directly receive messages from things which it does not even make sense to suppose we received a message from (in anything like the original sense of these words).

If the term 'awareness' ('sees' or 'perceives') is to have anything like its normal sense, anything like the sense it has in 'S is aware of (sees or perceives) the coffee pot', then it does not follow that S must be directly aware of something or see something directly when he sees the coffee pot. If one wishes to insist that he must be directly aware of something when he sees the coffee pot, then one must be prepared to admit that the statement 'S is directly aware of D' does not imply that D is even the sort of thing which it makes sense to suppose someone aware of (in the original sense of this term). D need not be the sort of thing which can be colored, or even look colored—anymore than radio waves need be the sort of thing which can compose messages. The only condition D must satisfy is that D must necessarily exist at the time when we (as we ordinarily say) see the coffee pot. And if we cast around for what this might be, it is not difficult to find the natural candidate: it is simply *the coffee pot's looking some way to S*. For this state of affairs is necessarily involved in S's seeing the coffee pot, it is simultaneous with his seeing the coffee pot (indeed, it is just an expression for the terminal stage of the causal sequence—e_n), and *it can occur when the coffee pot no longer exists*. This, in fact, is precisely what the scientific facts show us: that the coffee pot *can* continue to look some way to us *after* it has ceased to exist. The fact that the coffee pot's looking some way to S does not sound like the sort of thing of which S can be aware (it certainly is not colored or shaped like a coffee pot) should not disturb us; for there is nothing which should lead us to believe that being *directly aware* of this sort of thing is anything like being aware of something.

I conclude, then, that if someone wants to define a sense of 'direct awareness' ('immediate acquaintance', 'sensing') which has built into it the idea that the elements of which we are directly aware *must* exist at the time we are directly aware of them, then, in those cases which are ordinarily described by saying that we see a physical object, D, either (i) there is nothing of which we are directly aware or (ii) the meaning of the term 'aware' has been so shifted that the phrase 'S is directly aware of A' is but an alternative way of describing the state of affairs which I have expressed by saying that D looks some way to S. And there is nothing in all of this which should suggest the conclusion that when we see a coffee pot, this visual achievement is mediated by our direct awareness of something other than a coffee pot.

7. *Conclusion*

One occasionally hears it said that if one systematically strips away from a given perceptual act all the accretions due to past experience, all the collateral information, anticipations, interpretive and inferential elements, all the habitual or conditioned associations, then one will be left with a 'pure sensory core'—the *given of sense experience*. Such 'stripping operations' are taken very seriously by those who propose them. We begin by seeing a plump juicy tomato and finish by being told that all that is really *given* is a bulgy red patch, not really edible at all. What I have tried to show in this chapter is that we have a way of seeing plump juicy tomatoes which, when subjected to this 'stripping operation', leaves, as the sensory core or the directly given, *precisely the same plump juicy tomato with which we began*. If S, as we commonly say, sees a tomato, then we can supply him with the mentality of a one-year-old, take away all his past experience of tomatoes, subtract whatever beliefs he has about the tomato, allow him no inferences or interpretations, give him nothing that is not indubitable from the experience itself, and we are left with a simple residue: S's seeing a tomato. The tomato *is* the sensory core, the directly given, if these phrases are meant to signify what it is that S sees when this is purified of all inferential, interpretive, and discursive or associational elements.

What this suggests, and it has a way of appearing trivial when bluntly stated, is that what we see in this first way of seeing is a function solely of what there is to see and what, given our visual apparatus and the conditions in which we employ it, we are capable of visually differentiating. If the subtleties of epistemology are relevant to what we see, or what we directly see, they must be related to ways of seeing objects and events other than the way we have examined in this chapter. Such traditional areas of philosophical specialization as knowledge, certainty, illusion, the indubitable or incorrigible, justification, reasons, evidence, and so on must (if they are relevant at all) be related to whether we can see how a thing is behaving, *what* properties it has, *whether* it is changing, and so on. For what we see, in these latter ways, does seem to be inextricably related to a host of new variables, many of them epistemological in character, from which our first way of seeing is immune.

Nevertheless, a proper appreciation of this first way of seeing is absolutely essential; without it one cannot achieve a coherent picture of perception in general. For epistemic ways of seeing, the ways of seeing which will be examined in the following chapters, all have one feature in common: *viz.* nothing can be seen in these ways without acquiring some true belief about what is seen. For example, one cannot see that something is a table without at least believing that it is a table. What this suggests is that *what we see*, in an *epistemic* way, can be influenced by all those variables that are capable of influencing what we believe. If one's past experience, one's conceptual categories, modes of classification, and habits of association, have any influence on what one believes or what one can, in a given situation, come to believe, then they thereby have a commensurate influence on *what one can see* in the epistemic way of seeing. This, in turn, implies that *what one sees* (in the epistemic way) is relative to a greater or less extent on such factors. Therefore, if there was no non-epistemic way of seeing objects and events (seeing$_n$), one would be led to suppose that people who possessed radically different beliefs, or diverged significantly in conceptual orientation, did not, indeed could not, see the same things. The expert and the novice, the sophisticate and the savage, looking at the same thing, would see different things; and this is but a prelude to the view that we each have our *private* perceptual world.

Hopefully, the discussion in this chapter has provided an answer to this line of argument. One can freely acknowledge the relativity inherent in *other* ways of seeing, a relativity which depends on the conceptual background, past experience, and modes of association of the individual percipient, *without undermining the objectivity and publicity of what we see.* For the objectivity and publicity of this world resides in the fact that we can all, *regardless* of our conceptual background, associative talents, inferential skill, or past experience, see_n the same objects and events. However much we may differ from one another in what we can *see to be the case* in relation to these objects and events, almost all of us are similarly endowed to see (see_n) the objects and events themselves. The relativity of perception resides in those ways of seeing which provide us with *information* about what is seen, and it is to these 'epistemic' ways of seeing that we must now turn.

III

SEEING AND KNOWING

Although we can see the objects and events in our environment without recognizing or identifying them in any way, our sense of sight is generally credited with being one of our chief resources for discovering the content and character of our surroundings. Wherein, then, lies the epistemic importance of vision? If we can see the water (which is boiling) without seeing that it is boiling, without even seeing that it is water, what sort of additional achievement is reflected by our seeing that it is water and that it is boiling? Is this another distinctively visual ability, supplemental to seeing$_n$ the boiling water, which somehow informs us that what we are seeing is boiling water? Or does it, rather, reflect a purely conceptual achievement, some sort of mental manufacturing of the knowledge that the water is boiling out of the epistemically neutral results of seeing the boiling water?

1. *Primary Epistemic Seeing*

I shall proceed by describing a situation or state of affairs in which sentient beings, particularly human beings, often find themselves. When a sentient being is in this position, I shall say that he sees (or, occasionally, 'can see') that b is P in a *primary epistemic way*. In this chapter I confine my attention to what might be called non-relational states of affairs (i.e. that b is P, where 'P' is meant to be some non-relational predicate); in the first section of the following chapter I shall extend the notion of primary epistemic seeing to relational states of affairs (seeing that b is R to c). I shall also describe *other ways* of seeing things epistemically, but each of these can best be understood as an embellishment on, or extension of, the fundamental form of epistemic seeing described in this chapter and, for relations, the first section of the following chapter.

I shall state and discuss four conditions, numbering them for future reference. First, then, S sees that b is P in a primary epistemic way only if:

(i) b is P

The necessity of this condition does not preclude, of course, someone's (mistakenly) supposing he sees that b is P when b is not P. Nor does it preclude the possibility of S_1's seeing that b is P when S_2 sees that b is not P when S_1 and S_2 are using the term 'P' in different ways. For example, one might encounter this sort of divergence with respect to whether a person is pretty, bald, graceful, well dressed, and so on. I do not think there is any particular difficulty with such cases. It simply must be understood that in the sense of the words in which S sees that b is P, b must be P.

Secondly, S sees that b is P in a primary epistemic fashion only if:

(ii) S sees$_n$ b

The expression of this condition draws upon the entire discussion of Chapter II, and since I have already gone to considerable lengths to clarify what is, and what is not, involved in seeing something in a non-epistemic fashion (seeing$_n$), I shall confine my remarks to an explanation of why this condition is imposed.

There are a variety of uses of the construction 'see that' (and related expressions) which need not satisfy anything like condition (ii). One can see (by the newspapers) that the President is ill; one can see (by the gauge) that the battery is discharging, see (by her note) that she has gone shopping, and so on. At least we say such things, and it is fairly clear that we say them with a full realization that the President, the battery, and the person are not (or need not) themselves be seen. I can see that someone has been trampling on my daffodils without seeing anyone. I do not wish to legislate these cases out of existence; on the contrary, I shall undertake a full analysis of them in later chapters. I shall refer to such cases as instances of seeing that b is P in a *secondary* epistemic way, but I wish it to be clearly understood that the term 'secondary' is not being used in any philosophically pejorative sense. The terms 'primary' and 'secondary' are being used merely to contrast two different situations: the cases where we see that b is P *by seeing b itself*, and the cases where we see that *b* is P *without seeing b*.[1] I shall later argue that primary epistemic seeing is inextricably involved in secondary epistemic seeing, and in this sense it is more fundamental. But until we can go into this matter at greater length, I do not wish to suggest that secondary epistemic seeing is a-not-quite-fully-visual achievement or that to see that *b* is P in a secondary way is to be less secure in the knowledge that *b* is P. As things now stand, the terms 'primary' and 'secondary' refer simply to a differential satisfaction of condition (ii).

Furthermore, there are various epistemic uses of the verb 'to see' which have little or nothing to do with our visual endowments. We say (of a blind man) that he can see what we mean; a mother sees that her child has a fever by touching his forehead; and we might see how our friend's new high fidelity system sounds by (what else?) listening. I think it is undeniable that we talk this way. I think it is also undeniable that in such cases nothing resembling (ii) need be satisfied; there is no essential deployment of one's visual resources. And this brings us to the unmistakable fact that the 'seeing that' construction is not restricted to describing our *acquisition* of knowledge by *visual* means (nor are certain related expressions—e.g. seeing what, seeing whether). To say that *S* sees (or I see) that so-and-so is the case is frequently to suggest nothing more than that *S* realizes (I realize) that so-and-so is the case. We may quickly concede this point, however, without deflecting the thrust of the present discussion. For I am attempting (both in the present schema and in later schemata) to specify a type of situation which is *both* epistemic in character *and* essentially visual in nature, a type of situation which represents *the acquisition of knowledge by visual means*, a type of situation which is frequently, but certainly not always, described by the 'seeing that' construction.[2] In a cer-

---

[1] This method of expressing the contrast is not quite accurate, but it will do for the moment. The real contrast lies in whether or not it is the way *b* looks that is instrumental in our seeing that *b* is P.

[2] As suggested earlier (Section 3, Chapter II), the statement '*S* saw the *Queen Mary* arrive this morning' carries epistemic *utterance* implications unless qualifications are made to the reverse (i.e. our *saying* this about *S* suggests that he identified the event in the way described). Hence, this form of expression often replaces a more explicitly epistemic report (e.g. '*S* saw that . . .'). This has the advantage of emphasizing the fact that *S* saw that the *Queen Mary* was arriving *by seeing the Queen Mary itself*—i.e. in a *primary epistemic* way.

tain broad sense, a sense which should become clearer as the topic is developed, I am trying to provide an analytic description of those states of affairs which are described by statements of the form '*S* sees that *b* is *P*' *in so far as they tell us how S knows that b is P*. The present schema for *primary* epistemic seeing represents a particularly important sub-class in this group of cases—a sub-class which we are inclined to associate with such phrases as 'eye-witness report', 'first-hand observation', and 'direct testimony of the senses'.

This should help to explain the presence of (ii). Within what might be called *justificatory* contexts, settings in which the claim to have seen that *b* was *P* functions as an answer to the query '*How* do you know that *b* was *P*?', the *unqualified* response 'I saw that it was *P*' implies that (ii) was satisfied. If one never saw the flowers, and one purports to know that they were roses, then to the question 'How do you know they were roses?' one does not have available the *unqualified* answer 'I saw (or could see) that they were roses'. For in such justificatory contexts this answer, unqualified the way it is, inevitably suggests that one saw that they were roses *by seeing the flowers themselves*, that it was the way the flowers themselves looked that provided one with this piece of information.

I think, then, that condition (ii) becomes especially significant for subdividing the class of cases in which I am interested. This class of cases is, once again, those uses of the construction 'see that' which tell us *how S* knows that *b* is *P*. Hence, although I think it quite acceptable to say 'She could see that he had a fever' when she discovered this by *feeling* his hot forehead, this is not a use of the verb 'to see' in which I am interested; it is *not* a use of the verb which tells us *how* she knows he has a fever (although it tells us *that* she knows this). Furthermore, when the statement 'She could see that he had a fever' *is* designed to tell us how she knows he had a fever, we can distinguish two broad sub-classes. She might have seen that he had a fever *by looking at the thermometer*; this is what I have referred to as 'secondary epistemic seeing'. Or she might have seen that he had a fever by seeing (seeing$_n$) *him*—by the distinctive way *he* looked. It is this latter type of case which I am trying to depict by the schema for *primary* epistemic seeing; and for this form of seeing, for this way of knowing, it is essential to *seeing that b is P* that one see$_n$ *b* (this point will become clearer when we discuss clause (iii).) Even here, though, the situation is not always so simple; occasionally, even when condition (ii) is satisfied, we expect a more complete account. For example, 'I could see that you were angry *by* the expression on your face.' Here, even though the person who is angry is seen, and hence condition (ii) satisfied, we might demand a fuller explanation, the kind of explanation provided by the qualifying phrase 'by the expression on your face'.

I shall take these matters up again, both in reference to the third and fourth conditions and when discussing relationships in Chapter IV.[1] As things now stand we have an obviously incomplete account of what is involved in seeing that something is the case. If we take our first two conditions alone, the most that they entail is that S sees b which is P; they are quite consistent with S's not seeing that b is P. Our first two conditions, taken together, describe S's seeing a red barn; they do not tell us what additional elements are involved in S's seeing that the barn is red. The third and fourth conditions fill this gap.

S sees that b is P in a primary epistemic way only if:

(iii) The conditions under which S sees$_n$ b are such that b would not look, L, the way it now looks to S unless it was P.

I shall hereafter refer to the conditions mentioned in this clause as *background conditions*. B is a background condition if and only if (*a*) B is logically and causally independent of the (non-relational) features and properties of b itself (and, in particular, of b's being P), and (*b*) there are variations in B which affect the way b looks to S. The distance between S and b, the lighting conditions (*not* the reflected light—this is causally dependent on the properties of b itself), the angle from which S sees b, the medium through which S sees b, the state of S's eyes, nervous system, and brain (in so far as these are not causally dependent on his seeing b), what lies between S's eyes and b—all are, generally speaking, background condi-

[1] Section 1 of Chapter IV is concerned with the extension of the notion of primary epistemic seeing to relationships: seeing that b is R to c (e.g. seeing that the pencil is on the table). At that time I will discuss certain examples which might, at this point, be taken as counter-examples to what I have said about condition (ii). For instance, seeing that John is absent, that the money is gone, and that everyone has left do not involve (even in justificatory contexts) one's seeing John, the money, or everyone. I shall argue that these cases are best understood as seeing that some *relationship* does *not* obtain (where the analogue of (ii) is satisfied).

tions.[1] Normally, any one of these can be varied to produce a
corresponding alteration in the way b looks to S without altering the fact that b is P. This is not to say, of course, that every
variation in one of these background conditions produces
some corresponding variation in the way b looks to S; all that is
required is that there be some variation which produces such a
change.

We might think of this condition as an *enabling* condition. If it
is satisfied, S is, so to speak, in a position to see that b is P. He has
the opportunity although (see clause (iv)) he may not exploit it.
But if this clause is not satisfied, if the background conditions are
such that b somethimes looks this way (L) to S when it is not P,
or (in the event that b always happens to be P, or always happens
to be P when S sees it) might, by a suitable combination of other
features, still look the same to S under these conditions without
being P, then whatever S may think himself able to do, he is not
able to see that b is P (under these background conditions). For if
the background conditions are such that b might look the same to
S without being P, then (iii) is unsatisfied; it is not true that in
these conditions b *would not* look the way it does to S *unless* it were
P.[2]

It cannot be too strongly emphasized, however, that (iii) is
meant to express an empirical regularity between b's being P and
b's looking the way it does to S. It is not that in these background
conditions b must *logically* be P if it looks this way to S. It is rather
that, as a matter of the empirical uniformities which obtain in these
conditions, there is no other feature or combination of features

[1] Of course, if we see that b is *far away* (or *nearby*), the distance between
S and b is not, without restriction, a background condition. This, however,
is an example of a relational state of affairs, and I shall discuss these cases
later.

[2] Some values of 'P' call for special comment in this regard. When S sees
that *the* animal is a racoon or sees that *that* man is his father we cannot say
that *the animal* (or *that* man) would look different to S if it were not a racoon
(if it were not his father); for, of course, since *the* animal *is* a racoon, since
that man *is* his father, it is not altogether clear what could be meant by
supposing that the racoon was not a racoon or his father not his father. I
shall return to this particular matter again in relation to clause (iv), but it
should be understood that in such cases as this, clause (iii) is satisfied if
and only if, under these background conditions, no *animal* (no *man*) would
look the way *this* animal (*that* man) now looks to S unless it was a racoon
(unless it was his father).

which would result in b's looking the way it does to S *besides* b's being P. In these background conditions b's being P is a necessary (not logically necessary) condition for b's looking the way it does to S; and b's looking the way it does is, together with the prevailing background conditions, a sufficient (not logically sufficient) condition for b's being P. To illustrate the force of this clause, consider the following cases. Suppose that, as a matter of sheer coincidence, all the picket fences happen to be gray. Such a correlation between something's being a picket fence and its being gray, although it happens to be universal (there are no picket fences which are not gray), is not the kind of correlation which will permit a color-blind man who can recognize picket fences to see that the fence is gray (or, more precisely, to *know* that the fence is gray *by seeing* that it is gray). If he is acquainted with the above-mentioned correlation, he may of course realize that the fence is gray as soon as he sees that it is a picket fence. But he cannot see that it is gray, and the reason he cannot is that (iii) fails to be satisfied; it is simply not true that in these conditions (assuming them normal in every other respect) the fence would not look the way it does to him *unless* it was gray. For it *would* (given his color-blindness) look the same to him were it red or green. Or suppose a man is frowning, and he is frowning because he is worried about his medical bills. This fact *alone* does not permit us to see that he is worried (by the frown on his face); what must first be established (in relation to clause (iii) at least) is that in these visual (background) conditions he *would* not look this way (i.e. frowning) *unless* he was worried, that there are no *other* circumstances which would lead him to frown (e.g. perplexity), that he *only* frowns *when* he is worried. The man may *look as though* he is worried, but we cannot see that he is worried (and, thereby, *know* that he is worried) if he looks the same way when he is simply perplexed, or might look the same way for a variety of other reasons.

There are a number of different ways in which (iii) may fail to be satisfied. The background conditions may not be right; S may be too far away to see whether the animal is a racoon or not. Although it *is* a racoon, a beaver (or any number of other small animals) would look the same to S from this distance. Or the viewing conditions may be optimal, in a sense, but the fact is that b does not look any characteristic way (L) when it is P. The challenge 'How could you have seen that b was P?' is sometimes prompted by a suspicion of this sort. Granting that you saw her, and granting (as we now know) that she was ill, how could you have seen that she was ill. She looked the way she always looks—healthy and vigorous. You were just guessing.

Suppose there is some dispute about the object on the table. I pick it up, examine it, and announce that it is my lighter. When asked how I know this, I reply that I can see that it is ('Look, my initials are on it.'). Whether or not I do see what I claim to see depends on the satisfaction of condition (iii); given the conditions which affect the way the object looks to me (i.e. the background conditions), is it true that the object would not look the way it now looks to me unless it was my lighter? Clearly, the answer to this question will depend on just how my lighter now looks to me and on whether there are *other* objects which would look the same to me under these background conditions. If Francis Donovan, who also happens to own a Zippo lighter with his initials engraved on it, is present, we will have to answer this question in the negative. Perhaps it *is* my lighter; nonetheless, I cannot see that it is— at least not if L, the particular way it looked to me, is understood to involve nothing more distinctive about the way the object looked to me than its being a Zippo with the initials 'F.D.' engraved on its side.

I have been parenthetically inserting the symbol 'L' at various points in this discussion and I should now like to indicate its purpose. 'L' is meant to be a constant designating the *totality*, as it were, of b's appearance to S. In talking about the *way* b appears to S, we may, of course, be talking about any one of the mutually distinguishable aspects of the way b looks to S, or, possibly, a composite of such aspects. For example, we might say that b looks red, round, fuzzy, and far away; it could, of course, look fuzzy and round without looking red and far away. Call any one of these particular aspects (say, b's looking red) Lj. Now, it may turn out that condition (iii) is satisfied with respect to Lj alone; i.e. conditions are such that b would not look red (Lj) to S unless it was P (red). What I wish to point out is that if condition (iii) is satisfied with respect to one of these 'sub-aspects' of the way b looks to S, then it will *also* be satisfied with respect to L; for L designates the total appearance of b and this includes all of the sub-aspects which might be distinguished within the total appearance of b. In other words, if b would not look red unless it were red, then it will also be true that b would not look red, round, fuzzy, and far away unless it were red.

The point just mentioned is a somewhat technical point, and I shall have little cause to refer to it in the course of my exposition—with certain important exceptions (see the discussion of condition (iv)). For this reason I shall generally express (iii) by saying, simply, that in these background conditions b would not look the way it now does to S unless it was P. But when it becomes important to do so, I shall make explicit the fact that 'the way b now looks to S' is meant to refer to the totality of the way b looks to S—to that 'composite' formed out of all the mutually distinguishable sub-aspects of the way b looks to S.

While playing cards I may suppose myself able to see where the cards are coming from. Yet, I may be wrong in this supposition. True, the cards *are* coming from the top of the deck, but with *that* pair of hands, under these conditions, a card coming from the bottom looks the same as one coming from the top. *This* dealer is a very clever fellow; long hours of practice have enabled him to make one event indistinguishable from the other (to most casual card players). Hence, even though all the cards are coming from the top, even though one believes they are, even believes that one can see that they are, one may not, in fact, be able to see this. With *this* dealer condition (iii) fails to be satisfied. This should not be taken to imply, though, that it also fails to be satisfied when one's younger sister is dealing.

Whenever anyone purports to know that b is P by virtue of having seen that b is P, this person commits himself to the satisfaction of condition (iii) at the time at which he saw that b was P. That is, if he claims to have seen that b was P, and it is clear that he did this by seeing b itself, then his assertion implies that he saw b under the sort of conditions described in (iii). If these conditions did not obtain, and we have reason to believe they did not obtain, we may justifiably reject the perceptual claim. It may seem to some as if condition (iii) is much too strong. It may be supposed, for instance, that the conditions need only be such that it is *highly probable* that b is P or that b, when it looks the way it does under these conditions, is *most likely* P. If we substituted such a modified condition for the one I have provided, we would certainly make it easier to see what is the case. *But we would make it too easy.* It would be *too* easy, not because I am interested in imposing artificially tough standards on what we can truly say about what we see, but because I believe these tougher standards are already inherent in our ordinary use of the construction 'see that' in justificatory contexts. For example, suppose that you see b under a set of conditions, C, when it is, in fact, P. Furthermore, suppose that when b looks the way it now looks to you (under conditions C), nine times out of ten it is P. Occasionally (10% of the time) it looks this way, under these conditions, when it is not P. Could you, in such circumstances, see that it was P? Suppose we raise the ratio to ninety-nine out of one hundred. Now it is highly probable (99% probable) that, looking the way it does, b is P. Do you, in these conditions, see that b is P? We are assuming, of course, that b is P; the question is whether you can see that it is. I think one must answer 'No' to these questions. Seeing that b is P is not an achievement which leaves room for the qualification '. . . but, of course, b sometimes looks this way under these conditions when it is not P'. For such a qualification immediately raises the question: 'How, then, can you see that it is P under these conditions?' You may have excellent grounds, given these probabilities, for supposing that b *is* P, but you did not *see that it was*. When one asserts that one has seen that b was P, one does so with the firm conviction that the possibilities for b *not* being P have been ruled out. One may always be mistaken in this conviction, of course, but nonetheless, the conviction is there that something resembling condition (iii) has been satisfied and not simply some probabilistic alternative. And this suggests that condition (iii), and not some diluted form of it, is inherent in our ordinary use of 'seeing that' construction—especially those which occur in justificatory settings, settings in which the response 'I saw that b was P' is intended to tell one's listeners *how* one knows that b is P.

I shall have much more to say about this particular clause in later sections of this chapter. I want particularly to examine the philosophical query as to whether anything resembling (iii) *can* be satisfied in routine perceptual situations. And related to this point is another possible challenge to this condition: namely, that condition (iii) should be *even stronger*. That is, not only must the conditions be such that b only looks the way it does to S when it is P, but the conditions must be such that *nothing* looks to S the way b now looks unless it is P—or, stronger yet, nothing looks this way unless it is b which is P. For the moment, though, I think I have said enough about this third condition to justify its tentative inclusion as a necessary condition for seeing something in a primary epistemic way.

Finally, S sees that b is P in a primary epistemic way only if:

(iv) S, believing the conditions are as described in (iii), takes b to be P.

The statement of this final necessary condition completes the statement of the sufficient condition; (i)–(iv), taken together, are sufficient to truly say of S that he sees that b is P. My statement of this final condition, especially the phrase 'believing the conditions are as described in (iii)', has a good deal more packed into it than might be supposed. But before I 'unpack' it, let me illustrate the function of this fourth condition.

I think it is fairly clear that conditions (i)–(iii) do not themselves constitute a sufficient condition for seeing that b is P in any ordinary sense. It is not enough, for example, to see an empty bottle in conditions such that the bottle would not look the way it does to you unless it were empty. One might see it in these conditions and still not see that it was empty. If the bottle is sitting on the table across the room, and I believe (mistakenly) that it is the gin bottle, then I might believe myself unable to see whether it is empty or not from this distance. Someone else, however, knowing that it is the bourbon bottle, might quickly claim that he could see that it was empty. Leaving aside for the moment the question of whether he can *really* see what he claims to see, the fact is that both of us satisfy conditions (i)–(iii); we both see the bottle, it is empty, and we both see it under a set of background conditions such that if it were not empty (for all practical drinking purposes) it would not look the way it now does to us (bourbon being a brownish liquid and easily visible at this distance). The only difference between my companion and myself is that he satisfies condition (iv), or something like it, and I do not. I do not believe that the conditions are as described in (iii). I think it is the gin bottle, and, hence, believe that it would look the same to me (from this distance) whether it was full, partially full, or empty.

The source of many mistaken perceptual claims lies in the fulfillment of condition (iv) without a corresponding fulfillment of (iii). That is, the agent believes the conditions are as described in (iii), but, in point of fact, these conditions do not obtain. His mistaken belief leads him to take b as P, but the conditions under which he sees b are such that the way b looks to him is not reliably correlated with its being P. Even though b is P, we may convince him that his perceptual claim was extravagant; that is, he may not be mistaken in his belief that b is P, but he may be mistaken in believing that he sees that b is P. We might convince him of this by repeating the situation, by reconstructing the same circumstances, and showing him that although b still looks the same to him as it did on the previous occasion, it is not P this time. If someone supposes himself able to 'spot' F.B.I. agents, and he bases his extraordinary claim on one or two successful identifications, we may (if we care to take the trouble) attempt to show him that his discriminatory powers are not what he thinks them to be. Various men (and women) could be brought before him, and the man asked to identify the F.B.I. agents among them. Most of us (F.B.I. agents in particular) would expect only a random degree of success—a degree of success consistent with guessing. Conceivably, of course, the man could continue to score 100%. At this point we might begin to suspect that he could see what he claimed to see, and we might want to know what it was about the way these people looked that 'told' him they were agents of the F.B.I. On what sub-aspect Lj of the way they looked was he relying? He need not be able to tell us, of course (see Section 3), but we would no doubt be interested in knowing specifically, and in some detail, how condition (iii) was being fulfilled. That it *is* being fulfilled, and that he believes it to be fulfilled, seems to be supported by the fellow's extraordinary accuracy and by the fact that he believes himself able to *see* which persons are the agents.

The last example brings up a subtlety to which I have only briefly alluded in my discussion of clause (iii). Suppose that S, uncommonly ignorant of dogs, believes that any large brown dog is a boxer. He takes this set of features to be distinctive of boxers. Confronted, then, with a large brown dog (which *is* a boxer), S quickly identifies it as a boxer. When asked how he knows it is a boxer, he responds by saying he can see that it is a boxer. Question: does he see that the dog is a boxer? Conditions (i) and (ii) are satisfied, and since there is (let us say) a distinctive appearance to a boxer, it seems as though we must admit that (iii) is also satisfied. Under these background conditions (normal in every respect) the dog would not look, L, the way it now does to S unless it was a boxer.

Finally, it would seem that S satisfies something like condition (iv); believing that the conditions are such that the dog would not look the way it does to him unless it was a boxer, he takes it to be a boxer. But here we come to the point of this example. Condition (iii) is expressed in terms of L, the total appearance of the dog; S, however, believes (iii) is satisfied with respect to two non-distinctive aspects of the way the dog looks—those aspects of the way the dog looks which have to do, simply, with its color and its size. Nonetheless, it might be charged that since these latter two aspects are sub-aspects of the total appearance of the dog, L, S must believe that condition (iii) is satisfied with respect to L; that is, he must believe that conditions are as described in (iii). For if he believes that the dog would not look large and brown to him unless it was a boxer, he must also believe that it would not look the way it now does to him (in regard to its total appearance, L, which includes it looking large and brown) unless it was a boxer. Hence, it would seem that we can say that S, under the circumstances, satisfies condition (iv); and since the remaining three conditions are satisfied, we must conclude (according to this analysis) that S sees that the dog is a boxer. But surely this is wrong!

We are now in a position to partially 'unpack' the pertinent phrase in clause (iv). When it is said that S, *believing conditions are as described in* (iii), takes b to be P, the embedded phrase must be taken to mean not simply that S believes that the conditions are such that b would not look (in total appearance: L) the way it now does to him unless it were P but also that *if* S believes this in virtue of a belief that (iii) is satisfied with respect to some sub-aspect of L, call it Lj, then, in fact, condition (iii) must be satisfied with respect to Lj. By a sub-aspect of L, I simply mean any specific way in which b may be said to look to S which is such that b's looking L to S includes or comprehends b's looking this specific way to S, but not vice versa. This is simply another way of stipulating that S's belief in the satisfaction of (iii), a belief which condition (iv) describes him as having, must not be the result of, or in any way depend on, a mistaken belief in the distinctiveness of any sub-aspect of b's total appearance.

This talk of 'aspects' in contrast to the 'total appearance', and my use of subscripts to indicate the various 'sub-aspects', is, of course, artificial and highly idealized. When it comes to the question of actually describing what it is about the way a thing looks which 'tells us' that it is P, the majority of us are largely inarticulate. Generally, we can say little more than that it looks like a boxer or whatever. But the above discussion is not primarily concerned with the way people describe the way things look to them. It is concerned with what it is *on which* people rely as the significant aspects of the way b looks to them when they suppose themselves able to see that it is P. And what the discussion (admittedly over-formalized) is designed to make clear is that even when people are correct in taking b to be P, even when they suppose themselves able to see that b is P, even when conditions are completely routine and such that b would not have looked (L) the way it did to them unless it had been P, still a person may fail to see that b is P by virtue of a misplaced reliance on irrelevant aspects of the way b looks to them. This will not, as a rule, be manifest in what they say, but it can often be exhibited by an appropriate manipulation of what they see. In our example, we need only confront S with a large brown Labrador to reveal the defectiveness of his powers of detection; for he will suppose himself able to see that *this dog* is also a boxer. What I have tried to emphasize here is that when this occurs, S did not see that the dog was a boxer *even when it was a boxer*. Correct identification on visual grounds alone, even when condition (iii) is satisfied, is still not enough to allow us to say that S saw that b was P. He must also satisfy (iv), and (iv) entails that he not only believe that (iii) is satisfied with respect to L (the total appearance of b) but that he not believe this as a result of any mistaken belief in the distinctiveness of any sub-aspect of the way b looks to him.

There are other important features of clause (iv), but I must temporarily postpone their discussion (see Section 3 of this chapter).[1] For the present I would like to settle for one or two general remarks. First, it should be noted that S may *already* believe that b is P when he fulfills these four conditions. He may even have independently good reasons for so believing. S may have been told, before he entered the patient's room, that the patient was deathly ill. But this fact is irrelevant to whether S can see that the patient is deathly ill after he enters the room. We must still ask about the satisfaction of (iii) and (iv). S can see the patient, the patient can

[1] There is, in particular, another important restriction to be imposed on the phrase 'believing conditions are as described in (iii)', but this additional restriction can best be discussed after Section 2 of this chapter.

be deathly ill, S can believe this, even be prepared to say that he knows he is deathly ill (from what the doctors have told him), and S may even wish to say that the patient *looks as though* he is terribly ill. Still, given all of this, S may not be able to see that he is deathly ill. He may be prevented by a failure of (iii): e.g. the patient (a notorious fake) sometimes gives this appearance merely in order to elicit sympathy. Or (iii) may be satisfied (he simply could not get himself up to look *this* way unless he were really deathly ill), but S may be prevented from seeing that he is deathly ill through a failure of (iv): S simply does not believe (iii) satisfied. He (mistakenly) thinks that the fellow is such an accomplished fake that he could make himself appear this way, L, without being ill at all. Hence, whatever the actual status of (iii), and whatever my actual epistemic state in relation to the fact that the patient is ill (belief? knowledge?), I may fail to see that the patient is deathly ill because of my failure to satisfy (iv). Although I *take* the patient to be deathly ill, although I *know* he is deathly ill, I do not believe this or know this by virtue of a belief in the satisfaction of condition (iii).

A final comment. Let us suppose that people see$_n$ such things as after-images. Let us suppose, moreover, that it does not make much sense to suppose that an after-image is some other color than it appears to be, or some other shape than it appears to be. If we grant this much, then it follows that when we see an after-image we more or less automatically satisfy condition (i) through (iii) of our definition of primary epistemic seeing. That is, if S is having a purple after-image, then, according to the above assumptions, the following three things are true: (i) the after-image is purple; (ii) S sees$_n$ the after-image; and (iii) the conditions under which S sees$_n$ the after-image are such that the after-image only looks the way it does to S when it is purple. If it was not purple it would look different to S. From these facts (if they are facts) some philosophers have concluded that whenever we see an after-image we are always seeing it in some more or less excellent epistemic way, that we can always, without fear of mistake, see what color (or shape) the after-image is. Our discussion so far should have revealed why this conclusion is mistaken. For the 'having of an after-image' does *not* automatically imply that condition (iv) is satisfied. We can see the purple after-image and still not see that it is purple because we may fail to believe that the conditions are as described in (iii). It is quite possible, for instance, to (mistakenly) believe that the conditions are such that what we see *only* looks the way it does when it is red (and *not* purple). And it is possible to have this mistaken belief because it is possible to mistake the after-image for something quite different than an after-image—a textured area on the sofa, for instance. Hence, even if we admit that the seeing of certain things (after-images, hallucinatory images, etc.) implies an automatic satisfaction of conditions (i)–(iii), we still leave wide open the possibility of mistake, the possibility that the agent does not see what properties they have or mistakenly takes them to have properties they do not have. And these same remarks can be made about those entities which at one time figured so prominently in philosophical discussions of perceptions: *viz*. sense-data, sensa, or the given. Even if such things are the way the look, *by definition*, there is no automatic satisfaction of (i)–(iv). Seeing such things is no more mistake-free than is seeing a deathly-ill person who would not look the way he does unless he was deathly ill.

So much for general remarks. I would now like to raise an issue that has been (with some difficulty) kept below the surface throughout the preceding discussion: *viz*. the connection between seeing that b is P and our identification of b as b. Only after this has been fully clarified can we return to a discussion of the controversial elements in conditions (iii) and (iv).

2. *Proto-Knowledge*[1]

Our acquisition of knowledge by visual means is incremental in character, and it is the purpose of this section to illustrate this extremely important, but apparently overlooked, feature of epistemic seeing. In so doing we shall also gain a clearer understanding of one peculiar feature in clauses (iii) and (iv) of the schema in the previous section.

Consider the following dialogue:

Wife (from another room): I put some water on for tea; can you see whether it is boiling or not?

Husband (perfunctorily): Yes, it is.

Wife (suspiciously): Are you sure?

[1] An earlier, less developed, version of the material appearing in this section is contained in 'Seeing & Justification', a paper read to the Oberlin Philosophy Colloquium in 1967 and published in *Perception and Personal Identity*, edited by Norman S. Care and Robert H. Grimm, 1968.

Husband: Yes, I am sure. I can see that it is; I am looking right at it.
Wife: Are you sure that it is water?
Husband: ???

The last question is, to say the least, unusual. The husband was perfectly prepared to assure his wife that the water was boiling, and he felt no hestitation in assuring her of this since he could see that it was boiling. But he may not (from where he is standing) be able *to see that it is water*. It might, for all he is able to tell, be vodka or pear juice. Her original query is what led him to identify the liquid in the pan *as water*. It is on the basis of her original identifying reference that he is warranted in saying that he could see that *the water* was boiling.

This dialogue is meant to illustrate a single point. It can be put schematically as follows: within justificatory contexts the statement 'I can see that (this) *b* is *P*' although it entails that you know that (this) *b* is *P*, and although it tells us *how* you know that (this) *b* is *P*, *does not tell us* (*even in justificatory contexts*) *how you know that it is* (*a*) *b which you see to be* P. In the above dialogue we might admit that the husband knows that the water is boiling because he can see that it is boiling, but in saying this we do not commit ourselves to his having found out that it was water by having seen that it was water. If he knows that it (the liquid in the pan) is water, he presumably knows this because this is the way his wife referred to it and *she* ought to know what she put on the stove to boil.

Take a slightly different case. Suppose you convince yourself that the liquid in the bottle is, indeed, wine (and not just fruit juice or colored water) by tasting it. You then remark, half-way through the evening, that you can see that the wine is almost gone. Does this entail that you are able, or think yourself able, to see that the liquid in the bottle is wine? Of course not. You know it is wine by having *tasted* it, and you know that it (the wine) is almost gone because you can *see* that it is almost gone. One can see that the *b* is *P* without being able to see that it is *b* (or a *b*) which is *P*.[1]

The statement 'I can see that the *b* is *P*' is neutral with respect to *how* the percipient acquired the information which he exploits to make an identifying reference to what he sees to be *P*; it is neutral

[1] At this point a shift occurs in my use of the symbol '*b*'. Heretofore it was taken to include the articles 'a' and 'the' (or whatever term stood at the head of the noun phrase). I shall now make these explicit since their occurrence is especially significant to the point I am trying to make.

with respect to how he knows that it is a *b* which he sees to be *P*.[1]
The identification of the *b* as *b* (or a *b*) can be realized in any manner. I can run extensive investigations on the liquid in front of
me, subject it to chemical analysis, and listen to the findings of
experts as to its exact nature. When the results are in, and the
liquid has been positively identified as an acid, there is nothing to
prevent me from seeing (and saying that I see) that the acid is, say,
turning gray. The fact that I discovered that the liquid was an
acid by sniffing, listening, tasting, and feeling has nothing to do
with whether I can *see* that the acid is turning gray.

This point may strike some of my readers as rather trivial.
Nonetheless, I think it is of the utmost importance. For if we are
going to assess the validity of our commonsense perceptual claims,
as philosophers are wont to do, then we must be quite clear as to
what is, and what is not, being claimed in our commonsense perceptual reports. And if what I have just suggested is true, then we
must be extremely careful not to confuse *seeing that the water is
boiling* with *seeing that something is boiling water*. For if we conflate
these two achievements, if we treat them as a single achievement
described in alternative ways, then we will mistakenly suppose that
if someone cannot see that something is boiling water, neither can
he see that the water is boiling. And this is simply not true. Our
bemused husband could see that the water was boiling, but he
could not, from the same position and in the same circumstances,
see that it was boiling water. He could not see that it was boiling
water because he was unable, perhaps by his own admission, to
see whether it was *water* or not.

Why is it that someone may truly announce 'I can see that this
water is boiling' but not be able to truly announce, in the same
circumstances, 'I can see that this is boiling water'? I have already
given the reason. When we take the word 'water' out of the predicate position (this is *boiling water*) and place it into the subject position (this water is boiling), we thereby *alter* what it is we are claiming to have achieved. When I assert 'I can see that the water is
boiling' I am, in effect, telling you that I know it is water (but I am
not telling you *how* I know this), and I am telling you that I know
it is boiling (and I *am* telling you how I know this—I can see *that*
it is boiling). If, then, we put the word 'water' in the predicate

[1] For the moment I concentrate on reports in the first person, present tense.
This restriction shall be dropped later in the section.

position ('I can see that this is boiling water')[1] we are still telling the listener *that* we know it is water and *that* we know it is boiling, but we are also telling him *how* we know *both* of these things; we are telling him that we can both see that it is water and see that it is boiling. And this simple change makes all the difference. For I may, under certain circumstances, be able to see that the liquid (which I know to be water) is boiling without being able to *see that* the liquid is water. The fact that we can know that something is water in ways *other* than that of seeing that it is water is what makes it possible to see that the water is boiling without being able to see that it is boiling water.

In many cases, of course, we can see not only that the *b* is *P* but that it is, indeed, a *b* which is *P*. I can see not only that the dog is limping but that it is a dog which is limping. How do I know that the dog is limping? I can see that it is limping. How do I know that it is a dog which is limping? I can see that it is a dog. But the point which I am pressing is that our seeing that it is a dog, even our ability or capacity to see that it is a dog, is in no way involved in our ability to see that the dog is limping. I might *only* know that it is a dog because a committee of canine experts informed me that it was; up to this time I had never even seen a dog. Being completely ignorant of dogs and what they look like, I may be unable to *see that* anything is a dog; still, this does not prevent me from seeing that this dog is limping badly.

If I may be allowed the use of a special term, I would like to call *S*'s *proto-knowledge* that totality of information which *S* possesses about the identity or character of the *b* (which he sees to be *P*) at the time he sees that *b* is *P* minus only that increment in information whose *manner of acquisition* is described by saying that *S* can see that the *b* is *P*. It is this proto-knowledge that *S* exploits (in first-person, present-tensed, perceptual reports) to make identifying references to what he sees to be *P*.[2] Let my try to putt he matter diagramatically. These diagrams over simplify the case considerably, but I shall try to correct this in what follows.

[1] Without excessive emphasis on either the word 'boiling' or the word 'water'.
[2] I should point out that a person's proto-knowledge need not be something he knew *prior* to his seeing that *b* is *P*. *S* may see a brown dog and see (in one stroke, as it were) that it is a brown dog. If we say of him, however, that he could see that the dog was brown we *represent* the information that it was a dog he saw as part of his proto-knowledge since our statement does not describe the way he discovered this.

Diagram I: I can see that the water is boiling.

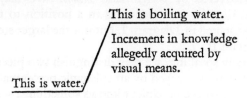

This is boiling water.

Increment in knowledge
allegedly acquired by
visual means.

This is water.

Diagram II: I can see that this (liquid) is boiling water.

This is boiling water.

Increment in knowledge
allegedly acquired by
visual means.

This is a liquid.

The lower (solid) horizontal line is, in each case, supposed to
reflect the percipient's level of proto-knowledge. In the first case
the statement does not tell us *how* the speaker identified the water
as water; it only tells us *how* the speaker discovered that the water
was *boiling*. In the second case the statement does tell us *how* the
percipient identified the liquid as water and, in particular, as
boiling water; it tells us that he could see that the liquid was both
water and boiling. Both statements depict the percipient as having
arrived at the same *terminal* point—the knowledge that what he is
seeing is boiling water—but they depict him as having arrived at
this terminal point *from* different starting points, from different
levels of proto-knowledge. Assuming for the moment that both
statements are true, the first statement represents the piece of information 'this is water' as part of the speaker's proto-knowledge
(since the first statement does not tell us *how* the speaker acquired
this information), whereas the second statement does not represent this information as part of the percipient's proto-knowledge
(since the second statement tells us *how* the speaker knows that it
is water). These statements describe different perceptual achievements, not because they embody different terminal points, but because they embody different starting points, and since the starting
points differ, the increments between differ. And it is the increments between which represent the substance of the visual achievement; it is the increment between the starting point and the

97

terminal point which represents what the percipient is alleged to have discovered *by purely visual means*.[1] We may believe, for example, that the percipient was in a position to take the small step represented in Diagram I, but not the larger step represented by Diagram II.

Generally speaking, we may distinguish two pieces of information which are conveyed by an epistemic perceptual report. First, it tells you that the percipient knows something; secondly, it tells you how part of that information was acquired. And it is this *part*, this increment in knowledge, for which our visual talents are held responsible in the sense that it is *only* this increment in knowledge which the perceptual report describes as having been acquired by distinctively visual means and, hence, as being justifiable on distinctively visual grounds. And this leads us to an important negative principle. Suppose that something cannot be a P unless it is also Q. Suppose, furthermore, that Q is the sort of feature or characteristic which we cannot, for some special reason, see that something possesses. With only this much information some philosophers might be tempted to conclude that, strictly speaking, one can never see that anything is P. For to see that anything is P one must be in a position to see that it has those properties without which it could not be P, and since, by hypothesis, we cannot see that anything is Q, neither can we (strictly speaking) see that anything is P (although we might infer that it was P on a diversity of other grounds). The discussion so far has shown us why this conclusion must be rejected. It must be rejected because if S sees that the *b* is P, where something's being a *b* *also* involves it's being Q, then the unobservability of Q is, strictly speaking, irrelevant to whether S can see that the *b* is P. It is irrelevant because the possession of Q by what S sees is *not* embodied in that increment of information which S's statement depicts him as having acquired in any distinctively visual manner. The fact that he cannot discover that anything is Q in any distinctively visual manner is, therefore, irrelevant to whether he can discover that something is P in a distinctively visual manner (i.e. see that something is P). An example or two may help to put some flesh on this skeleton.

We all know that tomatoes are physical objects and as such pos-

---

[1] Or, in the case in which S already knew (on independent grounds) that the *b* was P, the increment which the percipient has verified on purely visual grounds.

sess properties not possessed by reflections, mental images, and so on. That is to say, tomatoes have mass, an internal molecular structure, they persist through time, and they can be touched, squeezed, tasted, smelled, and, finally, eaten—not only by ourselves but by others as well. Call these 'properties' $Q_1, Q_2, \ldots Q_n$. Now if one is sceptical of our ability to see, in some straightforward visual sense of this term, that anything has the property Q_i (for any 'i'), one might (mistakenly) become sceptical of our ability to see that anything is a tomato. Consider, however, the following perceptual claim (made within a justificatory context): 'I can see that this piece of fruit is a tomato.' I think there is little question but that something's being a piece of fruit *also* involves it's having the properties $Q_1, Q_2, \ldots Q_n$. A piece of fruit has mass, an internal molecular structure, it persists through time, and it can be touched, squeezed, tasted, smelled, and, finally, eaten—not only by ourselves but by others as well. And what this perceptual report describes the percipient as having discovered in a distinctively visual fashion is that *the piece of fruit* was a tomato; it does not describe him as having discovered, as even being *able* to discover, in any characteristically visual manner, that what he was seeing was a piece of fruit. Hence, the perceptual report itself is conspicuously silent on the matter of how S found out that what he was seeing possessed the properties $Q_1, Q_2, \ldots Q_n$. It certainly does not entail that S knows, or could discover, that what he was seeing had the properties Q_1, Q_4, or Q_n by *seeing* that this was so. Therefore, with respect to this particular perceptual claim, questions of wax imitations, reflections, or hallucinations are totally irrelevant since there is nothing in S's achievement, as so described, which implies that he ruled out, or was capable of ruling out, these possibilities on any sort of visual grounds.

We cannot ask of a term or phrase, in isolation, whether it represents or expresses an observable feature of things or not. I shall have more to say about this matter in later chapters, but for the moment I would simply like to point out that such questions cannot be answered until we know *what it is* that is observed to have this feature, what increment in information it is of which this term or phrase expresses the terminus. And this will almost always vary from case to case. Suppose, for instance, that we could construct robots that were visually indistinguishable (externally) from real people. Now, what shall we say about the predicate 'is embarrassed'? Is it, as they say, an observational predicate or not? If we assume that mechanical robots are not really embarrassed (although they may look as though they are), it may seem that since, by hypothesis, we cannot see whether something is a real person or one of our remarkable robots, neither can we see whether something is really embarrassed. But this is simply false. There is nothing to prevent one from seeing that one's *wife, son,* or *friend*[1] is embarrassed. For in these cases the possibility of its being a robot that one sees, although it is ruled out (robots *cannot* be embarrassed), is not said to be ruled out on *visual grounds*. The possibility of its being a robot is already ruled out on the grounds that one's wife, son, and friend are not robots, and the perceptual claim mentioned above did not embody a claim to the effect that one could *see* that this thing was (really) one's wife, son, or friend. The increment in question here is (or may be) sufficiently small to acquire in a *purely* visual manner even though one is unable to tell, by visual means alone, that the thing one is seeing is the sort of thing which *could* be embarrassed.

One generally hears a good deal about hallucination and other sorts of visual delusion in philosophical treatments of perception. For the most part such matters are completely irrelevant to whether we possess the capacity to acquire knowledge by seeing that something is so. To suppose that the possibility of S's being visually hallucinated is epistemologically relevant to whether S really sees what he says he sees (e.g. that the flowers are wilted) is like supposing that the impossibility of walking on water is relevant to whether an African Chief, who we find in Times Square, really got there (as he insists) by walking. We must *first* find out where he *walked from*, since if he walked to Times Square *from* 32nd Street and Broadway, philosophical discussions about the impossibility of walking on water are hardly pertinent to whether he has done what he said he did. Likewise, if we want to know whether S can really see that the flowers are wilted, the question of whether he can *visually* distinguish his present experience from an hallucinatory one of a similar character is quite beside the point. He never said he could. He only claimed to be able to distinguish wilted flowers from fresh flowers on distinctively visual grounds.

I shall take a much longer look at the epistemology of these

[1] Unless, of course, one of these mechanical robots happened to be one's friend.

matters in a later section. At this point I simply want to stress the fact that most, perhaps *all*, epistemic perceptual claims do not even purport to claim what the occurrence of visual hallucinations, or the possibility of such delusions, tend to show could not be claimed with full and complete justification. The visual experience (*b*'s looking a certain way to *S*) is not supposed to be, nor is it generally alleged to be, a comprehensive support for what the percipient alleges himself to know (that this *b* is *P*). The report 'I can see that this *b* is *P*' (that these flowers are wilted) certainly implies that I believe I am not being deluded, but it does not tell you what grounds I have for so believing. It certainly does not imply that I can see that I am not being deluded (visually), that I can see that this (which I see to be *P*) is a *real b* in contrast to some hallucinatory *b*. Hence, the accusation that the visual experience associated with such epistemic achievements does not provide the percipient with a full and complete justification for what he alleges himself to know (or what his perceptual claim entails that he knows) is quite true; it is, in fact, but a simple reformulation of the point I have been making. But it is equally irrelevant to whether the percipient can see that this *b* is *P*, and, hence, to whether he *knows* that this *b* is *P*. The most that one can conclude from the occurrence (to *S*) of indistinguishable visual hallucinatory states is that when *S* (not just anyone) sees that the flowers are wilted, the information that they are flowers, real flowers, cannot itself be acquired *solely by visual means*.[1] But this neither shows that the percipient does not know that the flowers are wilted nor does it show that he does not see that they are wilted; for neither of these latter claims involves a commitment with respect to *how* the percipient knows they are real flowers.

It is interesting to look at situations in which there is a breakdown in what I have been calling the percipient's proto-knowledge. One can distinguish at least three different sorts of mistake that

[1] Even this much must be severely qualified. Whether *S* can see that something is a real flower will depend, again, on what this 'something' is which he sees to be a real flower. For example, there would be nothing preventing him from seeing that those things in the field are (real) flowers, that what you have in your buttonhole is a flower, or (as I shall indicate later in this section) that *this* is a flower or that *those* are flowers. In each of these cases *S*'s proto-knowledge embodies the fact that he is seeing something that is *public* and *objective*; the perceptual report does *not* tell us that *S* acquired, or was able to acquire, this kind of information on purely visual grounds.

can occur in relation to one's proto-beliefs (when they are mistaken, they can hardly be called 'proto-knowledge').

(1) S may misidentify what he sees to be P, but the mistake may extend no farther than this: i.e. it may be P, and he may see that it is P, but he is mistaken about what *it* is. For example,

> S: The captain is very young indeed.
> R. What makes you say that?
> S: I can see that he is; just look at him.
> R: That is the *porter,* not the captain.
> S: Oh, my wife told me he was the captain.

If we expand S's second statement into the perceptual claim 'I can see that the captain is a very young man' we might want to ask whether this statement is true or false. Well, in one respect it is clearly false; the captain is *not* (let us say) a very young man, and so S could scarcely be right in saying that he sees (or can see) that he *is* a young man. Still, there is the fact that the increment in knowledge which S alleges himself to have bridged by visual means *is*, in fact, an increment which he can easily bridge and in the present case *is* actually bridging with respect to that fellow over there (the porter). The mistake lies in his proto-beliefs. He ends at the wrong place because he began at the wrong place but his manner of transition was unexceptional and above reproach. In cases such as this we would naturally be inclined to correct S, but I think we would hesitate to classify his perceptual claim as false without a fuller story about the origin of the mistake. He is mistaken, yes, but his mistake does *not* reflect any deficiency in his visual talents to distinguish between young and old men.

(2) S's misidentification of what he sees may be more extreme. He may suppose himself able to see that some b is P, when nothing which he sees is P, *because* of his mistaken identification of what he sees *as* a b. For example,

> S: I see that this water is frozen already.
> R. That is *glass*, not water.
> S: Oh, really! Why is there glass in this tray and water in all the rest?

S's perceptual claim is, in this case, a non-starter. His mistake is real enough, but, once again, it does not reflect adversely on his *visual* talents. He is quite able to see, in such circumstances as now prevail, whether water is frozen or not. He is quite able to bridge the gap he thinks he is bridging, the gap between 'this is water' and 'this is frozen water'. He is simply not starting from where he thinks he is starting. But, and this is the prime consideration, the responsibility for being at the correct starting point is *not* a responsibility which rests solely on his sense of sight. All of his senses, his intellect, memory, and powers of inference, are equally implicated in this sort of mistake. And this is *not* because seeing involves inferring, remembering, sniffing, or what have you. Rather, it is because S's ability to see what is the case, in a purely visual sense of this term, is an ability the successful exercise of which depends on a successful deployment of these other forces in the acquisition of a correct set of proto-beliefs. Mistakes such as this show absolutely nothing about S's ability to see whether water is frozen or not (although it does say something about his ability to see whether something is frozen water). Such mistakes show only that this distinctively visual capacity which we possess, this capacity to discover and, hence, know that something is the case by seeing it to be the case, is a capacity which cannot, generally speaking, be exercised within an epistemic vacuum.

(3) In the most extreme case, S may be suffering from some visual delusion of a rather comprehensive sort. He says that he can see that some b is P, but there are no b's, let alone a b which is P, which he sees. If he purports to know that rats are following him around the room because he can see that they (the rats) are following him,[1] we have a rather gross mistake in S's proto-beliefs. But the same things can be said about this case that were said about the example in (2). The possibility of such mistakes shows nothing about S's ability to differentiate (visually) between rats standing placidly in the corner and rats following him around. Hence, it shows *nothing* about S's *ability* to find out, by purely visual means, what his statement depicts him as having found out *by visual means* (that the rats are following him around.) If S is afflicted with such delusions, the *most* that this shows is that when S sees that the rats are following him, *he* is not generally (because of *his* affliction) in a position to *see* that they are real rats. But, since his claim 'I can see that the rats are following me' is definitely *not*

---

[1] This claim must be carefully distinguished from the similarly expressed, but quite different perpetual claim 'I can see that *there are* rats following me around the room'. This latter claim is existential in nature, and I shall discuss these later.

a claim to know that the rats are real by virtue of *seeing* that they are real, these delusions, and the possibility of such delusions, is irrelevant to whether he can, on another occasion, in altered circumstances, *see* (in the strictest possible sense of this word) that the rats are following him around. *All* his mistaken perceptual statement claimed for his *visual* powers was that he could, by means of them, distinguish between rats that were following him and rats that were not, and for *this much* his visual resources were perfectly adequate. His statement went wrong, not in claiming too much for his visual powers but in presupposing too much about his other powers.

So much for the possibility of mistakes in one's proto-beliefs. I shall, in the next section, consider the sort of mistakes that can occur in that increment of knowledge which is allegedly acquired by visual means—i.e. those mistakes which *do* tend to show that the man cannot see what he supposes himself to see. I would like to turn now to another matter. I have been working with an over-simplified model up to this point. This was partially unavoidable. I cannot say everything at once, and I oversimplified matters in order to make a crucial point. Let me now step back and try to put things in better perspective.

There is, first, the fact that a considerable degree of freedom exists in the selection of a subject term for 'b' in the statement form 'S sees that b is P'. What we describe *ourselves* as seeing, what noun phrase or proper name we select to designate what it is that we have seen to be P, is a function of several variables. Among the most important variables is the level of identification (short of its being P) that we have achieved *at the time we make the report*. When the report is in the present tense, the subject term is often a rather accurate indicator to one's actual level of proto-knowledge. This is why I have, up to this point, been working largely with statements in the present tense. But when we move to statements in the past tense, the situation changes. I may, for example, say that I saw that John was acting silly even though, at the moment I saw him acting silly, I did not realize it was John. I found this out a moment later. Another important variable regulating the selection of a subject term are considerations relating to the ease with which we feel our listeners will be able to identify what it is that we saw to be P. For instance, I may have just been told that the blonde girl, the girl whose dancing ability I had been admiring, was

Harold's cousin. I might then express myself to Harold (who presumably knows who his cousin is) as having seen that his cousin was a good dancer. I would do so despite the fact that at the time I saw her dance I did not know that she was Harold's cousin. This information was not a part of my proto-knowledge. To another person (who, perhaps, does not know that the girl is Harold's cousin) I might select some noun phrase which allowed that person to easily identify who it was I saw to be a good dancer: e.g. that blonde, the girl who ate all the mixed nuts.

When we are describing what *someone else* has seen, or can now see, the situation becomes more irregular. Frequently, some attempt is made to select a subject term that approximates the percipient's presumed level of proto-knowledge. Even though *I* know that the person S saw to be approaching through the bushes was an enemy soldier, I will not, *not* if I believe S was unaware of his identity at the time he saw him, describe S as having seen that the enemy soldier was approaching through the bushes. To describe S's visual achievement in this way is to suggest that this is how S also identified what he saw coming through the bushes. It is to suggest that S's proto-knowledge included the information that what he saw was an enemy soldier.

As a loose general rule, then, we might say that a subject term is selected which it is believed approximates the percipient's actual level of proto-knowledge. But this is an extremely *loose* rule. Our ordinary conversation is swarming with exceptions. This is to be expected since, as I have already indicated, the selection of a subject term is partially governed by the ease with which we expect our listeners to identify what was seen to be P. I have said that perceptual reports are, in effect, progress reports; they tell us how the percipient got from one place (his proto-knowledge) to another (the knowledge that b is or was P). If I tell you that S arrived here on the train from the city where he resides, I am telling you *how* S arrived here from the city where he resides. What phrase or name I used to designate his starting point remains more or less inconsequential as long as it does not affect what I say he has done or how he has done it. If S happens to reside in Chicago, I could say that S arrived here on the train from Chicago. In some circumstances this might be a better way to describe what S has done and how he did it; at least it might be more informative to my listeners. Similarly with perceptual reports. I can substitute a variety of different phrases for '*b*' in my report of what someone has seen to be the case without materially altering my description of what he has done or how he has done it. For instance, whether I say that I can see that Harold's cousin is a good dancer or say that I can see that the blonde in the center of the floor is a good dancer makes little or no difference to what I have said I have done or how I did it. In both cases the subject terms reflect the same *relevant* level of proto-knowledge (this is a person). Whether or not that person in the center is a blonde, or whether or not she is Harold's cousin, makes no difference to the ease or difficulty with which one can see that she is a good dancer. Presumably, it is the fact that *she is a person* which is significantly involved in the satisfaction of clause (iii) of our schema for seeing that she is a good dancer. Hence, that increment in knowledge which my statement tells you I achieved by visual means remains substantially the same. The same *visual* achievement is described in both cases.

This is also why we can, on occasion, use a subject term which exceeds the level of identification achieved by that of the percipient himself. I can say that the man saw that the oscilloscope was smashed even though the man did not know that the instrument was an oscilloscope (he took it to be simply an electronic instrument of some sort). I may do this (whether I do it or not will depend on many variables) because, generally speaking, it is no easier, or no more difficult, to see that an electronic instrument is smashed when one knows that it is an oscilloscope. Both terms ('oscilloscope' and 'electronic instrument') reflect the same *relevant* level of proto-knowledge. That is to say, the truth or falsity of the subjunctive conditional in clause (iii) will not be affected by a substitution of the term 'oscilloscope' for the terms 'electronic instrument' at the place of '*b*'. The increment between 'this is an oscilloscope' and 'this oscilloscope is smashed' is no different (in terms of the satisfiability of clause (iii)) than the increment between 'this is an electronic instrument' and 'this electronic instrument is smashed'.[1] And since my description of what the man saw

---

[1] For the sake of those (if any) who wish to quibble about this statement, I will concede that the increment represented by these two pairs of statements *could* be different. If, for example, some electronic instruments looked (when they were *not* smashed) like smashed oscilloscopes, then it would be easier to go by visual means (roughly, from the way the thing looked) from 'this is an oscilloscope' to 'this is a smashed oscilloscope' than it would be to go

to be the case is a description of how he bridged this increment, my two descriptions are descriptions of substantially the *same* visual achievement.

One further point remains to be mentioned before we draw this discussion of proto-knowledge to a close. There are a variety of ways of expressing what we have seen to be the case that do not exactly fit the model with which I have been operating. Many of these variations will be discussed in subsequent chapters, especially Chapter IV, but I would like to pause a moment to remark on several of the most significant variations. What if we say, not that *S* saw that *the* instrument was smashed, but that *S* saw that *an* instrument was smashed? Does this not reflect a different sort of visual achievement? In some cases, yes; in other cases, no. In some settings the use of the indefinite article in the subject position gives the statement the force of '*S* saw that *one of the* instruments was smashed'. In this case I should want to make the same sorts of remarks as I have made about '*S* saw that *the* instrument was smashed'—*viz*. that the phrase 'one of the instruments' reflects *S*'s proto-knowledge; we are being told how *S* found out that one of the instruments was smashed; we are not being told how he discovered, or how he knew, that what he saw was an instrument of some sort or one among several instruments.[1] In other contexts, however, the use of the indefinite article has the

from 'this is an electronic instrument' to 'this is a smashed electronic instrument'. Or, in other words, it would be easier to tell (by visual means) whether something which one knew to be an oscilloscope was smashed than it would be to tell whether something which one only knew to be an electronic instrument of some sort was smashed. The fact that there are no electronic instruments which look (when they are not smashed) like smashed oscilloscopes is, however, what accounts for the equality in increment that I have alleged above.

[1] In some cases it is not even clear that we are being told *that* he knows this. As I have already indicated above, our selection of a subject term may occasionally exceed the indentificatory level of the percipient whose visual achievement we are describing. Just as we may say, on occasion, that *S* knows that John is nervous even though he does not know John (does not know that the person *is* John), we may also say that *S* sees that John is nervous even though *S* is unaware of the person's identity whom he sees to be nervous. This is the reason that I have consistently said that one's proto-knowledge is *reflected* by various phrases within the object of the verb 'to see'; these phrases do not infallibly indicate the percipient's actual level of proto-knowledge. They come closest to doing this, of course, in first-person, present-tensed, reports.

force of '*S* saw that *it was an* instrument which was smashed'. If the statement is understood in this way, then it is clear that the proto-knowledge is now being reflected by the phrase 'which was smashed'. That is, we are being told how *S* knows that *it was an instrument* which was smashed; we are *not* being told how he knows that *it was smashed* (although, of course, there may be a strong presumption that *S* could also see that it was smashed).

There are also certain existential clauses which I have scarcely mentioned. For example, *S* can see that *there are* flowers in the vase, *S* saw that *there was* someone in the room, and *S* saw that *there were* matches on the table. None of these statements fit the paradigm with which I have been working—*S* sees that *the b* is *P*. I fully agree with this accusation; there certainly are variations on my theme which I have not yet discussed. This particular variation will be examined at length in Section 1 of Chapter IV. I do not think that such 'existentials' can be adequately dealt with until we have first become clear on what is involved in seeing that certain *relationships* hold. That is to say, I wish to delay a discussion of such statements as those mentioned above until such time as we can clarify what is involved in seeing that the flowers are in the vase, seeing that the officers are in the room, and seeing that the matches are on the table. I shall argue that the 'existential' clauses mentioned above do represent an incremental epistemic attainment, and in this respect do not differ from the type of statements examined in this section, but this can only be made clear after the discussion of relations and statements of the form '*S* can see that the *b* is R to the (or a) *c*'.

There is also the fact that in place of '*b*' we may find a relative pronoun ('it', 'she', 'they',) or a demonstrative pronoun ('this', 'these', 'that'). I do not believe that these variations call for special attention. The statement 'He saw that it was *P*' must (if it is to be understood) occur in a context which makes clear what 'it' is (e.g. the thing I heard in the bushes, that speck in the sky, the man on the bridge). The only difference here is that one's proto-knowledge is reflected in the preceding context and is, therefore, deleted from the perceptual claim itself. In some cases 'it' may refer to one's after-image or an element of one's mental imagery. To say 'I can see that *it* (i.e. my after-image) is contracting' is, again, *not* to tell one's listeners how you know it is an after-image. Somewhat similar remarks can be made about the demonstrative pronouns. If I did not believe that my listener's attention could be directed to *this*, *that*, *these*, or *those*, if I did not believe that he could also see it (or them), I would not refer to what I see to be *P* in this purely demonstrative way. And these beliefs about the *objectivity* and *publicity* of what I am seeing, beliefs without which I would not employ a simple demonstrative, are proto-beliefs in first-person, present-tense, perceptual claims. When I say 'I can see that *these* are flowers' or 'I can see that *this* is a tomato', I am telling you how I know that they are flowers and it is a tomato, but I am not telling you how I know that what I see is something to which I can refer (and thereby call your attention) by using a simple gesture and the words 'these' and 'this'. The objectivity and publicity of what I see is *not* part of that increment in information which I purport to have acquired by visual means—hence, *not* part of that information which I need be prepared to justify on distinctively *visual* grounds. Hence, questions of visual hallucination are equally irrelevant to whether I can see that these are flowers or this is a tomato. But, of course, with respect to these particular perceptual claims, questions about the possibility of their being wax imitations *are* pertinent. When I see that this is a tomato, I must be in a position to see that it is a *real* tomato where it is understood that the word 'real' here contrasts with 'wax imitation'. In this sense the present claim is stronger than 'I can see that this piece of fruit is a tomato'.

Finally, and very briefly, there are the sorts of claims discussed in the last chapter. The statement '*S* saw some flowers', since it does not tell us *how* (or even *whether*) *S* knows they were flowers, does not indicate what *S*'s proto-knowledge might be. As I have defined 'proto-knowledge', *S*'s proto-knowledge in this case is simply that total body of information which *S* possesses about the flowers at the time he sees them. There is nothing to subtract from this body of knowledge since the above statement does not tell us how (or whether) *S* discovered anything about the flowers which he saw.

I think that I have said all that I can usefully say in a general way about the incremental character of our perceptual achievements. Specific illustrations of it will appear again and again in the following pages. We are, however, now in a position to understand why conditions (iii) and (iv) in the previous section received the formulation which they did. They were expressed as:

(iii) The conditions under which S sees$_n$ b are such that b would not look (L) the way it now looks to S unless it was P.

(iv) S, believing the conditions are as described in (iii), takes b to be P.

Notice, there is nothing in the expression of these two conditions which tells us how S knows, or what reason he has for believing, that it is b which he sees to be P. Indeed, it does not even appear necessary that S know that what he sees to be P is, specifically, b. What is presupposed in the formulation of these two conditions, and this will become clearer in the next section, is that S has identified b in a sufficiently determinate way (say, as an F) to make his belief in (iii) *true* when expressed in terms of 'an F' (instead of 'b'). That is, clause (iii) expresses a regularity concerning the way b looks and the way it is (i.e. its being P), and it is S's belief in *this* regularity which leads him to take b to be P. Therefore, the formulation of (iii) and (iv) presupposes that S has identified b, at least to the extent of believing that it is the sort of thing which would not look the way it does unless it were P. But (iii) and (iv) do not tell us *how* S has identified b. They certainly do not suggest that S can *see* that it is b. And this is as it should be. Clauses (iii) and (iv)—together with (i) and (ii), of course—describe the way S learns that b is P. They do not describe the way S learns that what he is seeing is b. They describe the way S bridges the increment between 'this is a b' and 'this b is P', and they describe him as bridging it (as I shall argue more fully in the next two sections) in a distinctively visual manner. In a word, these conditions describe S's seeing that b is P, and this is precisely what they were designed to describe.

If one does not appreciate the incremental character of our visual achievements, one might wish to adopt an altered version of (iii): *viz.*

(iii)′ The conditions under which S sees$_n$ b are such that *nothing* would look the way b now looks to S unless it were *both* b and P.

This is an extremely severe requirement. The only reason I can think why someone should wish to adopt it is if they confused seeing that the water was boiling with seeing that something was boiling water. For if one makes this confusion, one will suppose that S cannot see that the water is boiling unless he can see that it is boiling water—unless, that is, he can see that it is both water and boiling. And then one will make the mistake of supposing that if *anything* (e.g. boiling vodka) looks the way boiling water looks, then since (iii)' would be false, it would also be false that S could see that the water was boiling. If one selects a requirement such as (iii)', one is systematically misinterpreting every statement of the form 'S sees that this b is P' as of the form 'S sees that something (or other) is a b and also a P'. One is systematically misinterpreting our modest perceptual claims as descriptions of much more difficult, and sometimes, perhaps, unrealizable, perceptual achievements. And it is this sort of confusion which is partially responsible for the philosophical view that people do not *really* see what they commonly suppose themselves able to see.[1]

Incidentally, I do not wish to claim that something similar to (iii)' can never be satisfied. Whether it can or not is an empirical question. That is to say, whether a given individual can see that something is, say, a real tomato, where the word 'real' is meant to contrast not only with 'fake' and 'wax imitation' but also with 'hallucinatory tomato', is something that can only be decided by asking whether the conditions under which he is operating are such that *nothing* would look that way to him unless it was a real tomato (where the word 'real' is understood to have *all* of the above contrasts). When these optimal conditions are satisfied, and I see nothing strange about supposing that they are sometimes satisfied, we are in the position of not only knowing that the piece of fruit is a tomato because we can see that it is, but we also know

[1] There is a linguistic subtlety which might help to explain how this confusion is generated. There is, as I suggested earlier, a use of the construction 'sees that' which has something like the force of 'realizes that'; e.g. I could see that we were in for a long session (the lecturer was droning on over preliminary matters). In this use one does not commit oneself to having arrived at the realization that such-and-such is the case by any distinctively visual means (in the above example it is by listening, not looking, that I could see that we were in for a long session). If, then, we confuse these two uses we get the following results: when S says that he can see that the water is boiling, it follows that he sees that (i.e. *realizes that*) it is water which is boiling. The equivocation should be clear. S *knows* that the water is boiling because he can *see* that it is boiling, but he does not (or need not) know that it is water by seeing that it is water (although we might wish to say that he must see that it is water in the 'realize' sense of 'see that'). I have tried to keep this distinction clear by talking about justificatory contexts, contexts in which the 'seeing that' construction is designed to tell us *how* someone *knows* that something is so. It is this use of the 'seeing that' locution which I have attempted to capture by my definition of primary epistemic seeing (and which will later be extended when we discuss *secondary* epistemic seeing).

that it is, indeed, a (real) piece of fruit because we can see that it is.

Conditions (i)–(iv) describe, then, S's acquisition of that increment in knowledge which the statement 'S sees that b is P' depicts him as acquiring in a distinctively visual manner. What these conditions delete (the manner in which S learns that what he is seeing is b) is just the element which is also left out of our ordinary statements to the effect that S can see that b is P. In this respect our four conditions represent an adequate portrayal of the visual achievement described by such statements. They leave out what *should* be left out. Whether they include what *should* be included, and *only* what should be included, is the topic of the next two sections.

3. *Background Beliefs*

The fourth clause in our definition of primary epistemic seeing reads as follows:

> (iv) S, believing the conditions are as described in (iii), takes b to be P.

The bulk of this section will be devoted to a clarification of this clause and some related features of clause (iii) to which it refers.

The wording of (iv) is meant to imply *more than* that S takes or believes b to be P; it is meant to carry the additional implication that S's conviction that b is P is the result of, the outcome of, his belief that conditions are as described in (iii). This may not, of course, be the *only* source of his belief that b is P (since he may have other, independent, reasons for thinking this), but it must, if indeed he has seen that b was P, be *one* of his sources. It is not *enough* that S believe that b is P when clauses (i), (ii), and (iii) are satisfied; he must believe this (in part, at least) as a consequence of a belief that the conditions in which he sees$_n$ b are such that b would not look the way it does to him, L, unless it was P. He need not believe that *whenever anything* looks this way it is P; he need not believe that *whenever* b looks this way it is P. All he need believe is that the conditions are such that b would not look this way, L, unless it were P. If he believes this much, then, providing this belief is true (clause (iii) is satisfied) and he does not believe this as the result of any false belief about the distinctiveness of any sub-aspect of the way b looks to him, his consequent taking of b

to be P may be regarded as an instance of his seeing that b is P.[1]

This, at least in summary form, is the intent of condition (iv). I have earlier referred to the conditions mentioned in (iii) as *background conditions*: the conditions or factors which, although independent of the particular character and attributes of b itself (and, in particular, of b's being P), can, by being varied, affect the way b looks to S. The composition of the light which is incident upon b is a background condition because there are variations in this parameter which will affect the way b (while remaining P) looks to S. Let me, then, refer to S's belief that these background conditions are as described in (iii) as S's background belief. To say that S's background belief is true is now another way of saying that condition (iii) is satisfied (but see qualification in next paragraph). Of course, condition (iii) may be satisfied without S's believing it satisfied.

I think we are now in a position to state an important reservation about (iv) which could not have been expressed with any degree of clarity before our discussion of proto-knowledge in the preceding section. Suppose S sees a ripe yellow banana, and suppose (for the sake of the illustration) that bananas are only yellow when they are fully ripe. In other words, suppose (iii) is satisfied: conditions are such that the banana would not look the way it does to S (specifically: yellow) unless it was ripe. Suppose, moreover, that S does not know much about fruit and, in particular, has never seen a banana before. He has been told that this is a piece of fruit, but this is all the information he has about it. He has, however, a peculiar belief about fruit in general; he thinks that any piece of fruit that is yellow is ripe. Now this is false, of course, but nonetheless it is by virtue of the color of the banana that S purports to see that it is ripe. By hypothesis, S is relying on the distinctive aspect of the banana in telling whether it is ripe; hence, in this sense, his belief in the satisfaction of (iii) satisfies all the qualifications I have so far placed on (iv). (iii) and (iv) are *both* satisfied, *and* S does not believe (iii) to be satisfied by virtue of any false belief in the distinctiveness of any sub-aspect of the way the

---

[1] Assuming, of course, that (i) and (ii) are satisfied. It is clear, though, that my formulation of (iii) implies that (i) and (ii) are satisfied and, to this extent, (i) and (ii) are redundant. Nonetheless, I have included them, and will continue to do so in subsequent schemata, for the sake of being as explicit as I can about the implications of seeing that b is P.

fruit looks to him (the fact that it is yellow *is* the distinctive aspect with respect to whether the fruit is ripe). Now what shall we say about this case? Does he see that the piece of fruit is ripe or doesn't he? I do not think we can generalize about such cases too quickly. We may refer to such situations as cases of *over-generalization*. There is a regularity operating in these conditions, but the regularity has a much more restricted scope than S believes. He believes that *any* piece of fruit which looks this way (yellow) is ripe when, in point of fact, it is only a particular kind of fruit, bananas (let us say), for which this is true. The fact that he is operating with an over-generalized background belief will not of course be evident from this particular application of it since he is applying it in a situation, with respect to a particular piece of fruit, for which it happens to hold. Such a mistaken belief can be revealed, however, in other situations with respect to other pieces of fruit—pieces of fruit which, although yellow, are not ripe.

I say that it is difficult to generalize about such situations because it does not seem to be over-generalization itself which prevents one from seeing that b is P. Suppose that a child, accustomed only to its mother's characteristic expression of anger, over-generalized to the point of thinking that *anyone* who acted or looked that way was angry? Would this fact alone lead us to deny that the child could see when *its mother* was angry? I think not. It seems to be, rather, that the background belief which S actually manifests in seeing that b is P, the belief that conditions are as described in (iii), must not only be true with respect to the b which he sees, but he must not believe this in *virtue* of any false belief about the general character of b for which the regularity expressed in (iii) actually holds. In other words, conditions are such that *its mother* (but not just any person) would not look this way unless she was angry; and what we require of anyone who sees that the child's mother is angry is that he not only believe conditions are as so described, but that he not believe this in *virtue* of some false belief about *any person's* being angry who looks this way, or *any woman's* being angry who looks this way, etc. In the case of the child, we might say that it could see that its mother was angry because the background belief which is actually manifested (in these conditions my mother would not look this way unless she was angry), although it has been over-generalized (in these conditions any person who looked this way would be angry), is not held in virtue of, or as a result of, this over-generalized belief. Rather, it is the other way around; the child believes that anyone who looks this way is angry because, or as a (partial) result of, its (true) belief about its mother.

If I may make use of the type of diagram used in the previous section, the point can be made more easily. When one is operating with an over-generalized background belief, one mistakenly supposes that the regularities which prevail under these conditions are such that one can bridge the following increment (by purely visual means):

This is a ripe
piece of fruit.

This is a
piece of fruit.

Hence, one will suppose that the relevant level of protoknowledge required in seeing that this piece of fruit is ripe is, simply, that it is a piece of fruit one is seeing. But the regularity which in fact prevails is such that one can only successfully bridge the smaller increment:

This is a ripe
piece of fruit—
in particular, a
ripe banana.

This is a banana.

As a result of this over-generalization (not just bananas, but all pieces of fruit, are ripe when they look this way), one will often be in the position of supposing oneself to have seen that something was so when it is not so. But, what is more interesting for our present purposes, in those *coincidental* cases where the piece of fruit one happens to be seeing is a banana, then even though one is correct in believing of this piece of fruit (this banana) that it would not look the way it does unless it was ripe, nevertheless one does not see that it is ripe because one's background belief is the result of a false belief about the pertinent character of what one sees; one believes that this piece of fruit (perhaps one even knows it is a banana) would not look this way (yellow) unless it was ripe because one believes it is a piece of fruit, and pieces of fruit, in general, are ripe when they look this way. Part of the increment to be bridged is being bridged by the accidental fact that the piece of fruit one is seeing is a banana:

This is a ripe piece of fruit—in particular, a ripe banana.

Level of proto-knowledge *essentially* involved in seeing that this piece of fruit is ripe.

Increment which the actual back ground condition enables one to bridge by purely visual means (i.e. conditions are such that no banana would look this way unless ripe).

This is a banana.

That portion of the increment which (in our example) is bridged by the accidental fact that the piece of fruit S is seeing *happens* to be a banana.

This is a piece of fruit.

The point of the current restriction on one's background beliefs is that the actual increment which the regularities (in these conditions) allow one to bridge must be no smaller than the increment which S believes himself bridging by virtue of such regularities.

If I may summarize, then, the two essential reservations which have been imposed on condition (iv) can be put as follows. S's background belief, his belief that conditions are as described in (iii), must be such that (1) it is not the result of, does not in any way depend on, a false belief in the distinctiveness of any sub-aspect of the way b looks to him. When this condition is violated we may refer to it as an instance of *under-specification* (or misplaced specification) *of the way b looks to S*. Secondly: (2) If the regularity expressed in (iii) holds because of the special character of b (e.g. because it is a banana, a piece of fruit, a physical object, etc.), then S must not believe that (iii) is satisfied in virtue of some false belief about the special character of b which is relevant to the satisfaction of (iii). Failures in this respect may be referred to as instances of *under-specification* (or over-generalization) of *the relevant character of b*. The word 'relevant' is added to indicate that even if S knows that the piece of fruit is a banana, he violates this restriction if he believes condition (iii) satified, with respect to *this* piece of fruit, *because* he believes that, in these conditions, *any piece of fruit* which looked this way (yellow) would be ripe.

Two things must be avoided: (1) *under* (or misplaced) specificity with regard to the appearance of b, and (2) *under* (or misplaced) specificity with regard to the pertinent character of what it is that appears. One's background belief must be true, and it must be true by virtue of no mistaken under-specification of the pertinent variables ('L' and 'b') in the expression of (iii).[1] And hereafter I ask the reader to understand that these two essential qualifications are part of what I mean in saying of S that he possesses a true background belief, part of what I mean in saying that condition (iv) is satisfied—that S, believing conditions to be as described in (iii), takes b to be P.

Turning now to other features, let us suppose that conditions are as described in (iii), and that the prevailing background conditions are $B_1, B_2, \ldots B_n$. It is important to notice that S may have a true background belief *without* believing of any particular background condition, or any set of such conditions, that it or they are among the relevant background conditions. For example, B_3 may be a condition relating to the refractive index of the intervening medium (the air or gas between S and b). S may never have heard of such matters; he may not know what 'refractive index' is or how variations in it can affect the way things look to him. In this sense he does not know that B_3 is one of the relevant background conditions. Nonetheless, he may still possess a *true* background belief. His ignorance does not prevent him from believing that the background conditions (whatever they are) are as described in (iii), nor does his ignorance prevent (iii) from being true. It is the business of physics, physiology, and psychology to tell us, in some systematic and comprehensive manner, *what* the background conditions are, and just *how* they affect the way something looks to us. An ignorance of these facts may prevent one from appreciating *what* constitutes the rightness of conditions, but it

---

[1] Over-specification with respect to either variable will not prevent one from seeing that b is P when conditions (i)–(iv) are satisfied; it will merely result in a more frequent satisfaction of (i)–(iii) without (iv) being satisfied, and, hence, a more frequent failure to see that b is P when one is in a position to do so.

does not prevent one from truly believing that the conditions are right (as described in (iii)). Compare the farmer who believes that the time is right for planting his potatoes (if he plants now, he will obtain the greatest yield). He can believe that the conditions (whatever they are) are most favorable, and he can believe this truly, without being able to describe the nature of those conditions or just how they affect his potato crop.

Of course, most adults are reasonably familiar with some of the more routine conditions which affect the satisfiability of (iii). We are familiar with the way a non-homogeneous medium, a peculiar angle, or the distance affects the way a thing looks to us. The chief difference between an experienced observer and an inexperienced observer (a small child, say) is that the latter will be less cautious in his *belief* that condition (iii) is satisfied; the unsophisticated observer will more frequently satisfy condition (iv) when condition (iii) remains unsatisfied. In such cases the child must be cautioned that he cannot, not in *these* circumstances, see what he thinks he can see: 'No, Jimmy, it isn't that A is much larger than B, B is farther away', 'No, Jimmy, Mother isn't always angry when she looks that way', 'No, Jimmy, it only looks bent because part of it is submerged in water', and 'No, Jimmy, the clouds are moving, not the sun'. The variety and complexity of the conditions mentioned in (iii) do not prevent anyone from believing that conditions *are* as described in (iii), nor do they prevent anyone from believing this truly. Hence, the variety and complexity of background conditions need have nothing to do with the satisfiability of conditions (iii) and (iv).

This brings us to another important feature of (iv). I do not wish to suggest that S's background belief is something which S is turning over in his mind, something which he is uttering, *sotto voce*, as it were, when he sees that b is P. Quite the reverse. This background belief is, in a fairly literal sense, part of the background. Compare, if you will, a situation in which an old card-playing friend tells you that he just dropped eighty dollars in an all-night poker game. Such a communication may provoke a number of different responses: 'Serves you right', 'Who was the big winner?' or 'What did your wife have to say about that?' It seems clear that on many occasions such responses are not mediated by any intellectual deliberations concerning the veracity of the speaker. That is to say, we do not indulge in a bit of covert reasoning which *begins* with the premise (1) he has just said that he lost eighty dollars in a poker game, and *moves* to the conclusion (3) he *has* lost eighty dollars in a poker game by virtue of some belief to the effect that (2) he generally tells the truth about such matters. Yet, although nothing of this sort is happening, or need happen on any conscious level, it would be quite proper to say that you responded the way you did *because* you believed that he was telling the truth. In such cases as this, although we say of someone that he would not have done (or said) X when he heard Y unless he believed Z, there is no question of this belief operating as a conscious intermediate link between his hearing X and his doing (or saying) Y. Rather, his doing Y upon hearing X *manifests* his belief that Z.

Perceptual situations are no different in this respect.[1] Background beliefs are *manifested* in perceptual achievements of the sort we are concerned with in this chapter; they are not *used* as premises or principles of inference. When S sees that b is P, he achieves a degree of certainty about b's being P which we expect of someone who knows that b is P. We want to say that S would not have achieved this degree of confidence about the character of b as a result of seeing b if he had believed that the conditions in which he saw b were such that b might have looked that way (L) to him without its being P. S's arrival at this state of confidence about the character of b in a situation in which he sees$_n$ b *manifests* a belief of the sort described in the first part of (iv). Hence, we ascribe such a background belief to S when S sees that b is P, *not* on the grounds that part of what S is *doing* when he sees that b is P is rehearsing this belief, appealing to this belief, or inferring from or in accordance with this belief, but because what S did do (see that b was P) evinces such a belief. If S does not believe that the way b looks to him *is* a reliable index to its being P, from whence springs his conviction that it is P. In short, S's conviction (a feature of his knowing) that b is P in response to b's looking a certain way to him manifests a (background) belief on S's part that, in these conditions, b would not look the particular way it does to him unless it were P. This belief ascription, then, has the same

---

[1] Throughout this section I will be using the construction 'S sees that b is P' as it would be used in a justificatory context without qualification: i.e. as an answer, direct or indirect, to the question 'How does S know that b is P?' I shall assume, therefore, that condition (ii) (S sees$_n$ b) is satisfied and that the statement 'S saw that b was P' tells us how S knows that b was P.

logic as that in which we would say of you, when you responded sympathetically to your friend's reported poker losses, that you must believe that he tells the truth on such matters—to you, at least, under these conditions.

Let me carry the analogy a step farther. When asked how I know that my friend lost eighty dollars in a poker game, I might naturally reply that he told me he did. This is my reason for believing he lost eighty dollars, but in citing this as my reason I certainly do not wish to suggest that when he told me about his unfortunate luck I went through any process of reasoning, deliberating, or inferring that he lost eighty dollars. I have a reason to believe, yes, but I did not do any reasoning in acquiring that belief. I did not even *take* what he said *as* a reason if this is meant to imply that I first listened to what he had to say and then *used* this *as* a reason (a rational inducement) in arriving at my belief that he had lost eighty dollars. He told me, and I believed him. The response was unmediated by any intellectual deliberations; there was no passage from premises to conclusion, no swift inferences, no rapid reasoning from what he said to the truth of what he said. Nonetheless, although I did not arrive at my belief by any process of reasoning, I do have a reason (in the sense of a justification) for believing as I do.

Another look at condition (iv) will reveal that it does not suggest that S takes b to be P *by virtue* of any process of reasoning. The only things our four conditions describe S as *doing*, in any reasonable sense of the word 'do', is (1) seeing b and (2) taking b to be P. What these four conditions do describe is the *circumstances* in which S takes b to be P. And these circumstances are described in such a way that, although S need not arrive at his belief that b is P by any process of reasoning, inferring, or deliberating, he nevertheless *has*, in the way b looks to him, a *reason* to believe that b is P. These conditions describe S as taking b to be P in circumstances in which he *has* a reason (in the way b looks to him) to believe that b is P, but they do not describe him as *using* the way b looks to him *as* a reason, *as* a premise for concluding, that b is P. If S *does* do some rapid (automatic? unconscious?) reasoning in arriving at his conviction that b is P, this is immaterial; for if he arrives at this belief in the circumstances described by (i)–(iv), then he does see that b is P, and if he subconsciously reasons his way to this conclusion when the circumstances are not as described in (i)–(iv), then he does not see that b is P. This definition is independent of what view we adopt as to the psychological or physiological mechanisms which bring about in S, when he sees b, the conviction that b is P. We can, if we like, simply regard this as a matter of conditioning: S, in virtue of his past conditioning, simply takes b to be P whenever b looks this way to him under these conditions. We can then leave the explanation of how this conditioning operates to the relevant specialists. If we adopt this view (and I do not think it an unreasonable view) we must understand that what conditions (i)–(iv) tell us is that this conditioned response only *counts* as seeing that b is P when the response occurs in the circumstances described by these four conditions. For it is only when these four conditions are satisfied that S not only sees$_n$ b, and truly takes it to be P, but also fulfills those *epistemic* requirements implied by the use of the 'seeing that' locution.[1] It is only when these four conditions are satisfied that S meets *both* the *visual* and the *epistemic* requirements necessitated by our saying of him that he knows that b is P because he can see that b is P. And if he meets these requirements, it is immaterial whether he arrived at his conviction that b is P by unconscious inferences, lightning swift reasonings, automatic inductions, or by absolutely no intellectual or discursive process at all.

I have just said that when conditions (i)–(iv) are fulfilled, S *has*, in the way b looks to him, a reason for believing it P. It is this feature which confers upon the perceptual state of affairs its epistemic quality, which converts S's *taking* b to be P into S's *knowing* that b is P. I shall justify this at much greater length in the next section. Before doing so, however, I would like to look briefly at two other features of clauses (iii) and (iv).

It should be clear, in the first place, that the satisfaction of (iii) alone does not allow us to say that S has, in the way b looks to him, a reason to believe that b is P—much less that this reason is good enough to say that S *knows* that b is P. S must, in addition, believe that conditions are as described in (iii). If S does not believe that conditions are as described in (iii), then although (iii) is satisfied, and even though he believes (with a high degree of certainty) that b is P, we cannot say that he sees that b is P in answer to the question 'How does S know that b is P?' Unless S believes that

[1] That it does satisfactorily fulfill the epistemic requirements of the 'seeing that' construction will be argued in the following section.

(iii) is satisfied, the source of his certainty that b is P cannot be traced to the way b looks to him, and if it cannot be traced here we cannot say that he knows *because* he can see that it is so. We might say that he knows that b is P on other grounds; perhaps everyone, competent experts included, have testified that b is P. *This* is how he knows. Hence, even though conditions (i), (ii), and (iii) are satisfied, and even though I *know* that b is P, I still may not see that it is P because I do not believe that the way b looks provides *any* grounds, much less the sort of grounds available through the satisfaction of (iii), for believing it to be P. If it is difficult to imagine these circumstances arising, simply consider the case of a child who sees his uncle under conditions described in (iii). Does the child see that the man is his uncle if he believes him to be his uncle *because* (and only because) his parents told him it was? Of course not. If the child lacks the background belief depicted in the first part of (iv), he may have a variety of different reasons for believing the man to be his uncle, perhaps he even knows that the man is his uncle, but he does not *see* that he is. This is not *how* he knows. If the child has seen a few old photographs of his uncle, we might wish to say that he has *some* reason (in the way the man looks) to believe that he is his uncle: 'The man certainly looks like my Uncle Bob.' But to see that the man is his uncle it is not enough that the child have *some* reason, not even enough that he have *good* reasons, in the way the man looks to believe that he is his uncle. He must have, in a sense to be discussed shortly, *conclusive* reasons; only then does he know that it is his uncle by seeing that it is his uncle.

One further preliminary point before we come to the philosophical 'heart' of this matter. I have, up to this point, been speaking of a state of affairs (b's looking so-and-so to S) as a reason. I have said that S has, in the way b looks to him, a reason (indeed, when (iii) and (iv) are satisfied, a conclusive reason) for believing b to be P. I do not think it strange to speak of a state of affairs as a reason. A man can *have* reasons without being able to *give* reasons. We sometimes lack the verbal sophistication requisite to articulating our reasons. We cannot describe the condition or state of affairs whose presence we take as making it more likely that so-and-so is the case. For instance, S may feel a certain characteristic way prior to each of his recurrent attacks of the gout. He may not know how to describe the way he feels except by saying that he feels the

way he always does prior to such an attack. He may not even be
able to *say* this much; this will depend on whether he has learned
that *these* words, or indeed any comparable words in any other language, correctly describe the situation as he is now experiencing
it. Yet, granting that the correlation has been consistently uniform
throughout his past experience, I think it perfectly acceptable to
to use the word 'reason' in saying of him that he has, in the way he
feels, some reason to believe that an attack of the gout is imminent.
Similarly, S may have, in the particular way an animal looks to
him, a reason for believing it to be a cat. I shall go on to argue that
this reason may be conclusive. But this should not be misunder-
stood to mean that S need be in any kind of position to describe
the way the animal looks to him or to state what particular aspect
of the animal's appearance, if any, it was that led him to believe it
was a cat. In some situations we would say that it looked like a
cat (or like a cat looks under these conditions);[1] in other situations
we would say, simply, that we could see that it was a cat. In no
case, however, is the ability to describe how something looks, or
to specify the significant aspects of the way a thing looks, presupposed in our having in the way a thing looks a reason to believe
something about it.

Also, in saying that S has, in the way b looks to him, a reason
for believing it P, I should not be taken to mean that it is always
appropriate for S to cite this as his reason for believing that b is P.
This will depend. *If* condition (iv) is satisfied, S is not likely to say
'It looks P' or to say anything else about the way it looks—especially not if he is responding to a question, or supplying information,
about *how he knows* it is P. For *if* our four conditions are satisfied,
S has a much stronger way of expressing himself: 'I can see that it
is P.' This answer is stronger because it not only invokes the way b
looks to S, but it does so within the framework of a belief, S's
background belief, which tells us that S is invoking this reason as
a *conclusive* reason—as the sort of reason which entitles him to say
he *knows*. In a certain loose sense, 'It looks P' or 'It looks as though

---

[1] We use the phrase 'look like a cat' to mean both (*a*) looks as a cat looks
under normal conditions, and (*b*) looks as a cat looks under *these* conditions—
where these conditions may be quite extraordinary. In this sense, then,
b and c may both look like cats to S, but not look at all the same (see Richard
Wollheim's discussion in 'The Difference between Sensing and Observing',
in the Aristotelian Society Supplementary Volume, XXVIII, 1954).

it were P' stands to 'I can see that it is P' as 'Check' stands to 'Checkmate'; in each case the latter formula is our way of expressing the fact that something which might *otherwise* be signaled by the first formula has occurred in a particularly decisive set of circumstances.

There remains only one topic to be discussed, and I have chosen to give it separate attention in the following section because of its crucial philosophical significance. Up to this point I have been speaking of the way b looks to S as a reason for S's believing that b is P. I have said that S *has*, in the way b looks, a reason for believing that b is P, and it was this reason which conferred on the situation its epistemic quality. As hinted above, I wish to go even further than this. I wish to say that, when condition (iii) is satisfied, and S believes it satisfied, S has in the way b looks to him a *conclusive reason* for believing that b is P, and it is the conclusiveness of this reason which supports the entailment between 'S sees that b is P' and 'S knows that b is P'. When I refer to this as a conclusive reason I have something very simple in mind: *viz.* b's looking L to S is a conclusive reason for S to believe that b is P in the sense that if b was *not* P, b would not look the particular way it does to S. That is, the truth of (iii) and (iv) support the statement, expressed in the subjunctive mood, that if b were not P, S would not have the reason for believing it to be P which he in fact has; hence, his having that reason implies that b is P.

I have no doubt but that the philosophically oriented reader will be dismayed at this series of assertions. In what possible sense (he might ask) is the way b looks to S a *conclusive* reason for S to believe that it is P? I have just answered this question; it is conclusive in the sense that in the circumstances in which S is described as seeing$_n$ b (clause (iii) being satisfied), b *only* looks the way it does to S *when it is* P. But it is at precisely this point that my challenger wishes to object. The way b looks to S is a conclusive reason for S to believe that it is P *on the condition that (iii) is satisfied*. That is to say, the way b looks to S can function as a conclusive reason for S to believe that b is P only if he is *given* the satisfaction of (iii), only if he is somehow *given* the truth of his background belief. We are told (in clause (iv)) that S believes (iii) is satisfied, but who *gives* him this information? Is not S's background belief (referring to the satisfaction of condition (iii)) in reality *part* of his reason for believing b to be P? If one is seeking conclusive reasons for believing that b is P, then something like the following premises are required:

(1) In these conditions b only looks L when it is P.
(2) b *looks* L.
    Hence, b is P.

But you (my challenger continues) have been referring to the second premise *alone* as a conclusive reason *on the assumption that the first premise is true*. The first premise, however, is also required in any statement of *conclusive* reasons, and since the first premise is but an expression of S's background belief, this background belief must be included as part of S's reasons for believing that b is P. And now the trouble begins. For if both (1) and (2) are part of S's reason for believing that b is P, then S does not really know that b is P unless he knows that both (1) and (2) are true. Now, perhaps, we may give him premise (2); he is, after all, described (in clause (iv)) as believing something about the particular way, L, b looks to him, and it is difficult to see how he could be mistaken about the particular way something looks to him.[1] But what about (1)? S is described as believing this, but he is not described as *knowing* it to be true. And if he does not, or cannot, know that this is true, then his reasons for believing that b is P are, in that respect, inconclusive. These four conditions do not even describe S as having any reason to believe that his background belief (premise (1) above) is true. In what sense, then, can S be described as having conclusive reasons to believe that b is P? Clearly, the conclusion to be drawn from this is that either the above four conditions do not adequately portray our ordinary (justificatory) use of the 'seeing that' construction (since they are not strong enough to capture the essentially epistemic character of this construction), or if we suppose that these four conditions do faithfully reflect the ordinary situations in which we correctly employ the 'seeing that' locution in telling someone how we know, we must admit that in these ordinary situations we do not *really* pull off what we think we have pulled off—we do not really know what our statement implies

---

[1] He could, of course, be mistaken about the fact that *it is b* which looks L to him. I think, however, that the previous section has shown why this possibility is irrelevant to whether S is able to see that b is P—i.e. irrelevant to whether S has the 'capacity' to acquire that increment of information (on purely visual grounds) which such a statement depicts him as acquiring.

that we know. And this means that we do not really see what we think we have seen.

The following section is an attempt to expose the fallacy in this line of reasoning. In this sense, the next section will support my contention that when S satisfies conditions (i)–(iv), *he thereby knows that b is P*. Indirectly, then, the final section of this chapter is a justification of my claim that when anyone satisfies the four conditions defining primary epistemic seeing, conditions which are frequently and routinely fulfilled in countless everyday settings, his achievement is not only a visual achievement but is also, in the fullest possible sense of this term, an epistemic achievement. Conditions (i)–(iv) are adequate to the epistemic implications of 'seeing that'; they describe someone who *knows* that b is P.

4. *Reasons and Justification*

There is a doctrine which has long been associated with the philosophy of perception, a doctrine which denies to the ordinary man the ability to see, in routine perceptual situations, what he supposes himself able to see. I have already, in the second chapter, examined and rejected this doctrine in relation to non-epistemic seeing. What we see$_n$, in routine perceptual situations, is a function of what there is to be seen and what, given our individual visual endowments and the circumstances in which we exercise them, we are able to visually differentiate. It is, in short, an empirical question for which there is overwhelming evidence that we see$_n$, in as direct and unmediated a manner as this way of seeing permits, the everyday objects and events (among other things) which we commonly suppose ourselves to see. But we now find this sceptical doctrine reasserting itself in reference to epistemic seeing. And, once again, we shall find that it is fundamentally mistaken.

Those who have become sceptical of man's perceptual abilities have not, of course, wished to deny that people often believe that so-and-so is the case as a result of believing that they have seen, or can see, that so-and-so is the case. Nor have they been so foolish as to issue the blanket denial that so-and-so is *ever* the case, regardless of time, place, and percipient. The sceptic may wish to re-interpret what it means to say that so-and-so is the case in order to salvage something from his own sceptical critique, but, generally speaking, he has not insisted that whenever and wherever a man believes himself to have seen that *b* was *P*, *b* was not, in fact, *P*. When philosophers deny us the benefit of being able (really!) to see that, say, the rear tire on our automobile is flat, they do so, not because they are convinced that we are never really certain that the tire is flat, in some subjective sense of certainty, not because the philosopher has some (secret) reasons to believe that no tire is ever flat, but because he believes that the visual experience on which we rely (when we allege ourselves able to see that the tire is flat) does not contain the elements essential to an adequate *justification* of our belief that the tire is flat. We may be certain that the tire is flat, yes, but we are not *entitled* to this certainty. One cannot, by appealing to the way the tire looks to one, *adequately justify* one's belief that the tire is flat; and in this sense one does not really know that the tire is flat. And if one does not know that the tire is flat, one does not (strictly speaking) see that it is flat.

The sceptically minded philosopher might admit, then, that our four conditions perhaps describe the circumstances under which we ordinarily issue, and accept, perceptual claims. But this, he will urge, only proves his point. For the four conditions do not describe *S* as having an *adequate justification* for his belief that *b* is *P*. These four conditions can be fulfilled without *S*'s being able to justify his background belief, they can be satisfied without *S*'s *knowing* that condition (iii) is fulfilled. Hence, they can be satisfied without *S*'s being able to justify, on the basis of the way *b* looks to him, that *b* is indeed *P*. Therefore, these four conditions do not describe *S* as knowing that *b* is *P*.

Such arguments embody a mistake, but the mistake is not altogether simple-minded. Before attempting to expose it, let us get clear about what we have already established. Conditions (i)–(iv) do not describe *S* as *using* the way *b* looks to him *as* a reason for concluding that *b* is *P*. The most that they say is that *S has* a conclusive reason for believing *b* to be *P in the sense* that, in these background conditions, *b* only looks the way it does to him when it is *P* (condition (iii)), and *S* believes this (condition (iv)). The actual psychological process (if any) which *S* goes through in taking *b* to be *P* may not involve reasoning or inferring at all; indeed, if *S* does *consciously* reason or infer, one is inclined to say that he does so because he does *not* see that *b* is *P*. The *immediacy* associated with seeing arises precisely because no intermediate discursive process mediates the seeing of b (which is P) and the consequent conviction (in cases of seeing that b is P) that b is P.

Secondly, our discussion of proto-knowledge should have eliminated one other possible source of confusion. When S sees that his rear tire is flat, he is not committed to having (although we might naturally expect him to have), *in the way the tire looks to him*, a reason, much less a conclusive reason, for believing that it is a tire, a rear tire, or a rear tire on his automobile. He need only have, in the way the tire looks to him, a conclusive reason to believe of his rear tire (proto-knowledge) that it is flat (visual increment). His ability to see that his rear tire is flat is not an ability to *see* that what appears flat is really a *rear* tire, is really *his* tire, or is a *real* tire and not, say, a clever imitation.

With this much understood, let us consider the actual situation with respect to the possibilities of knowing, let us even say 'knowing *for* certain', that b is P when conditions (i)–(iv) are fulfilled. I think it will help in this matter if we consider a sequence of three 'experiments'. The third 'experiment' is the one of interest, at least to the sceptically minded philosopher, but it can be best appreciated by viewing it in the context of the first two.

Experiment #1: Suppose we take S into a specially prepared room, a room that looks normal in all respects, but a room which is equipped with a rather elaborate lighting system. The wallpaper is beige, but by means of our well-concealed lighting system we can make the wallpaper appear to be various other colors.[1] Before entering the room with S we arrange to have the lights adjusted so as to make the wallpaper appear dark green. Then, without arousing S's suspicion about our intentions, we try to elicit from him an observation concerning the color of the wallpaper. Suppose we succeed and S naïvely asserts that he can see that the wallpaper is green. A mistake, of course; we have fooled him. There is nothing very interesting about this state of affairs. Common sense would agree with the philosopher in saying that, in these circumstances, S did not see what he purported to see. S was convinced that the wallpaper was green; if asked how he knew it was green, he might naturally reply that he could see that it was. We have here, however, a failure of condition (iii) (and hence a failure of condition

---

[1] I do not wish to argue the 'objectivity' or 'subjectivity' of color properties. I use this only as an example, but the same point could be made with such characteristics as 'size', 'length', and so on.

(i)—*viz*. the wallpaper *is* green). *S* does *not* see that the wallpaper is green because the background conditions under which he sees it are *not* such that it only looks the way it does to him when it is green.

Experiment #2: We inform *S* about the clever lighting arrangements. We vary the light and show him how the wallpaper can be made to appear different colors. Then, *without* telling him that the wallpaper is really beige, and *without* telling him how we are presently illuminating the walls, we diffuse the room with ordinary incandescent light. That is, we switch to a lighting arrangement which is normal in the sense that most rooms are so illuminated, and it is the sort of illumination under which beige walls look beige (to normal observers). Assuming, then, that everything else is normal (*S* is not color-blind), we once again attempt to elicit from *S* an observation about the color of the wallpaper. I think there is little doubt but *S* will not, in these circumstances see that the wallpaper is beige. Even though it is beige, he sees it, and the conditions under which he sees it are such that the wallpaper would not look beige to him unless it was beige, he nevertheless does not see that it is beige. The reason for this is simple: *viz*. although (i), (ii), and (iii) are fulfilled, (iv) is not satisfied. *S* does not believe that the conditions are as described in (iii). He doesn't disbelieve it either; he just does not know what the present state of illumination is, and he therefore does not believe the walls to be beige simply *because* they happen to look beige to him at the moment. He might volunteer the comment that they *look* beige, but he will hardly suppose himself able to *see* that they are beige.

Once again, this state of affairs does not contain much to excite the philosophical imagination. Common sense would agree that under such circumstances *S* does not see what color the wallpaper is, and *S*'s failure is represented in our four conditions by a failure of (iv). But our first two experiments suggest a third, and it is this third situation which has traditionally inspired philosophical controversy.

Experiment #3: *S*'s state of mind being what it now is, we wait several weeks, several months, or as long as necessary to allow *S* to forget what has happened or, at least, to become reassured of our good (non-deceptive) intentions toward him. We then introduce him into a room with beige walls with *normal* lighting arrangements. The room is different (so as not to arouse *S*'s suspicions), and we cautiously try to elicit from him another observation about the color of the wallpaper. We must be careful how we set about this, of course, since we are attempting to construct a situation in which *all* four conditions are satisfied. Hence, we must not arouse S's suspicion about our intentions else he begin to doubt that conditions are as he normally supposes them to be. In other words, we want a situation in which he *does* believe that conditions are as described in (iii), and so we must not jeopardize the fulfillment of this condition by allowing S to doubt our intentions and, hence, the sort of conditions which prevail in the room. Suppose that we are very clever and we succeed in getting S to commit himself.[1] S (naïvely?) asserts that he can see that the wallpaper is beige. The question we must now answer is: does S see what he purports to see? Conditions (i)–(iv) are all fulfilled. Yet, can we say that S *knows* that the walls are beige? Can he really be certain of this? Is he in any position to justify this belief to the degree of conclusiveness which we ordinarily demand of someone who alleges himself to *know*. How can he possibly justify this? He may, for all he knows, be in the position depicted in Experiment #1. He has naïvely taken the walls to be beige without checking the lighting arrangements. And if we generalize from this case we can see that in a vast assortment of common perceptual situations we are in precisely the same circumstances as that depicted in this third experiment; we *say* we see this and that, but we seldom, if ever, take the precautions requisite to saying we *know* that the background conditions are as described in (iii); generally speaking, we take these conditions for granted. Even if we wanted to justify our background belief, the obstacles in our way would become insurmountable; for aside from their being an indefinite number of background conditions which are relevant to conditions being as they are in (iii), our ability to determine that these conditions are appropriate would presumably rely on our sense of sight once again (assisted by our other senses), and the problem re-emerges all over again since how can one see that anything else is the case (e.g. that the lighting is normal) without having another (different) background belief concerning this state of affairs. And then

---

[1] If the reader feels that this would be incredibly naïve on S's part, we can think of the third experiment as being performed on a different person, someone who did not participate in #1 and #2. This will not affect the conclusion to be drawn from the experiment.

we have the difficulty of trying to justify the truth of these other background beliefs. The whole enterprise can hardly get off the ground—not, at least, when one is talking about physical objects and their properties.

This argument, or some variation on it, has struck many people as a formidable objection to the view that common sense, and the claims which it inspires, is in a satisfactory epistemological state. The reaction has often been to either (i) insist that common sense has its own (diluted) standards, and hence cannot be criticized for failing to measure up to the stricter standards of epistemology, or (ii) reject common sense and the sorts of knowledge claims it embodies as a totally unrealistic reflection of what we really do know about this world around us. I think both approaches mistaken.

In the first place, we should not be misled by the fact that we might easily (in Experiment #3) persuade S to renounce his claim to know that the walls are beige. That is, we might remind S (or anyone else) of our prior ingenuity in deceiving people, and (with a smirk on our face) ask him whether he still wishes to say that he *knows* that the walls are beige. Such remarks might well induce S to respond more cautiously. He might admit that he did not check the lighting arrangements; he can no longer *be sure* about that which he originally took for granted when he alleged himself able to see that the walls were beige—*viz.* that the conditions under which he saw the walls were such that they would not have looked beige unless they were beige. And once S's suspicions are aroused about the ingredients of the perceptual situation, his preparedness to say that he knows that the walls are beige is commensurately diminished since it was on the basis of the perceptual situation that the knowledge claim was originally advanced. Although this might well occur, I say we should not be misled by it because it shows *nothing* about whether S, *when* he said he could see that the walls were beige, knew *then* that the walls were beige. There is a degree of conviction associated with knowing something, and because we have deprived S of this degree of conviction and, hence, brought him to the state where he is *no longer* willing to assert that he knows, this alone does not show that he did not *previously* know. We might easily maintain that the reason S no longer knows is that he has been deprived of that degree of certainty, that degree of conviction, which is characteristic of *knowing* that something is the case. Nonetheless, *when* he was certain, *when* he did possess the requisite degree of conviction, he *did* know. Our success in making *S* doubt, or become uncertain of, what he previously claimed to know is not an indication that what he previously claimed to know he did not really know. The *most* that this shows is that *S* cannot be said to know that *b* is *P* *when* he actively doubts whether *b* is *P* or not, or when he actively questions the reliability of the method by means of which he originally arrived at the belief that *b* was *P*. But since *neither* of these questioning attitudes characterized *S* *at the time* he alleged that he saw that the walls were beige, his subsequent uncertainty does not show that he did not formerly know that the walls were beige.

The ease with which a clever sceptic can induce a person to renounce (or suspend judgment about) what he formerly claimed to know shows nothing (by itself) about what that person formerly knew. A good crack on the head might achieve the same results as a sceptic's blandishments, but this should not mislead us into believing that what a person *now* doubts he *never* knew. There is nothing odd about a person knowing that *b* is *P* and later, mistakenly, coming to the belief that his reasons were not good enough and, hence, denying that he ever knew. Knowing that *b* is *P* does not entail that the knower *always* knows that *b* is (was) *P* or that the knower always believes that he *knew* that *b* was *P*. Hence, we should not conclude from the gullibility of our subject in Experiment #3 that he did not really know what he implied he knew when he said that he could see that the walls were beige.

What the sceptic must show in relation to our subject, *S*, in Experiment #3 is that *S* did not know that the walls were beige *even at the time* when he saw the walls, the walls were beige, the conditions under which *S* saw them were such that they would not have looked *L* (beige) to him unless they were beige, and, *S*, believing the conditions were such, was thereby certain that the walls were beige. And how might a sceptic attempt to demonstrate this? Well, he might proceed by arguing that since *S* did not actually check all the relevant background conditions, since, for example, he did not actually verify the presence of normal illumination, he could not be certain that his background belief was true, he could not be certain that condition (iii) was satisfied. And without the assurance that condition (iii) is satisfied, *S* cannot be certain that the walls *are* beige just because they look the way they now do to

him. In one quite clear sense this sceptical objection is mistaken.
Obviously S *could* be certain that conditions were as described in
(iii) because, as a matter of fact, he *was* certain; he manifested this
certainty; at least he manifested an unquestioning acceptance of
the satisfaction of (iii) by his belief that he could *see* that the walls
were beige.[1] No, the sceptic must not say that S *could not be certain*
that conditions were as described in (iii) without a full justification; he must, instead, maintain that S *was not entitled to his certainty* without a full justification. And when S sees that b is P, S
does not know for certain that b is P unless he is *entitled* to his certainty that in these conditions b only looks the way it does when it
is P. And, in so far as S is not entitled to this certainty, he does not,
strictly speaking, see that b is P.

I think it must be conceded that, whatever the sceptic might
mean by an 'entitlement' to certainty, in situations like that depicted in Experiments #1 and #3, S has *some* justification for the
background belief which he manifests in alleging himself able to
see that the walls are beige. We might say that, among other things,
normal conditions are those which it is reasonable to assume prevail unless there is something to suggest otherwise. S's reason for
believing the conditions normal (in #1 and #3) is that rooms of
this sort are generally illuminated by light of the conventional
incandescent variety, and there is nothing to suggest (to him) that
this room deviates from the norm. But our sceptic will be quick
to point out that S's degree of justification for his background belief is obviously not good enough. One need only be reminded
that in Experiment #1 S was mistaken, and he was mistaken because, although he possessed the same justification for his background belief as he possessed in #3, the justification was not
good enough to insure that the background conditions were as
described in (iii). In neither case, then, does S have a *sufficient*
justification to entitle him to the certainty which he (naïvely)
manifests in alleging himself able to see that the walls are beige.

I think with these preliminaries out of the way we are now in a
position to answer the sceptic's demands. *Why* should one suppose
that S cannot know, or cannot know for certain, that b is P when
he sees b under conditions (i)–(iv) *unless* he meets the sceptic's demands for a full justification of his background belief? What does

[1] I am using the word 'certain' in what I take to be one of its accepted
senses: *viz.* having no doubt, assured, or sure.

such a justification *add* that is not *already* present in the fulfillment of (i)–(iv)? Will S's having such a justification mean that he will not make a mistake in taking b to be P? But conditions (i) and (iii) already tell us that S will not make a mistake in taking b to be P. Will S's having such a justification give him a greater degree of assurance (conviction, certainty) that b is P? But S is *already* provided with this assurance by virtue of his belief that conditions are as described in (iii). His belief in the satisfaction of (iii) is what generates in S the conviction that b, given the way it looks, *must be* P. Will S's having such a justification provide S with a better (more conclusive) reason for believing that b is P? But the fulfillment of condition (iii) already tells us that the way b looks to S is a conclusive reason for taking b to be P in the sense that b's looking the way it does is, in these conditions, a perfectly reliable index to its being P. A full justification for S's background belief will not make this reason any *more* conclusive. The only thing that S's having a justification for his background belief lends to this situation is an *assurance* to S that the way b looks *is* a conclusive reason in the above sense. But S does not *need* this assurance since he already (see condition (iv)) believes that conditions are as described in (iii) and, hence, believes that the way b looks *is* a conclusive reason in the above sense. He would need the type of assurance which such a justification could provide only if he did not believe, doubted, or was reluctant to admit that conditions were as described in (iii).

Furthermore, it should be noticed that once S satisfies conditions (i)–(iv), whether or not he has indulged in any antecedent precautionary checks in relation to the background conditions, we cannot reasonably object to S's having seen that b was P on the basis of his actual or potential performance in discovering that b is P (on visual grounds). That is to say, we can never demonstrate to S, or to anyone else, that S could not have seen that b was P in these conditions by reconstructing another situation in which S *fails* to perform satisfactorily. For if we are to reconstruct a situation in which S's failure to perform satisfactorily is to be relevant, we must reconstruct a situation in which the background conditions *are the same* as they were on the occasion in question, and this means constructing a situation in which (iii) is once again satisfied. But if (iii) is satisfied, S cannot *mistakenly* take b to be P when it looks the way it formerly looked to him (L). We cannot change the background conditions and expect to show anything that is at all relevant because the most that will be shown by S's failure in *altered* background conditons is that S cannot see that b is P under *any* and *all* conditions. And this is irrelevant to whether he saw that b was P under the conditions that originally obtained. We cannot prove that S does not see that the car is, say, a Chevrolet *at three paces* by showing that he cannot (although he might think that he can) see that it is a Chevrolet *at three hundred paces*.

The last point is interesting because it shows that when S satisfies (i)–(iv) he is, in a certain sense, *always able to justify his background belief*. He is able to justify it, not in the sense that he has actually performed any antecedent tests or checks in confirmation of it, but in the sense that any subsequent tests on his accuracy in telling whether b is P (on visual grounds alone) will automatically confirm the background belief which he originally manifested in supposing himself able to see that b was P. His infallible performance on subsequent occasions, occasions on which the same background conditions prevail, should provide ample justification for the belief which he manifested on the first occasion—i.e. that conditions were such that b would not look L to him unless it was P. And since (i)–(iv) tells us that S is able to justify his background belief, at least to this extent, we can say that whatever the actual degree of justification which S has at the time he sees that b is P, he is certainly able to (subsequently) justify this background belief.

I am by no means suggesting that a degree of justification for one's background beliefs is unnecessary or superfluous. All I am suggesting is that, in relation to background beliefs, the relevance of justification is a psychological, not a logical, relevance. Most men require some degree of justification before they believe something, but what makes a background belief effective in allowing us to see what is the case is not its justification, or how (antecedently) justified we are in having it, but the fact that it is a *belief* and the fact that it is *true*. In so far as we do not believe something without justification, then justification is relevant to the effective operation of background beliefs because it is relevant to their *being beliefs*. But the only *degree* of justification which is relevant is that degree of justification which is sufficient to engender in the percipient the belief that conditions are as described in (iii). Once he has that belief, with whatever justification he holds it, then providing that our other conditions are fulfilled, he knows that *b* is *P*. He knows it because he not only truly believes it, but he has, and he believes he has, in the particular way *b* looks to him, a conclusive reason for so believing.

The sceptical standards of justification would only be relevant if *no one* would believe anything until they met these high standards. If, for example, *S* (in Experiment #3) did not believe that conditions were as described in (iii), and *would not believe* it until he had personally checked every possible background condition, then, of course, he would not see that the walls were beige *until* he had completed (*if* he could complete) this elaborate procedure. But the existence of *S*'s impeccable standards would not mean that only *he* could really see that the walls were beige; nor would it mean that if he relaxed these standards he would be unable to see that the walls were beige.

It is important to understand what I am *not* asserting. I am not suggesting that *S* can know that *b* is *P* without having any reason to believe it. With respect to *seeing* that *b* is *P* I am, in fact, maintaining just the reverse. If *S* knows that *b* is *P*, and he knows this because he sees that *b* is *P*, then, in this instance, *S* has (in the required sense) a conclusive reason for believing that *b* is *P*. And I am suggesting, furthermore, that when *S* satisfies the four conditions defining primary epistemic seeing, he has, in the way *b* looks to him, a conclusive reason for believing that *b* is *P*, and it is this conclusive reason that is invoked by the utterance 'I can see that *b* is *P*'.

Neither am I suggesting that one can ignore the justification of one's background beliefs. With most individuals it is necessary to their believing *X* that there be some grounds for believing *X*. Very often, when we are dealing with pervasive uniformities, these grounds will consist of no more than that there is nothing to suggest that the circumstances are not normal—i.e. as they have always been in the past. Generally speaking, it is this minimal form of justification which is sufficient, on numerous occasions, to prompt the percipient to manifest a belief in the normality of the conditions by putting forward an epistemic perceptual claim. What I am suggesting is that the *degree* of justification which the percipient has for his background beliefs is quite irrelevant to the effective operation of these beliefs in transforming *S*'s seeing beige walls into *S*'s seeing that the walls are beige. What is alone relevant to this achievement is the *having* of the background belief (iv) and the *truth* of this belief (iii).

Nor am I denying that mistakes could be prevented by indulging in more elaborate precautions, the sorts of precautions which the sceptic suggests. Mistakes could be avoided because one would less often find oneself *believing* that conditions were as described in (iii) when conditions were *not* as described in (iii); that is, one would less often operate with false background beliefs. What I am arguing is that *if* (iii) *is fulfilled*, then the absence of a justification for one's background belief does not, by itself, prevent one from seeing what is the case. If we take the sceptic's remarks as a warning, a caution that unless we take greater care in ascertaining that conditions are as described in (iii) we will make a greater number of mistakes in what we suppose ourselves able to see, we can accept his warning as salutary. For, of course, he is quite right. But the fact that we would make fewer mistakes by taking greater precautions does not mean that when we do not take precautions we are *also* making a mistake. One cannot conclude that I do not see that the walls are beige by *correctly* assuming that the conditions are as described in (iii) *because* on other occasions, in different circumstances, I mistakenly suppose myself able to see that the walls are beige by *incorrectly* assuming that the conditions were as described in (iii).

What an elaborate justification of one's background beliefs gives one is a rather impregnable defense against subsequent sceptical queries. One is better prepared to cope with such questions as 'Are you sure the lighting was normal?' and 'Are you sure it wasn't just the funny angle from which you saw it?' And being better able to cope with these queries means that one is in a better position to justify the fact that one did see what one claims to have seen. Hence, one is in a better position to *persist*, as it were, in the claim that one knows. In what I take to be one acceptable sense of this iterated construction, *one knows that one knows*. But if this is what one means by 'knowing that one knows', one can know that *b* is P *without* knowing that one knows it. An inability to justify the claim that one saw, by virtue of an inability to give any elaborate defense of one's background belief, does not mean that one did not see what one claimed to have seen while possessing that background belief. Hence, it does not mean that one did not, at the time one saw, know what one claimed to have seen (to be the case). Justification of one's background beliefs lends *durability* to the knowledge which one achieves by visual means (and, thereby, relative immunity from sceptical questioning), but it is not a necessary ingredient to that knowledge itself.

I should want to say, then, that in Experiment #3 *S did* know that the walls were beige *when* he satisfied the four conditions defining primary epistemic seeing. *At that time* he satisfied all the conditions which we expect of someone who knows something to be the case. His inadequate ('inadequate' on sceptical standards) justification for his background belief (he did not check the lighting arrangements) merely exposes him to *subsequent* uncertainty as to whether he really did what he supposes himself to have done (i.e. leads him to doubt whether he really did see what color the walls were). But given the truth of (iii), there is no reason why he cannot subsequently verify the fact that conditions were as he supposed them to be, and, hence, verify the fact that he did do what he thought he did: namely, see that the walls were, indeed, beige.

Later chapters will provide dozens of examples to illustrate and, hopefully, confirm the characterization which I have given in this chapter of primary epistemic seeing. If the reader is still doubtful about the sense in which conditions (i)–(iv) allow us to say that *S* knows that *b* is *P*, I can only ask him to keep the following points in mind:

(1) *S*'s knowing that *b* is *P* does not entail that *S* can justify the claim that *b* is *P* to *your* satisfaction or even to *his own* satisfaction at some later date.

(2) *S*'s knowing that *b* is *P* does not entail that *S* must always remain convinced that he did know that *b* was *P*; it does not entail that *S* cannot be brought to doubt that *b* is (or was) *P* or brought to doubt the adequacy of those reasons which he originally had for believing *b* was *P*.

(3) If *S*'s *knowing* that he *knows* that *b* is *P* means, simply, that *S* is *convinced* that he knows that *b* is *P*, that he believes *truly* and without question that the grounds he has for believing that *b* is *P* would not have been available to him unless *b* was *P*, then conditions (i)–(iv) describe a person who knows that he knows that *b* is *P*. If, on the other hand, *S*'s knowing that he knows that *b* is *P* means not only that *S* has a conclusive reason (in the above sense) for believing that *b* is *P* but is *also* able to provide conclusive evidence (in the above sense) for its *being* a conclusive reason (i.e. able

to conclusively justify his background belief to the effect that b would not look the way it does to him, under these conditions, unless it was P), then our four conditions do *not* describe S as knowing that he knows that b is P. But I should want to say in this case that S's seeing that b is P, and thereby knowing that b is P, does not entail that S knows that he knows that b is P.

If these points are kept in mind, I believe that conditions (i)–(iv) describe a situation in which it is true to say that S knows that b is P and knows this *because* he can see that b is P.

IV

RELATIONS, EVENTS, AND SECONDARY SEEING

The next four sections extend the analysis begun in the last chapter. Certain related uses of the verb 'to see' are examined, uses which bear a direct connection with our ability to discover something by using our eyes. I shall have little or nothing to say about a number of important affiliated notions (e.g. recognition, identification), and I shall no doubt miss some of the significant nuances which can be found in those uses of the verb 'to see' which I do discuss, but I think the analysis will approach completeness in a more fundamental sense. This chapter, together with the preceding two, represent, I hope, a satisfactory description of the sorts of achievement, both epistemic and otherwise, associated with our sense of sight. If some of the ways we have of describing these achievements is neglected the neglect is inspired by a conviction that the distinctively visual achievements reflected in these assorted descriptions has already been adequately characterized. What is missing is a detailed description of the different circumstances, attitudes, motives, and intentions which combine to give these achievements a different quality and, hence, which make these achievements more appropriately expressed in one way rather than another as their composition varies.

1. *Relationships*

When we see that our pencil is longer than our pen, we might, following the pattern established in the last chapter, say that this is a case of seeing that two objects, *b* and *c*, bear a certain relation, R, to one another: *S* sees that *b* is R to *c*. The relation 'longer than' is what logicians call a *dyadic* relation; it requires two things to exemplify it. There are higher-order relations: triadic (S saw that Jimmy was standing between his mother and father), tetradic (S saw Harry kick the ball between the two goalposts)[1] and so on.

We can adjust our schema for primary epistemic seeing to these new cases in a fairly straightforward way:

S sees that b is R to c in a primary epistemic way:
  (i) b is R to c.
  (ii) S sees$_n$ b and S sees$_n$ c.
  (iii) Conditions are such that b and c would not look the way they do, L, relative to one another to S unless b was R to c.[2]
  (iv) S, believing the conditions are as described in (iii), takes b to be R to c.[3]

It should be emphasized that these four conditions are not designed as an analysis of our ordinary use of the 'seeing that' construction. At best they provide a partial analysis, an analysis which will be extended even further in the following section (when 'secondary seeing' is discussed). The above four conditions are sufficient to truly say of S that he sees that b is R to c (and thereby knows that b is R to c), although there are other ways of expressing this same state of affairs, and, in justificatory contexts ('How does S know that b was R to c?'), these four conditions are individually

---

[1] Note the absence of the 'that' in this statement. Epistemic visual achievements are often described without the use of an explicit 'that' clause, and I shall discuss such cases at greater length in Section 3 of this chapter.

[2] The conditions mentioned in this clause are, again, what I shall refer to as *background conditions:* B is a background condition in this (relational) case if and only if (*a*) B is logically and causally independent of the particular character and properties of b and c and of the relationships which obtain between them; and (*b*) there are variations in B which affect the way b and c look to S individually and relative to one another.

[3] Once again it must be understood that S's background belief, his belief that conditions are as described in (iii), must not be the result of, or in any way depend on a false belief in the distinctiveness of any sub-aspect of the way b and c look to him. For example, suppose the twins Tom and Jerry are dressed alike, and S mistakenly believes that any two people who are dressed alike are siblings. If, then, S believes himself able to see that Tom and Jerry are siblings *by virtue of this mistaken reliance* on the significance of their dress, then, although (iii) is satisfied (they would not be this similar in physiological appearance unless they were brothers), S does not see that they are siblings or brothers. Similar remarks must also be made about the possibility of S's possessing an over-generalized background belief (see Section 3, Chapter III) about the relevant character of b and c in virtue of which the regularity in (iii) holds.

necessary for truly saying of S, without qualification (i.e. 'by . . .'), that he saw that b was R to c. To repeat, there is nothing odd or incorrect about saying that one can see that b is R to c without seeing either b or c: e.g. one can see *by the map* that one road is longer than the other, one can see *by the gauge* that material A is harder than material B, and one can see *by a photograph* that one's nephew and niece are about the same height. One might also see that b is R to c by seeing only *one* term of the relation; e.g. S can see that Harold is far ahead of the other runner (who has not yet even appeared around the curve), S could see that someone *had* painted the chair, and she could see that the color *would* clash with her curtains. Such examples will be examined in the following section where there is a discussion of seeing something in a secondary epistemic way—seeing that b is P (or that b is R to c) without necessarily seeing b (or both b and c). And then, of course, we have the usual examples which need have little or nothing to do with our sense of sight: I can see (hear?) that these fellows are never going to agree on anything, or he saw (realized?) immediately that my conclusion did not follow from my premises. This is only to say that there are hundreds of examples which do not fit the schemata I have provided for *primary* epistemic seeing, but, as I have pointed out earlier, these schemata are not designed for universal application. The schemata for *primary* epistemic seeing are descriptions of a particular class of situations, a class in which the 'seeing that' locution functions in such a way as to answer the question 'How does S know that b is P (or that b is R to c)?' Descriptions of what we have seen in a secondary manner also function in this way, but, generally speaking, it is only when we have seen something in a primary way that explanations of how we have seen (i.e. 'by . . .') can be deleted without in any way impairing the completeness or correctness of our answer (although we may occasionally insert such an explanation, 'by the look on his face', 'by the way it was behaving', etc., to anticipate a sceptical or curious listener). It is this use of the 'seeing that' locution which primary epistemic seeing is meant to reflect, and it is for this reason that the four conditions on the right are taken as sufficient and necessary for *primary* epistemic seeing. If S knows that the screwdriver is on the workbench, and he knows this because he can see that it is on the workbench, then S's visual achievement satisfies the four conditions listed above.

Relations tend to complicate the picture in several respects. When there are *two* objects (or events) that must be seen, the possibility exists of seeing them at *different* times. I saw that Harry was taller than Jimmy, not by seeing Harry and Jimmy simultaneously but by seeing, first Harry, then Jimmy. Is this to count as a satisfaction of condition (ii)? Ordinarily, given an 'obvious' difference in height, we would have little hesitation in saying we saw that one was taller than the other—especially if we saw them within a few minutes (or few hours, weeks, or even a few years if both Harry and Jimmy were full-grown adults) of each other. If the case could rest with ordinary examples, I think the case would be complete: *b* and *c* *need* not be seen simultaneously. But the case does not rest here. For I am not *now* trying to describe what we do and what we do not see to be the case, or what we say and what we do not say we see to be the case, but rather what we see to be the case in some fundamental (primary) epistemic way. And it may be argued that when we see *b* and *c* at different times, the situation is analogous to, say, successive measurements with a yardstick. That is, we first see that the table is longer than the yardstick, and then see that the yardstick is longer than the doorway, and then, by virtue of these two operations, we 'see that' the doorway is too narrow for the table. In other words, it may be supposed that when *b* and *c* are seen at different times, we should classify this way of seeing their relationship to each other as a form of *secondary* epistemic seeing, or, perhaps, not even as a form of seeing at all but as a way of determining that *b* is R to *c* *on the basis of what we have seen.* When one sees that Harry is taller than Jimmy by seeing them at different times, one always (??) utilizes some third object (reference object), perhaps the background, perhaps one's own body, to gauge successively the height of the two men. One sees that the first is taller than that lamp, say, and that the second is not. Then, by utilizing (assuming) certain principles, one concludes (infers?) that the first man is taller than the second. These principles include such things as the presumed constancy in the height of the lamp, the presumed constancy in the height of the two men between the occasions when they were compared with the lamp, and so on.

I think that if this is meant as a description of the psychological processes in which *everyone* engages *whenever* they truly say that they have seen that two men differ in height (when the two men were seen at different times), I think it is factually false. Certainly there are background conditions which must obtain before we can truly be said to have seen that the men differed in height, but this does make the present state of affairs different than *any* other perceptual state of affairs. Certain background conditions must also obtain if we are to see that they differ in height when we see them at the *same* time. The increased complexity of these background conditions (involving certain temporal considerations) does not, by itself, show that we do not see what we allege ourselves to see. The background conditions which must obtain if we are to see that some person is an *old* woman are also, in a sense, more complex than those which must obtain for us to see that some person is a woman; but this alone does not mean that we cannot see that a person is an old woman.

I think the manner in which we answer this question is somewhat arbitrary. The question is whether we should treat such cases as instances of primary epistemic perception or as instances of secondary epistemic perception (to be discussed in the following section), and I do not see that it makes much difference *how* we classify it. For reasons of convenience, I have chosen to treat those cases of seeing that b is R to c, when b and c are seen at different times, as cases of secondary epistemic perception, but I do not regard this choice as particularly significant. I am not (as I shall argue in the next section) assigning these cases to any second-rate epistemological citizenship. All my choice amounts to, in the last analysis, is a decision to define my own technical term (*primary* epistemic seeing) in one way rather than another.

Having said this much, I shall henceforth restrict clause (ii) to situations in which b and c are seen at roughly the same time. The qualifier 'roughly' is prefixed in order to suggest a degree of looseness in the interpretation of this clause. I do not mean to interpret the phrase 'the same time' as signifying some instant, some mathematical point, in the time continuum. Clause (ii) will be kept flexible enough so that it makes sense to say, of two events which occurred within a very short time of one another, that S saw (in a *primary* way) that the one event *preceded* the other: e.g. I saw that Bill fired before his opponent. This is not very precise, but, as we shall see later, the borderline between primary and secondary epistemic seeing is not a very precise line; and it cannot be made very precise without making a host of *arbitrary* decisions. And since these arbitrary decisions do not affect what is seen, when it is seen, or the epistemological significance of seeing it, I think we can proceed without making them.

Many of the same remarks can be made about our new schema that were made in the last chapter about seeing that b is P. Once again there are background conditions (the ones mentioned in (iii)) and a background belief (mentioned in (iv)) about the satisfaction of condition (iii). One significant new development is the slightly altered status of S's proto-knowledge. When S sees that b is R to c, both 'b' and 'c' reflect S's proto-knowledge. When S knows that the pen is longer than the pencil, and he knows this because (as he testifies) he could see that the one was longer than the other, his perceptual claim tells us *how* he discovered that the pen was longer than the pencil; it does not tell us how he discovered that one was a pencil and the other a pen. In many circumstances, of course, we would expect him to be able to see that the one on the left, say, was a pen and the one on the right a pencil, but S's capacity to do this is certainly not entailed by his capacity to see that the pen is longer than the pencil. He may have been told which was the pen and which the pencil, or he may first have determined which was which in a variety of different ways. Seeing that the pen is longer than the pencil represents an increment in knowledge in the sense that it tells us how the percipient went from (i) this is a pen, and (ii) that is a pencil, to (iii) the pen is longer than the pencil. Of course, (i) and (ii) may not represent S's actual proto-knowledge at the time he saw that the pen was longer than the pencil; he may, at the time, have only identified one as the blue object and the other as the red object (and discovered which was the pen and which was the pencil later, or if *we* are describing what S did, S may still not know which was which). The important point is, however, that if we are going to assess whether S could see what it is claimed he saw, we must not get sidetracked into the totally irrelevant issue of whether he could, in those conditions, see that the two things which differed in length were, indeed, a pen and a pencil or were, indeed, a red object and a blue object, or (the ultimate in irrelevance) two real objects (in contrast to figments of his own imagination). If we are going to ask whether S did (or could) see what he claims (or we claim) he saw, then we must ask whether the conditions were such that *the pen* and *the pencil* (or the red object and the blue object) only look the way they did to S when the one he took to be longer *is* longer. That is, we must ask whether condition (iii) is satisfied.

Relations bring with them other possibilities. What I discover may sometimes be described, not by saying that I saw that *the pen* was longer than the pencil, but by saying that I could see that *it was a pen* that was longer than the pencil. And this is but a way of introducing what might be called an existential form of epistemic seeing: e.g. S saw that there was some beer in the refrigerator, S could see that there was someone in the room, and S could see that there was some money in the jar. Such statements describe significantly different achievements than those we have so far considered, and this difference is reflected primarily in a corresponding alteration of condition (iii). Nevertheless, no major revisions are necessitated; what I have said about proto-knowledge, background conditions, and background beliefs remains essentially the same. What changes is the *increment* in knowledge which the statement depicts the percipient as having acquired by visual means.

A complete description of the subtle variations on this theme would be a vast undertaking, one which would require another book for its satisfactory completion. Therefore, let me simply try to illustrate the salient features of what I have just called 'existential epistemic seeing'. Consider the statement (said in a justificatory context) 'S saw that there was a rabbit in the garden'. This tells us how S knew there was a rabbit in the garden. Does it also tell us *how* S knew that what the rabbit was in was a garden? Certainly it suggests that S knew that it was a garden which the rabbit was in, but does it tell us that S could see that what the rabbit was in was a garden? I think the answer to this is clearly 'No'. If a comparative stranger asks to show you his garden, and during the guided tour you remark to yourself, 'Funniest looking garden I ever saw; not a flower or plant in sight,' you are not thereby prevented from seeing that there is a rabbit in his garden. You have reason to believe it is a garden (he said it was his garden), but your reason for believing it to be a garden is surely not that you can see that it is a garden. Yet, there is nothing extraordinary about expressing yourself by saying that you can see that there is a rabbit in his garden. There is nothing extravagant about this perceptual claim since 'This is his garden' is part of your proto-knowledge; at least it is depicted as such by the claim that you can see that there is a rabbit in his garden. This information is *not* included within that increment which your statement describes you as having acquired by *visual* means. Hence, if we wish to formulate our four defining conditions for primary epistemic seeing in a way that is appropriate for this particular example of existential seeing, they should read:

(i) There is a rabbit in his garden.
(ii) S sees$_n$ both the rabbit and the garden.
(iii) Conditions are such that his garden would not look the way it does to S unless there was a rabbit in it.[1]
(iv) S, believing conditions are as described in (iii), believes that there is a rabbit in his garden.

S's proto-knowledge is here reflected in the formulation of (iii). It is not that *anything* which looks this particular way to S (under these background conditions) is a garden with a rabbit in it or is *his garden* with a rabbit in it. Rather, given S's proto-knowledge, he sees that there is a rabbit in his garden if the conditions are such that *his garden* (not just *any* garden or not just anything) would not look the way it now does to S unless it had a rabbit in it. The generalized form of these four conditions (see footnote) represent, then, the defining schema for seeing that *there is a b* which is R to *c* in a primary epistemic way.

Of course, one may object that the object which S sees may not be a rabbit at all; it *might* be a clever mechanical contrivance of some sort. If this 'might' is to be understood as simply a way of calling attention to the fact that (iii) is not a logical truth, then we can quickly agree. For it is indeed logically possible that the conditions are not as described in (iii). But the fact that conditions

---

[1] Considerable care must be taken in the formulation of this condition with certain relations. For example, if S sees that there is a dog *next to* the tree, we can hardly say that the conditions are such that *the tree* would not look the way it does to S unless there was a dog next to it. *The tree* might look the same whether it has a dog next to it or not. In such cases (this will depend on the relation involved) we must say that the tree and its environment would not look the way they do to S in these conditions unless there was a dog next to the tree. Or, to put in its most general form, conditions are such that *c* and its environment would not look the way they now do (L) to S unless there was a *b* which was R to *c*. In this general case the word 'environment' is meant to comprehend everything (other than *c*) which S sees$_n$, and 'L' is meant to signify, as it did previously, the 'total look' of *c* and its environment and not simply some special aspect of the way *c* and its environment look to S.

might not be as described in (iii), in the sense of this word which is appropriate to logic, does not mean that they are not as described in (iii). And what is essential to S's visual achievement is not that (iii) be *necessarily* true, but that it be *true*. For if it is true, we can say that the garden would not have looked the way it did to S unless it had a rabbit in it and, hence, S had, in the way the garden looked to him, a conclusive reason (in the sense discussed in the preceding chapter) for believing that there was a rabbit in the garden. To the best of my knowledge, there are no imitation rabbits scampering about gardens, imitations which cannot, at ten paces, be distinguished from a genuine frightened rabbit. Hence, to the best of my knowledge, there is nothing unusual about supposing that in relation to many gardens clause (iii) is frequently satisfied. *If* such clever imitations someday become available, and *if* people start putting them in their garden, then it will turn out that in *these* conditions (the conditions under which S saw the garden and the rabbit) gardens will not *only* look the way this garden now looks to S when there is a (real) rabbit in them. *If* this happens, *then* condition (iii) will no longer be satisfied, and we will say that S cannot, not under *these* conditions (i.e. from ten paces away), see whether there is a (real) rabbit in the garden.[1] But until such time as people start behaving in this extraordinary manner, there is nothing to suggest that clause (iii) is not frequently satisfied with respect to gardens. Therefore, there is nothing to suggest that S cannot see that there is a rabbit in this garden. Whether he does or does not see this depends on the actual truth of (iii); it does not depend on whether it *could* be false in some logical sense of 'could'.

I think that most 'existential' seeings will exhibit the same pattern. A certain element of proto-knowledge is reflected in the accompanying phrase. We see that there is a b on, over, in, next to, near, behind, to the left of, talking to, following, watching, shaking hands with, so-and-so. When we report what we have seen to be the case in this manner, we tell our listeners how we know that there is a b which is R to c, but we do not tell them how

[1] This would still not prevent me from seeing whether there was a rabbit in *my garden*, since the regularities governing the appearance of things in my garden may be quite different than gardens in general. I may quite truly believe that in these conditions *my garden* would not look the way it does to me unless there was a rabbit in it (whatever may be true of *other* gardens).

we know that it is *c* to which *b* is related by R. I may not be able to tell whether someone is a widow or not by seeing whether they are; such an identification may exceed the limits of what we can discover by purely visual means. Nonetheless, this does not prevent me from seeing that there is someone talking to the widow. And once this pattern becomes familiar, it is an easy step to appreciating the subtle difference between such statements as (*a*) *S* saw that *there was* a rabbit in the garden, and (*b*) *S* saw that *it was* a rabbit that was in the garden. If *S* is given over to eidetic imagery of a special sort (visual images projected onto a normal landscape with the eyes open), we might wish to deny him the ability represented by (*a*), but concede him the ability represented by (*b*). To see why this is so, simply consider the way condition (iii) would be expressed in relation to these respective claims:

(*a*) Conditions are such that *the garden* would not look this way to *S* unless there was a rabbit in it.
(*b*) Conditions are such that *something in the garden* would not look this way to *S* unless it was a rabbit.

That is, these two claims reflect different levels of proto-knowledge, and, given *S*'s affliction, we may wish to say that conditions might be as described in (*b*) but not as described in (*a*). For instance, if other people had been pointing at the rabbit and asking 'What is that thing in the garden?', *S*'s affliction does not stand in the way of his seeing that it is a rabbit that is in the garden (for its being something in the garden, and not an eidetic image, is given here in *S*'s proto-knowledge). But we may wish to say that under these conditions, *S* is still not able to see that there is a rabbit in the garden since the conditions described in (*a*) above are not satisfied: the garden *would* (or *might*) look this way to *S* when there was no rabbit in it (but, rather, an eidetic projection of one).

The complications could, perhaps, be multiplied indefinitely by subtle shifts in the syntax of the 'that' clause (e.g. by playing with definite and indefinite articles). What, for instance, is the difference between seeing that it was a cat that had fallen from the ledge into the well and seeing that the cat had fallen from a ledge into a well? I will not pause long enough to answer my own question. I think I have said enough to suggest the general approach, and I would now like to shift attention to some other important facets of seeing something relational in nature.

It may be trivial, but I should like to point out that a failure to see, or to be able to see, that a certain relationship holds in one set of circumstances, with respect to certain elements, does not mean that one is thereby prevented from seeing that it holds in altered circumstances with different elements. Some things are longer than others, but the difference in length is too minute to be visible to the naked eye. Clearly this fact is irrelevant to whether I can see that this fishing pole is longer than that pencil. I cannot see which of those two cars is moving faster, but I can see that both are moving faster than the wagon. I cannot see any difference in color between these two samples, but I can certainly see that they both differ in color from this third sample. Trivial as this point may be, it sometimes seems to be overlooked. Because I cannot see when any two people are in love does not mean, by itself, that I cannot see that *these* two people are in love. Because I cannot, given any two objects, see which is heavier does not mean that I cannot, in *these* circumstances, see that *this* object is heavier than *that* object. If I cannot see these things, in the strictly visual sense now in question, it is not because the ability to see them fails to be universally applicable to all sets of objects (or persons) in all circumstances. For this argument, if accepted, could be used to show that *nothing* relational in nature was *ever* seen.

These same remarks apply, of course, to seeing that something has a particular (non-relational) property. Some things (e.g. fleas) are very small; we cannot see what shape they are with the un-aided eye. I shall say more about this later, but the same is true of people. Some people are not very demonstrative; I cannot tell whether they are angry or not. This does not mean, however, that I cannot see that my best friend is angry. And this does not imply that I can *always* see when he is angry; it simply means that *he* would not behave *this* way unless he were angry. If, for some reason, I cannot see that my friend is angry in the same sense in which I see that his face is getting red and his teeth are clenched, it is not because he *could* (logically) do this without being angry or that certain actors might look this way without being angry. The question is: could my friend (not just anyone) ever, in fact, behave this way in these circumstances without being angry? For it is a negative answer to this question which is what allows me, when the assumption is true, to see that he is angry.

Another significant feature of relations—significant, that is, with respect to our ability to see that they are exemplified—is the explicitness with which they are expressed in our statements about what is seen. Sometimes the relation is given explicit expression: e.g. *S* saw that Harold was standing between the sofa and the table. At other times it is less explicit: *S* saw where Harold was standing, that Harold had a good position (spot, location, vantage point, etc.). Occasionally the relation is almost totally concealed. For instance, we can say that *S* saw that the length of remaining cord was only three feet. If one chooses to construe this statement as of the form '*S* sees that *b* is *P*', difficulties are unavoidable. For the next step is to construe 'the length of something' as a non-relational property of things on the model of 'the color of something'. Given this interpretation, it is a quick slide to the conclusion that this property, the length of something, is unobservable. For although we can tell what the color of something is just by looking at it (in the right conditions), we cannot tell what the length of something is just by looking at *it* (no matter how close we are or how good the lighting may be). We need a yardstick (or some other measuring device) for this; somehow the yardstick allows us to determine the numerical value of this non-observable property. Or so one might argue if one insists on interpreting the statement in this manner. If, however, one realizes that to see that something is three feet long is to see that it is *the same length* as something else which one knows (proto-knowledge) to be three feet, there is no longer any reason to regard length as a non-observable property of things. Instead one will treat it, correctly, I think, as an observable relation between things.[1]

Indirectly related to the question of implicit relations is the matter of seeing that something is *not* the case. With some relations (and non-relational properties) this offers no difficulty. I see little Susan and her brother and see that her brother is not taller than she. Conditions (i)–(iv) can be applied to this case with only minor and perfectly straightforward adjustments (the inclusion of a 'not' in (i) and (iii)). With some relations, however, especially *spatial* relations, one can see that *b* is not R to *c* without seeing both *b* and

---

[1] I prefer not to speak of properties and relations as being 'observable' and 'unobservable'. This can be extremely misleading, and I shall indicate why this is so when I take up the question again in Section #2 and #4 of the final chapter. I ask the reader, therefore, not to put too much pressure on my use of the term 'observable' at this point.

c; yet what is seen seems to be seen in as *primary* a way as is possible. For example, I could see that Susan was not in her room; I saw the room, but did not see Susan. Or I saw Susan (playing outside), but did not see her room. In such cases the second clause of our schema (S sees *both* b and c) is not satisfied. Are we, for this reason alone, to count such cases as instances of secondary epistemic seeing (whatever that may turn out to be)? I think not. Although classification is always somewhat arbitrary, I believe such cases can best be understood as seeing that so-and-so is not R to such-and-such in a primary epistemic way. We can achieve this inclusion by understanding that when S sees that b is *not* R to c, he can do this without satisfying (i)–(iv) as they now stand. Rather, he *may* (depending on the relation involved) satisfy the slightly modified conditions:

(i) b is not R to c.
(ii) S sees$_n$ b (or c).
(iii) Conditions are such that if b were R to c, b (or c) would not look the way it now does (L) relative to its environment to S.
(iv) S, believing conditions are as described in (iii), believes that b is not R to c.

Generally speaking, we may say that S's seeing that b is *not* R to c is an instance of primary epistemic seeing only if under these same background conditions, S could see that b is R to c in a primary way if, contrary to fact, b was R to c.

This matter is related to the question of implicit relations by the fact that certain instances of seeing that b is not R to c are described by statements in which the relationships are well concealed, and when this happens we get something which may appear puzzling on superficial analysis. For example, 'I saw that Susan was gone' looks, on the face of it, like a case of 'seeing that b is P' *without* seeing b. The word 'gone', however, simply means 'not here' or, better yet (because more explicit), 'not *in* this region (where 'this region' is determined by the context)'. Seeing that Susan is gone is, therefore, an instance of seeing that Susan is not in her room (or not in the vicinity, or whatever). There are dozens of such cases, but I do not believe they call for individual treatment. Seeing that everyone has left, that Harold is absent, that his index finger is missing, that there is nothing to eat, that the rain has stopped, and that one's wallet is gone are each (given the right circumstances—see the above schema) instances of primary epistemic seeing. Which is not to say that they are *always* instances of primary seeing. I might see that his wallet is gone by seeing neither his wallet *nor* the place where his wallet would be if it were not gone. I might see that his wallet was gone by observing his frantic movements, the look of panic in his eyes, as the waiter stood impatiently in front of him with the bill. But this is a case of seeing that *b* is not R to *c* in a *secondary* epistemic way, a manner of seeing to which we must now turn.

2. *Secondary Epistemic Seeing*

Quite frequently, we see that *b* is *P*, not in virtue of the way *b* looks or behaves, but in virtue of the way other objects look or behave when *b* is *P*. A cook may place a toothpick into her cake to see if it is done; if it emerges with batter on it, the cake is not yet ready to remove from the oven; if it is dry, the cake is done. The traffic officer can, by examining the length of the tire marks produced by the sudden braking action, see whether the driver was exceeding the speed limit. And the way I tell whether my cigarette lighter is low on fluid is by observing the flame.

In such cases, although we may see$_n$ *b* when we see that it is *P*, seeing *b* is, as it were, incidental; it is the way other things look, or the way other things are behaving, the leads us to say that we can see that *b* is *P*. I would like to call these situations instances of seeing that something is the case in a secondary epistemic manner. More precisely:

S sees that *b* is *P* in a secondary epistemic way:
  (i) *b* is *P*.
  (ii) *S* sees *c* (*c* ≠ *b*) and sees (primarily) that *c* is *Q*.
  (iii) Conditions are such that *c* would not be *Q* unless *b* were *P*.[1]
  (iv) *S*, believing the conditions are as described in (iii), takes *b* to be *P*.

[1] The background conditions for secondary seeing may be defined thus: *B* is a background condition if and only if (*a*) *B* is logically and causally independent of the particular character and properties of *b* itself (and, in particular, of *b*'s being *P*); and (*b*) there are variations in *B* which affect (i.e. can alter) *c*'s being *Q*. For example, in seeing that you still have some gasoline in your fuel tank by glancing at your gauge, a background condition is the strength of your automobile battery (for electrically operated gauges), since variations in the strength of your battery will affect the reading of your fuel gauge without affecting the fuel tank itself (and, in particular, without affecting the amount of gasoline you have in your tank).

By introducing relations this schema can be extended in rather obvious ways. For example, S may see that b is P by seeing that c_1 is R to c_2 or by seeing that c is R to b. Let me illustrate some of this variety by a few examples. If I see that the piece of metal is hot by seeing it glow in the way characteristic of hot metal, then I see that it is hot in a primary epistemic manner. If I see that the metal is hot by observing that the solder (which is in contact with it) is rapidly melting, then I am seeing that b (the metal) is P (hot) in a secondary way by seeing that c (the solder on the metal) is Q (melting rapidly). If I see that the metal is hot by noting the reading on a (properly connected) thermometer, then I am also seeing that the metal is hot in a secondary way by seeing that c_1 (the mercury in the thermometer) is R (beyond) to c_2 (the 300° mark). The variations here are almost endless, and I do not intend (even if I were able) to exhibit them all. I would, however, like to display one more schema since we will have occasion to refer to it in what follows. This is the schema for seeing something relational in nature in a secondary epistemic way:

> S sees that b_1 is R to b_2 in a secondary epistemic way:
> (i) b_1 is R to b_2.
> (ii) S sees b_1 and sees (primarily) that b_1 is Q or S sees b_2 and sees (primarily) that b_2 is U or S sees c_1 and sees (primarily) that c_1 is T or S sees c_1 and c_2 and sees (primarily) that c_1 is M to c_2. . . . . . .
> (iii) Conditions are such that b_1 would not be Q unless b_1 was R to b_2 or . . . . .
> (iv) S, believing the conditions are as described in (iii), takes b_1 to be R to b_2.

I have by no means exhausted the possibilities, but we are, I think, reaching the point of diminishing returns. Additional complications can only confuse the basic underlying pattern of all these schemata. Let me, therefore, give just one example of each of the four possibilities mentioned in clauses (ii) and (iii). S might see that the house was occupied, that someone was *in* the house, by observing the house and watching the lights go on and off in various rooms, smoke issue from the chimney, and so on. That is, he sees that b_1 (the house) is R (is occupied) to b_2 (by someone) by seeing that b_1 (the house) is Q (has various windows lit and smoke ascending from its chimney). The second alternative in the above schema is simply the same as the first with the order of the terms reversed: e.g. S can see that the chair (b_1) is covered (R) with a blanket (b_2) by seeing, simply, the blanket (with its revealing bulges) but not the chair. The third alternative might be illustrated by a variety of detection devices: a light flashes (c_1 becomes T) when a certain relational state of affairs obtains—say, the water level descends below a certain point (b_1 is R to b_2). The remaining case is, perhaps, the most significant for some purposes since it is very often exemplified in measuring procedures: seeing how fast the vehicle is moving relative to the ground by reading the speedometer, or seeing who is heaviest by looking at the dial on the scale.

Notice, each instance of secondary seeing embodies a primary epistemic achievement (clause (ii)). There is reason to suppose that this is not essential; one may see that b is P (or see that b_1 is R to b_2) without seeing that c is Q (or that b_1 is Q, etc.) in any primary way. It may turn out that one sees that b is P, not by seeing that c is Q, but simply in virtue of the way c itself *looks*. For example, I may see that someone is fooling around with the lights *by the way the actors and objects on the stage look* (they look first blue, then red, and so on). I do not, of course, see that the actors (and objects) are changing color, nor does there seem to be any necessity for saying that I see that anything *is* the case besides the fact that someone is fooling with the lights. Here, then, we have a limiting case: S sees that b is P *by the way c looks* (not by the way *c is*), and I shall henceforth understand that the various schemata for secondary seeing have this as a possible limiting case. That is, (ii) may become 'S sees$_n$ c' and (iii) becomes 'Conditions are such that c would not look the way it does to S unless b were P'.

One must be careful to distinguish between seeing that b is P in a secondary way and seeing that b_1 is R to b_2 in a primary way. Simply because one must look at something else (besides b) to determine whether b is P does not automatically mean that b is seen to be P in a secondary way. It may mean that P is implicitly relational. To use a previous example, we do not, when using a yardstick, see that the table is three feet long *in a secondary way*; rather it is (as I shall argue more fully in Chapter VI) to see primarily that a certain relationship holds between the yardstick and the table. Conversely, to see that the letter came from Germany, by examining its postmark, is most plausibly construed, I think as a case of seeing that b_1 is R to b_2 (the letter was sent from somewhere in Germany) by seeing that b_1 (the letter) has a German postmark (is Q)—i.e. the first alternative in the above schema for seeing that a certain relation holds in a secondary manner.

Instances of seeing that b is P (or that b_1 is R to b_2) in a secondary fashion give some impetus to the idea that the verb 'to see', when it is followed by a 'that' clause, does not signify a *visual* achievement at all—or, if it does, it is only incidentally visual. Once the visual tie (see$_n$) with b (or b_1 and b_2) is broken, as we have broken it in our last several schemata for secondary seeing, there seems to be no limit to the extremes to which one can go. If we can see that the metal is hot by watching the behavior of a thermometer in the presence of the metal, then we should also be able to see that it is hot by observing the behavior of a *properly connected* thermometer in the absence of the metal. And if we can *see* this, why not say that we can see that the metal *was* hot by reading a continuously recording temperature graph? And why not go even further? Why not see that it was hot by reading the report of the man who, say, read the graph. And as the ultimate in disassociation, why not say that we can see that the metal was hot when we have only *heard* the report of the man who *felt* that it was hot. And what does all of this have to do with the eyes?

Well, it has very little (or nothing) to do with our sense of sight. Yet, I think it is undeniable that we sometimes *say* we see that so-and-so is (was) the case even in such extreme situations as the last mentioned. I do not think it extraordinary to hear someone say (when he hears the clatter from his engine) that he can see that his valves are acting up again, that he can see that his neighbors are at it again (when he hears the dishes breaking), or that he can see how it works (by actually placing his hand near the suction nozzle). Somewhere, of course, we draw a line, but I think it would be impossible to say, in a general way, where this line is or how often it gets shifted or how much it depends on context. As I have said before, if we try to ascertain the meaning of the construction 'sees that b is P', and all of its variants, by taking the *common denominator* of all its uses, the inevitable result is going to be that this construction will lose all of its visual impact. The expression will merge with 'realizing (or understanding) that b is P' and there will be nothing of a visual nature left to discuss.

I must emphasize again, however, that I am not proposing an analysis of this linguistic construction in all its uses. I am not attempting to describe, on some general level, a type of achievement expressed by *every* epistemic use of the verb 'to see'. I am attempting to describe only one special sort of achievement (in Chapters III and IV) which this verb is frequently used to describe, an achievement which is both *visual* in nature and *epistemic* in character, an achievement which is constituted by the *visual* acquisition of knowledge. In a word, I am interested in the construction '*S* can see (saw) that *b* is (was) *P*' in so far as it can be used to answer the question '*How* does *S* know that *b* is (was) *P*?' The fact that this form of words often tells us *only* that *S* does know, or has reason to believe, that *b* is *P*, and not *how* he knows or what his reasons are, is, for my purposes, irrelevant. Seeing something in a primary epistemic way represents a particularly favored position in which we sometimes find ourselves for answering the question 'How do you know that *b* is *P*?' The position is favored, epistemologically speaking, because we have available the reply 'I can see that it is *P*', not *by* the newspapers, not *by* the gauge, not *by* seeing that something else is *Q*, but *by* seeing *b* itself.[1] But secondary seeing *also* gives us an answer to the 'How' question. Generally speaking, however, we are expected to qualify our reports of secondary epistemic perceptions with an appropriate 'by ...' phrase. How do you know someone has been in your garden? I can see by these footprints that someone has been here. How do you know there is someone in the house? I can see by the lights and smoke that there is. How do you know she wrote this letter? I can see by the handwriting. Primary and secondary epistemic seeing, taken together, as defined by our assorted schemata in this and the last chapter, comprehend the distinctively visual ways we have of acquiring knowledge, and in this sense they exhaust the epistemic senses of 'to see' which are *essentially* visual in nature.

Primary epistemic seeing earns the epithet 'primary' in virtue of its fundamental epistemological status. The respect in which it is fundamental is revealed in clauses (ii) and (iii) in our various schemata for secondary seeing. Unless we could see that *c* was *Q*, for some value of '*c*' and some value of '*Q*', in a *primary* fashion, we could never see that anything was the case in *any* way (that was essentially visual). The only exception to this is the limiting case,

---

[1] The favored status of primary seeing is often reflected in a deletion of the 'that'; e.g. we say, 'I saw Jimmy getting ready to leave' and not (always) 'I saw that Jimmy was getting ready to leave'. See next section for a fuller discussion of this feature.

mentioned earlier, in which S sees that b is P by the way c *looks* (without seeing that c *is* Q for any value of 'Q'). It would be of little help to assume that state S_1 (c's being Q) was an infallible sign of state S_2 (b's being P) in these conditions if one could never, in these conditions, see whether c was Q. Wind socks permit us to see in which direction the wind is blowing because we can see the wind sock itself and see what it is doing. The reverse is not the case, however. Someone (a child, say) might see what the wind sock was doing and not, thereby, see from which direction the wind was blowing.

Secondary epistemic seeing involves a more extensive set of background conditions and, therefore, a more comprehensive background belief. It requires that the background conditions not only be such as to allow one to see that c is Q (primarily) but also such as to insure the relationship or connection between c's being Q and b's being P. In this respect, secondary epistemic seeing exposes itself, at a greater number of points, to the possibility of error. Since it depends for its successful realization on the presence (in these conditions) of a regularity between c's being Q and b's being P, it is vulnerable at a point where the embodied primary achievement is not. This is why, when confronted with a sceptical query concerning our perceptual report (when they are secondary), we 'fall back' to what we have seen primarily: I could see by the ashtrays, disarray of the furniture, etc., that someone had been here; and we generally include such information in our perceptual reports, not only to anticipate such queries (whether they be sceptical or merely prompted by curiosity) but also to indicate our *credentials*, the course of our assurance, that b is P. Such a practice reveals to our listeners what regular connection it was on which we were relying and it has the effect of focusing subsequent questions, if there are any, on the issue of whether or not, in those conditions, such a regularity can be taken for granted.

Although the primary form of epistemic seeing is more fundamental in this sense, one should not conclude from this that the secondary form does not represent a purely visual achievement of an epistemic sort. For despite the fact that a more elaborate system of background conditions is necessitated in secondary seeing, the belief that they are as described in (iii) is still a *background belief*, still a belief which is *manifested* in seeing by c's being Q that b is P and not a belief which is *used* in any discursive process of *concluding* that b is P; and one still has, by virtue of this belief's being true, a conclusive reason (in the sense previously discussed) in what one sees for believing that b is P. Secondary seeing does not, any more than primary seeing, involve a reasoning or inferring that b is P on the basis of what one has seen to be the case or on the basis of how something looks. I am not, of course, denying that we often do *infer* that something is the case *on the basis* of what we have seen. But it seems clear to me that when this does happen, we have done something quite different than what is normally described by the formula 'I saw by . . . that so-and-so was the case'. In studying a man's behavior I might *infer*, on the *basis* of what I see, that he loves horses; but although this might be an adequate description of what makes me *think* he loves horses, it hardly suffices to tell you *how* (or even *whether*) I *know* that he loves horses (since it, unlike the 'seeing that' locution, does not even imply the truth of what I consequently believe). What I am trying to describe with the various schemata for primary and secondary epistemic seeing is a certain class of situations in which we sometimes find ourselves, a class of situations which make available to us, when we are in them, a kind of answer to the question 'How do you know that b is P?' that is distinctively visual. Secondary seeing, as I am now trying to characterize it, shares with primary seeing the feature of being unmediated by conscious intellectual *processes*; in both cases the most that one is described as doing, in any reasonable sense of the word 'do', is *seeing* (in the case of primary seeing, seeing$_n$ b; in the case of secondary seeing, seeing that c is Q) and coming to (or verifying) the belief that b is P. The *presumption* that certain regularities obtain transforms what could (in *other* circumstances, circumstances in which the pertinent regularities were *not* taken for granted) have been an exercise in inference into an attainment which short-circuits those discursive processes which might otherwise stand between the seeing and the believing. And the same remarks that were made about background beliefs in connection with primary epistemic seeing apply to those in secondary seeing. What makes these beliefs effective, what gives them the power to broaden the scope of what we can see to be the case, is (i) their truth, and (ii) their *being* beliefs. Questions concerning their degree of justification, whether they occur in primary or secondary seeing, are relevant only to the extent that they affect the percipient's willingness or capacity to assume them true. If they are true, then the percipient is, so to speak, in a position to see that b is P by seeing that c is Q; and if he assumes them true, then he *does* see that b is P by seeing that c is Q. If he sees that c is Q without an appropriate background belief (in the satisfaction of condition (iii)), then he may, by virtue of certain other procedures (inferring, interpreting, etc.), come to the belief that b is P *on the basis* of what he has seen. But when this happens his seeing that c was Q functions as only *one* of the stages in the process by which he arrived at his belief that b was P. And the presence of *other* elements (inference, interpretation, accumulation of further evidence, etc.) means that the percipient did not arrive at his belief that b was P *simply* by seeing that c was Q. Rather, he arrived at this belief by at least two psychologically distinguishable steps: seeing that c was Q *and* inferring or interpreting this as a sign that b was P.

Secondary seeing also exemplifies a more extensive application of proto-knowledge. When S sees (by c's being Q) that b is P, both 'c' and 'b' reflect S's proto-knowledge. When S says that he can see (by the water level) that the drain is plugged, he is not testifying to his ability to see that it is water which has backed up into the sink or his ability to see that what is plugged is a drain. This visual achievement, as so reported, only tells us how S knows that the water is backed-up, *what* he is assuming about the connection between the water level and a plugged drain, and, hence, *how* he knows that the drain is plugged. The function of proto-knowledge is, in fact, most easily seen in the case of secondary seeing. For in the example just mentioned it is clear that S need not even see (see$_n$) the drain itself, or any part of it, to see that it is plugged. Hence, he may not be in a position to say that he knows it is a drain which is plugged since he can see that it (what is plugged) is a drain. To object to S's visual report on the basis of the undeniable fact that the sink (which he does see) may not even have a drain (without things looking any different to S) is to make a totally misplaced objection. For the fact that the sink *has* a drain is not part of what S has described himself as finding out by visual means. Hence, this fact (that S is in no position to see that the sink has a drain) is irrelevant to whether S did achieve, *visually*, what he described himself as having achieved. It is, therefore, irrelevant to whether S does know what his perceptual report commits him to knowing.

I conclude, therefore, that although we have two distinguishable forms of epistemic seeing, and although one is, in certain respects, more fundamental, *both* forms represent a purely visual epistemic achievement. Both represent a direct (i.e. non-mediated) way of acquiring knowledge about our environment by using our eyes. If one wishes to object that secondary seeing is not a *purely* visual achievement because it involves too many conceptual elements, I think such an objection would spring from a simple confusion between *what one is doing* and the *conditions under which it is done*. All epistemic seeing, both secondary and primary, presupposes the satisfaction of certain conditions; some of these are physical and physiological in nature (condition (iii)) and some conceptual in nature (condition (iv)—the belief that (iii) is satisfied). But the fact that the visual achievement can only be engineered in certain conditions does not imply that it is any the less visual. The fact that one cannot set a record in the broad jump without meeting certain competitive standards (e.g. wind velocity below a certain level) does not mean that one must do something in addition to *jumping*, say, twenty-nine feet; one must simply do this *under* competitive conditions and *in* regulation circumstances. In both primary and secondary epistemic seeing a belief is generated (or, if one already possessed the belief, it is verified) as a direct result of a visual experience occurring within a certain set of conditions, and when this occurs one has seen that something was the case however complex may be the conditions which made this result possible.

The chief difference between primary and secondary seeing is that, under critical pressure, we can more easily be brought to qualify, hedge, or even retract our latter perceptual claims; and this is so because the achievement which we report depends, for its successful realization, on a more elaborate network of regularities (background conditions being such that c would not be Q unless b were P). But this does not imply that what we see in a secondary fashion we did not (at the time we alleged ourselves to have seen it) really know it to be the case or that we did not really see it to be the case. Admittedly, condition (iii) in secondary seeing may, generally speaking, be more difficult to satisfy than the corresponding condition in most cases of primary epistemic seeing. But that it frequently *is* satisfied, and we frequently assume it satisfied, is undeniable. For to deny it would be to deny the most well-established regularities which dominate our physical environment. It would, for example, be tantamount to denying that there are conditions under which certain thermometers in water only read 200° F. when the water is hot, and *would* not read such unless the water was hot. For this is all that need be satisfied to see (by the thermometer) that the water is hot.

What is interesting in relation to secondary perceptual achievements is that the 'by' phrase which normally accompanies them acts as a *signal* to one's listeners. Assuming them to be reasonably well informed about the regularities which prevail within the relevant environment, this qualifying phrase tells them what kind of 'weight' they can place on the implied claim to knowledge, and thus protects the speaker from the possible charge of being misleading. In saying 'I see by *The Times* that oil has been discovered in Hashabar' I am allowing my listeners to decide *for themselves* to what degree they may depend on the facts I report. Would *The Times* have printed such a story if it were not true? Is (iii) satisfied? My listeners can decide this question as they please, but they should not later accuse me of having misled them by implying that I knew something which was not true (or for which I had insufficient grounds for saying I knew). But at this point, as the assurance in the satisfaction of condition (iii) becomes less and less secure, and we consequently take greater and greater pains to tell our listeners *by what it was* that we saw that so-and-so was the case, secondary seeing begins to merge with 'learning that . . . by such-and-such means' and the description of the *means* begins to assume the important role and the 'seeing that' locution no longer functions as an adequate answer to the question '*How* do you know?' This, then, is the borderline between secondary epistemic seeing and epistemic achievements *in general*; and just as the borderline between primary and secondary seeing is indistinct and obscure (see following chapters), the point at which secondary seeing merges with something no longer distinctively visual in character is impossible to locate with any precision.

The subject of seeing something in a secondary epistemic fashion will arise again, especially in connection with perceptual relativity (Chapter V) and scientific practice (Chapter VI), and in these discussions there will be ample illustrations of the schemata provided in this section. It will be shown that this form of seeing can take us quite far, indeed, into the regions customarily reserved for 'inductive inference'.

3. *Events and States*

A state (or state of affairs) is something's being in a certain condition, one thing's having a certain property, or two or more things standing in certain relations to each other. We generally think of a state as persisting for a certain period of time, but they can also be quite transitory. When a match is wet, the match's being wet is a state of the match, and since it normally takes some time for the match to dry, this state persists for a time. But when Clyde is confused, we speak of Clyde's state of confusion however temporary it might be.

When there is an alteration in state, and the alteration is more or less abrupt, we have an *occurrence* or a *happening*. We sometimes speak of the occurrence or happening as an *event*, although it seems that this latter term is reserved for those occurrences which are particularly significant to those who are describing it. History books are filled with descriptions of events: those changes which are found significant enough to be mentioned in such a book. Nevertheless, every alteration in state is, as it were, potentially an event in the sense that we need only regard it as being important (e.g. as a signal or a cause) in order to classify it, along with births, deaths, ceremonies, and battles, as an event. Roughly speaking, we can say that an event is a change of some sort; it is constituted by a succession of *different* states. If everything should remain in its present state, nothing would happen; no events would occur.

There are several pertinent aspects of our talk about events and states which I should like to mention. One such aspect involves the way we have of referring to such things. Suppose that the book is in a tattered condition, and Harold sees that it is. There are alternative ways of describing what Harold sees. We can say that he sees that the book is tattered, or we can say that he sees the tattered condition of the book. The tattered condition of the book is something that presumably has a cause, it is something that came into being, as it were, after the book was published. The condition of the book is something we might try to change by carefully repairing the torn pages and rebinding them. On the other hand, the phrase 'that the book is tattered' is not a phrase which we use to refer to the tattered condition of the book. That the book is tattered is, if you will, a *fact*; the tattered condition of the book is a state (of the book). States succeed one another (they are temporally related); one state is replaced by another. This is not true of facts.[1]

The differences between the language of facts and the language of states (or states of affairs) is both real and important. Nonetheless, when we are describing what Harold has seen, or can see to be the case, I believe that we tend to use these two constructions interchangeably. For many purposes we say, simply, that Harold saw the tattered condition of the book, and it is clear that what we are saying might equally well have been said: Harold saw that the book was tattered. Perhaps this is obvious in the case of the book, and the state of the book, but it seems to be less obvious when we turn our attention to another class of examples. When one sees that someone is depressed, angry, or embarrassed, one sees that they are in a certain state. Sometimes we have occasion to *refer* to this state in order to say something about it: e.g. 'His depression was caused by her indifference', 'His anger subsided after a few moments', and 'She could not conceal her embarrassment'. This makes it more or less natural, on some occasions, to *refer* to what is seen (when one sees that he is depressed, that he is angry, or that she is embarrassed) with the noun phrases 'his depression', 'his anger', and 'her embarrassment'. I do not think there is anything exceptional in this as long as we understand that what it is to which we are referring with these noun phrases is the state or condition which the person is in whom we have seen to be depressed, angry, or embarrassed. Nevertheless, the substitution of a referring phrase ('his anger') for the factive nominal ('that he is angry') seems to inevitably produce philosophical perplexity. How can we (so the question goes) see someone's anger, depression, or embarrassment? These are private goings-on, and although we may see the *symptoms* of someone's anger, depression, or embarrassment, we do not see the anger, depression, or embarrassment themselves. I do not, at the moment, wish to argue this point.[2] All I wish to point out is that *if* these referring phrases ('his anger', 'her embarrassment', etc.) are used to refer to a state or condition of the person, the state or condition which is expressed by the

[1] For a discussion of the distinction between facts and events or states of affairs see Peter Herbst, 'The Nature of Facts', reprinted in *Essays in Conceptual Analysis,* Antony Flew (ed.) (London, 1956).
[2] I return to it again in the following chapter.

propositional clauses 'that he is angry', 'that she is embarrassed', etc., then to say that one can see his anger (or her embarrassment) is nothing but an alternative way of expressing the fact that one can see that he is angry and that she is embarrassed. And this being so, the question of whether his anger or her embarrassment is observable or not will depend on how we answer the question 'Can we see that he or she is angry or embarrassed?' One will not, therefore, make the mistake of supposing that seeing his anger or her embarrassment is like seeing his wallet or her appendix. If I see his wallet and her appendix, *his wallet* and *her appendix* must look some way to me; but if the phrases 'his anger' and 'her embarrassment' are understood to refer to the states which are expressed by 'that he is angry' and 'that she is embarrassed', then *he* and *she* must look some way to me. Asking how his anger looks is like asking how the tattered condition of the book looks; all one can do is describe how *he* looks and how *the book* looks. For one is, in both cases, seeing that something is in a certain state; 'his anger' and 'the tattered condition of the book' are simply noun phrases which allow us to *refer* to the state of affairs which is seen to obtain when we see that he is angry and that the book is tattered. 'That he is angry' and 'that the book is tattered' are not available for this purpose; for they do not *refer* to the corresponding state. Rather, they describe the thing as being in that state. Under this interpretation of what is referred to with the phrase 'his anger' we can say that his anger cannot be seen if *he* cannot be seen, or if the conditions are *never* as described in (iii) of our first schema. Under these circumstances we could never see that he was angry (his anger) in a primary epistemic way. But this is quite a different matter than supposing that his anger cannot be seen because it (in contrast to the *person* who is angry) does not look some way to us. This latter approach is simply a confusion of the *state* which a person is in with a *thing* to which he is related; it is to interpret the phrase 'his anger' as *always* being used to refer to 'the feeling he has when he is angry' and *never* to the state which *he* is in when he is angry. And although we may sometimes perhaps be referring to his (private) feelings when we use the phrase 'his anger', I think it is clear that we are frequently referring to the state or condition which he is in which makes the statement 'He is angry' true. And to observe *this* condition it is only necessary that *he* look some way to us (under conditions described in (iii) of our schema) for us to see his anger.

Events, as I have said, are constituted by an alteration in state; they are occurrences or happenings of appreciable significance. When Harold *becomes* angry, that is an event; or, at least, it could be so classified if Harold were a king and the occasion was critical. We also witness events, and we have a good many terms to classify the sort of event seen: an accident, a battle, a wedding, a birth, a death, an arrival, a departure, a collision, a signal, a gesture, a robbery, and so on. I have already indicated (Chapter II) that such things can be seen in a non-epistemic way; we can see an accident or a collision without realizing that it was an accident or a collision which we witnessed. But we can also see these events in an epistemic way; we can see a robbery committed or a wedding take place and in so doing satisfy conditions (i)–(iv) of our original schema (Chapter III). I may see not only Harold *while* he is waving to his friend, but see Harold and see *that* he is waving to his friend. I see (sometimes) not only an object which is beginning to move, but I see the object and see that it is beginning to move. In such cases we are seeing, in an epistemic way, an event take place, and the achievement is, I believe, subject to the same kind of analysis which has already been given in this, and the preceding, chapter. One sees the constitutents of the event and sees them alter their state in a specified manner; moreover, one sees *that* they do this. One sees, in a primary epistemic fashion, one runner overtake another when one sees the runners, and the conditions are such that they would not look this way (in this case, over a period of time) unless one was overtaking the other; when these conditions are satisfied, and when one believes them satisfied, one sees that one runner is overtaking the other.

There are various ways of reporting these epistemic achievements. Frequently, such reports do not utilize a 'that' clause. We say, simply, that he saw Harold signaling his friend, kissing his old sweetheart, and preparing to leave home. If we consider such reports *in isolation*, there is nothing in the report itself which requires us to interpret the visual achievement as an *epistemic* achievement. After all, one can see Harold signaling his friend and *not* realize what he is doing. I do not have to believe that Harold is preparing to leave home in order to see him preparing to leave home. I would not, of course, *say* I saw these things if I did not believe that this is what I saw, but I could *see* them without such a belief. Third-person reports, and past-tense reports, amply testify to this fact: 'I saw him preparing to leave, but I thought, at the time, that he was merely straightening his room', 'He saw Harold signaling his friend, but he mistook the gesture for a sign of relief', and so on.

Nevertheless, despite the fact that such sentences do not, in isolation, carry with them epistemic implications, they are frequently used to describe an epistemic achievement. Let us consider an example. How does Barbara know that the chair was moved? She saw them moving it. Now, if we consider the latter statement ('She saw them moving it') *in isolation*, there is nothing inconsistent about her having seen this and not known that they were moving the chair. She might have believed at the time (she still might believe) that they were moving a different article of furniture, or she might have believed that they were moving nothing at all (they did it so cleverly). But in the context of answering the question 'How does she know?', and in a great many other contexts in which there is no explicit qualification to the contrary, the response 'She saw them moving it' functions perfectly well to convey the idea that she came to know that the chair had been moved in this way. That is to say, in most contexts, unless explicit qualifications are made to the reverse, such a statement carries with it the implication that she not only saw them moving the chair but also saw *that* they were moving it. The fact that this implication can be suspended by an explicit qualification ('She saw them moving the chair, but she did not realize until later that that is what they were doing') shows that the implication in question is not of a logical sort. For one cannot qualify the statement 'She saw that they were moving the chair' in the same way; if one sees that they are moving the chair, one cannot realize, only later, that they were moving the chair.[1]

I think, then, that the perceptual situations in which I am interested, situations in which conditions (i)–(iv) of our schema are satisfied, are frequently described by constructions which do not themselves entail that these conditions are satisfied. Such constructions emphasize the satisfaction of condition (ii) of our various schemata at the expense of conditions (iii) and (iv) and are, therefore, frequently used in situations where one wishes to make clear

[1] Not to be confused with 'that it was the chair they were moving', a confusion which might arise by emphasizing 'the chair' in the last clause in the text.

that what was seen was seen in a *primary* epistemic way. 'S saw them moving the chair' signifies that he saw that they were moving the chair *by seeing them* while they were moving the chair, and if no explicit qualifications are made to the reverse, this is what we take such a statement to mean. This same practice is found in a variety of different cases. How do you know he was wearing his hat? I saw him. This way of answering the question is a way of saying that I saw that he was wearing his hat *by seeing him*—not in any secondary way.

There is one further characteristic of events which I must mention briefly. We sometimes say we see that b is P when 'b' is some phrase which we use to refer to an event and 'P' is some feature of the event. For example, I might have seen that the battle was fierce, that the game was interrupted, or that the delivery was Caesarian. Or, slightly more complicated, the 'b' and 'c' in seeing that b is R to c may both be event-expressions: S saw that the right cross landed before their heads collided, that the throw to first base was not in time to beat the runner, and that his antics caused her considerable embarrassment. Such cases demand no essential modification of the schemata already provided.[1] Condition (ii) specifies that the event or events in question must be seen$_n$ if the achievement is to be classified as one of a *primary* nature. And, once again, the percipient's proto-knowledge is reflected in the choice of words used to refer to b or to b and c.

4. *Selector Words*

Can you see who that is on the road down there? Can you see how many there are? Can you see what they are carrying and where they are going? Can you see whether they have crossed the bridge yet and why they are making so much dust?

Such questions are designed to elicit specific information about a particular situation; they select, as it were, the various sorts of information which the addressee is presumably in a position to supply by virtue of his favored or privileged visual vantage point. Whatever details one might be able to see, the question 'Can you see *who* . . . ?' is a request for a particular sort of detail: *viz.* the identity, on some more or less specific level, of the persons specified in the remainder of the clause. Are they friends or enemies,

[1] The topic of seeing that one thing *caused* another, or what *caused* something to happen, will be taken up in Section 3 of Chapter VI.

soldiers or civilians, men or women, the group we have been expecting or not? I call such words 'selector words' because they determine, on an extremely general level, the *sort* of thing that can be seen. The phrases 'who ...', 'whether ...', 'when ...', 'what ...', 'if ...', 'how ...', 'which ...', 'why ...', and so on are used to select aspects of a situation; when such phrases occur in the context of the verb 'to see' they function to restrict attention to what can be seen *within the range of that aspect*.

One cannot see what *b* is if one cannot see that *b* is *P* for *some* value of '*P*'. Neither can one see who she is if one cannot see that she is *P* for *some* value of '*P*'. The same is true of all selector words. It is not true, however, that if one can see that *b* is *P*, for some value of '*P*', then one can see who or what *b* is. I can see that an object is red without seeing *what* it is; I can see that a person is walking without seeing who it is. Of course, I see *what color* it is, and what the person *is doing*, but this is something else again. The selector words, if I may express it this way, compartmentalize our ability to see *that* something is the case. They presuppose this ability, and they constitute a rough classification of the ways in which this ability is exercised, or can be exercised. Within each classification there are sub-classifications corresponding to the various ways we have of filling out the selector word phrase 'what (who, when, etc.) ...' We can see what color, what shape, and what size a thing is. We can see who they are, who they are talking to, and who they are looking at. We can see where the man is, where he came from, and where he is headed. All of these abilities presuppose the ability to *see that* in the sense that if we could never see that something was the case, as this has been characterized in this and the preceding chapter, we could never see who, what, when, where, whether, how, or why. There would, of course, still be the non-visual uses of these terms corresponding to the non-visual (or, better, not-necessarily-visual) use of the construction 'see that'. For example, we could still see *whether* he was home by listening outside his door. But without the strictly visual capacity to see that something is the case, as this has been described in our several schemata, the achievements reflected by the locutions 'see whether', 'see who', and 'see what' could never be *visual* achievements.

I think that the primary use of these selector words, and their associated phrases, when they occur within the context of the verb 'to see', is in questions, commands, and reports of a failure to see. *Question:* Can you see whether they are finished? *Command:* Go see if they are finished. *Response:* I could not see whether they were finished or not. If we saw that they were finished, the natural expression would be 'Yes, they are finished; I could see that they were'. The 'that' clause is particularly ill-suited to questions, commands, and negative responses. For instance, the question 'Can you see that they are finished?' suggests that the speaker can see that they are finished, or already knows that they are, and wants to know whether *you* can see it. The imperative 'Go see that they are finished' is scarcely intelligible unless it is interpreted as a request to expedite their work. And the negative response 'I could not see that they were finished' suggests, as does the interrogative form, that the speaker has some reason to suppose that they are finished, but is simply unable to see that they are. The selector words, on the other hand, are ideally suited for these roles; they allow us to select an aspect of the situation without the necessity of specifying, one way or the other, a determinate value for this aspect. They allow us to specify a *level* of discrimination without the necessity of specifying what is, or is not, discriminated at this level. 'No, I cannot see *how many* men there are.' This is simply a way of denying that we can see *that* there are precisely n men, for any value of 'n'.

The selector words, then, serve a useful (perhaps an indispensable) role in giving and receiving information, requesting and supplying data, on what can and cannot be seen. They do not, however, in any of their uses, reflect a visual achievement, or a visual ability, that is distinct from the ability to see that something is the case. They serve a communicative purpose, but they do not, within the context of the verb 'to see', represent any distinctive visual ability on the part of human beings. They do not, in other words, reflect an ability, or a successful exercise of an ability, that has not already been thoroughly discussed in the preceding pages. For this reason I leave them without further comment.

V

PERCEPTUAL RELATIVITY

By and large no one needs to be told that perception is relative. It is already sufficiently obvious. Jim and Judy have not seen (seen$_n$) all the same things; Hans and Yoshira have seen few of the same things. Even when people do see the same item, it might look different to them. They see it from different distances, different angles, and under different lighting conditions. Physiologically, they are differently equipped; one sees details that his near-sighted friend does not. Psychologically, one is more attentive than the other. They bring to the experience different training and different interests. They look at the same thing and see it differently.

Most of the variability between individuals is familiar. In this chapter I would like to discuss only one form of relativity: the differential ability of individuals, and groups of individuals, to see that something is the case. Specifically, I am interested in their differential ability to satisfy the four conditions of our schemata for *primary* epistemic seeing. Any relativity exhibited here will infect the very heart of our ability to find out about the world by means of our sense of sight; it will be a form of relativity which will, in its turn, be magnified in secondary perception.

1. *The Parameters*

The second condition in our schemata for primary seeing embodies a use of the verb 'to see' (see$_n$) which is not itself epistemic. Since a differential satisfaction of this condition will result in a difference in what people can see to be the case, it will first be necessary to briefly review the sorts of variables which are pertinent to this way of seeing objects and events.

When S sees a horsefly, no alteration in what he believes or knows, no change in what he says or thinks, no improvement or decline in inferential or associative dexterity will, by itself, alter the fact that he sees a horsefly. Seeing$_n$ the fly is something which does not depend on such conceptual conditions for its realization. The only variables that are relevant are those which are relevant to his being able to visually differentiate it from its immediate environment, those which are influential in allowing or preventing the fly from looking *some* way to S. The most obvious variables of this sort are those which are physical and physiological in nature: *viz*. the location of the fly relative to S, lighting conditions, the opacity of the intervening medium, the condition of S's retinae, the state of his central nervous system, and so on. I say these are the most obvious variables. There are others which are less obvious, and I do not doubt but that there are some of which I am totally unaware. It may be that certain psychological parameters are indirectly relevant. It seems likely, especially when one is concerned with the less conspicuous details of certain objects, that one's attention, interests, motivation, and past training will help to determine what is, and what is not, visually differentiated. It may be that certain past experiences, the remembrance of these, or the conditioning brought about by them, is capable of enhancing or inhibiting one's discriminatory powers. I do not wish to deny these facts, if they are facts, nor do I wish to legislate about matters which are best left to experimental determination. The sole point I wish to emphasize is that the variables relevant to whether S can see the fly are those which are capable of affecting S's ability to visually differentiate it from its surroundings. Given what we know about human beings and their limitations, this makes certain physical and physiological variables obviously relevant. Psychological conditions may also be relevant but only to the extent to which they affect S's discriminatory powers. In this respect, seeing the fly is, indeed, like stepping on it. Both 'abilities' are acquired in the normal process of maturation, and the successful exercise of both involve the satisfaction of various physical and physiological conditions. Still, one's ability to see the fly, just as one's ability to step on it, may be affected by what one believes, what one has been trained to do, and the experiences which one has had. Such factors assume an importance when they affect S's discriminatory capacity or when they affect S's ability to move his legs in the appropriate fashion. But if these latter abilities are not affected, the psychological factors are irrelevant.

Aside, then, from those variables which affect an individual's ability to see_n something, conditions (iii) and (iv) in our schemata for primary epistemic seeing constitute the only remaining source of variability between individuals. I will not attempt to discuss these conditions separately; rather, I will simply state what I take to be the relevant parameters which are involved in a differential satisfaction of these two conditions taken jointly. In order to hold other factors constant, let us proceed by discussing two individuals S_1 and S_2, who possess a comparable level of visual acuity. That is to say, whatever S_1 can see_n (under specified conditions), S_2 can also see_n (under the same conditions), and vice versa. We will suppose that in each case S_1 and S_2 see_n the same things including the 'details' of the objects which they do see_n. This assumption merely allows us to say that if S_1 and S_2 differ with respect to what they can see to be the case, this difference must be attributed to something other than a difference in what they see_n. Since (i) is constant, the difference will therefore lie in a differential satisfaction of (iii) and (iv).

I shall number the parameters for future reference. First, a difference between what S_1 and S_2 see to be the case may be attributable to their difference in proto-knowledge:

(P-1) S_1 and S_2 differ with respect to their relevant level of proto-knowledge of b (or, in the case of a relationship, of b and/or c).

A difference of this sort may arise in a variety of ways. There may be a certain class of objects, C, having a certain sub-class, C_1, such that condition (iii) is satisfied for the members of C_1 but not, in general, for the members of C. That is to say, conditions are such that a C_1 would not look this way to S unless it was P, but these conditions are not such that a C (in general) would not look this way unless it were P. If, then, S_1 has antecedently identified what he sees as a C_1, but S_2 has not, then S_1 may well see that *this* C (which he knows to be a C_1) is P while S_2 does not. For example, S_1, knowing the wood is a species of birch (and, hence, light in color), can see that it has been stained while S_2, ignorant of the species of wood (it could be walnut or a dark mahogany), may not see this. A case could arise, of course, where S_2, uncommonly ignorant of the various types of wood, thinks he can see that the wood has been stained in virtue of the false background belief that no piece of wood would look this way (dark brown) unless it had been stained. Here we have a case, mentioned earlier, of an *over-generalized* background belief and therefore a failure of condition (iv). The aspect of the wood's appearance on which S_2 depends is, of course, the crucial aspect (its color), but S_2's background belief is *under-specified* with respect to the pertinent character of that which he sees—of the piece of wood—which displays this distinctive aspect. It is not that *any* wood which looks this way is stained; rather, any *piece of birch* which looks this way is stained. Hence, whatever S_2 supposes himself able to do in this case, S_1's greater information about the special character of what he sees, his greater proto-knowledge, allows him to see that something is the case which S_2 cannot.

P-1 also covers such 'artificial' situations as the following: S_1 is *told* that this b is either a P or a Q where P's and Q's are easily distinguished by S. Then, on the basis of this antecedent information, S sees *which* it is—that it is a P, not a Q. In such a case he can see that this b is P even though he cannot, in general, distinguish P's from non-P's. For instance, if I am told that the piece of fruit I am about to be shown will be either an orange or an apple, I should have no difficulty in seeing which it is—that it is an orange, say. If, however, I am told that the piece of fruit will be either an orange or a tangerine, I may not be able to see which it is. One's proto-knowledge is enhanced to the point where the regularities that do prevail (in these background conditions) are capable of allowing one (when one has the appropriate background belief) to acquire an increment of information which one could not have acquired without possessing that level of proto-knowledge.

Relational examples are easy to find. S_1 can see that the table is slightly under three feet in length *because* he knows that the window in front of which it is situated is exactly three feet in width (having measured it on a previous occasion). S_2 sees$_n$ the same things as S_1 (the table and the window), and he sees them in the same background conditions, but a deficiency in proto-knowledge prevents him from seeing that the table is less than three feet in length. The most that he sees is that the table is slightly shorter than the window. To cite a routine sort of case, why is it that S_1 can see, with just a hurried glance, that there is still some beer in the refrigerator while his guest, S_2, does not? Clearly, S_1 knows before he looks that if there are any cans at all in the refrigerator they are cans of beer. *He* stocked the refrigerator, and he knows that there is nothing in it except a few frankfurters, a bottle of catsup, and, hopefully, still a few cans of beer. He knows something about the refrigerator and its contents which S_2 does not, and it is this difference in proto-knowledge which allows S_1 to exploit the regularity between the way this refrigerator now looks to him and its having some beer in it, Admittedly, this regularity is of rather restricted scope—applying, if it applies at all, to this refrigerator on this particular evening. Nonetheless, it is S_1's *specialized* proto-knowledge about the refrigerator and its possible contents which permits him to 'travel' from his proto-knowledge (this is my refrigerator) to the information that there is some beer in the refrigerator on the basis, simply, of its looking to him in the particular way it now does. Seeing a few cans is sufficient for S_1 to see that there is still some beer in the refrigerator while S_2, under these same background conditions, can only see (without closer examination) that there are a few unidentifiable cans in the refrigerator. In a certain sense it is quite true that the refrigerator *would* look the same to S_1 were it to contain several cans of soda pop instead of cans of beer, and in this respect one might suppose that condition (iii) was not satisfied. But the point to be made here is that what S_1 has claimed he discovered, on visual grounds alone, is that a refrigerator which, if it contains any cans at all, contains cans of beer has some beer in it; it is *this* increment for which condition (iii) is satisfied, and it is *this* increment which S_1's specialized proto-knowledge puts him in a position to bridge by purely visual means—by the way the refrigerator looks to him. If we interpret S_1's perceptual achievement as something of a more substantial sort, as representing the acquisition of a larger increment of information, then there is no alternative but to deny that he could see (by such a hurried glance) what he purports to have seen by a hurried glance in the refrigerator.

The variability generated by P-1 arises because, although condition (iii) is satisfied for both S_1 and S_2, they differ with respect to condition (iv); S_1 believes (iii) to be satisfied *because* he has already identified what he is seeing *as something* for which condition (iii) is true. S_2 may also have identified it in some way, but he has not identified it in a determinate enough fashion; he has not correctly identified it as something which only looks this way when it is P. And this difference in proto-knowledge makes a difference in what they see to be the case.

Secondly, a difference between what S_1 and S_2 see to be the case may be attributed to a difference in background beliefs:

> (P-2) S_1 and S_2, although possessing the same relevant proto-knowledge, differ with respect to the belief that conditions are as described in (iii).

Such a difference is most often referred to by saying that S_1 knows what P's look like and S_2 does not. The simplest illustration of this difference is found in the contrast between what children can see and what adults can see. Even if a child knows what a badger is, he may not know what badgers look like. Even if a child knows that a badger is a sturdy burrowing animal, this information scarcely helps him to recognize a badger when he sees one. The child can see an animal under roughly the same background conditions as his father; yet his father can see that the animal is a badger and the child cannot. The father manifests a belief that, under these conditions, the only animal which looks this way is a badger. What leads him to believe this is obviously his past experience with badgers. What prevents the child from believing this is clearly his lack of experience of the same sort. In this case the proto-knowledge of the two individuals might well be the same; both of them know it is an animal of some sort. The difference in what they see to be the case (that the animal is a badger) is a manifestation of only one thing: *viz.* a difference in background beliefs. And the difference here is amply accounted for, in most cases at least, by differences in past experience. The child does not believe that condition (iii) is satisfied because either: (*a*) he does not know what a badger is; (*b*) he knows what a badger is, but does not know what badgers look like; or (*c*) he knows what a badger is, and knows what they look like, but does not believe that *these conditions* are such that the *only* animal which looks this way is a badger (he mistakenly thinks that in these conditions gophers also look the way this animal now looks).

Notice, (*a*)–(*c*) do not constitute differences in proto-knowledge. The father may be said to know something that the child does not, but this information is not about the identity or character of what they both see$_n$. Prior to his seeing that it was a badger, the father knew no more about the animal (which they both saw) than did the child. Admittedly, he knew something about badgers which the child did not know; if nothing else, he was familiar enough with badgers to know what they looked like (or what they looked like under these conditions). But this is not a difference in proto-knowledge; if anything, it is a difference in their *disposition* to take something as a badger in certain visual circumstances (such as the ones they are now in).

Having said this much, however, it must be conceded that the differences between P-1 and P-2 can become quite subtle. To illustrate this, suppose that S_1 sees that the word 'transmorgify' is misspelled, but S_2 does not. To what shall we attribute this difference? Much depends on how we construe S_1's visual achievement. Shall we say that S_1 has seen that this token or instance of the word 'transmogrify' is misspelled? If so, we are including, as part of S's proto-knowledge, the fact that this (misspelled) word is an instance or token of the word 'transmogrify'. Hence, his *visual* achievement is quite consistent with *his being told* by the person who was attempting to spell the word that this set of letters was supposed to be the word 'transmogrify'. That is, S_1 could (in these circumstances) see that the word was misspelled even though he was unable to *see that* it was an instance of the word 'transmogrify'. He could see this even though he was ignorant of whether there was another word, unknown to him, which was correctly spelled 'transmorgify'. Or shall we construe S_1's visual achievement as seeing that *this word* (without specifying *what* word it is supposed to be) is misspelled. Here the proto-knowledge is not represented as including the crucial piece of information that this word is (supposed to be) 'transmogrify'. And *this* is an increment which S_2 may not be able to bridge even though he knows (can see that) this set of letters is not a correct spelling of the word 'transmogrify'.

The difference, here, is our old difference between seeing that the water is boiling and seeing that the liquid is boiling water. Our discussion may sound somewhat academic because we are trying to pinpoint the source of a difference when, ordinarily, most people are interested only in the fact that there is a difference.

Finally, S_1 and S_2 may differ with respect to the way things look to them:

(P-3) S_1 and S_2 differ with respect to the way b looks to them under a specified set of physical conditions and, hence, they differ with respect to the occasions on which they satisfy condition (iii).

Color-blindness is an example of this difference. If S_2 has a serious case of color-blindness, then although S_1 and S_2 see the same objects, possess the same relevant degree of proto-knowledge, and see these objects under precisely the same physical conditions (distance, lighting, etc.), S_1 may see what color the objects are while S_2 will not. If b is gray, for instance, and S_2 (unaware of his perceptual deficiency) mistakenly believes that conditions are as described in (iii), then both S_1 and S_2 will suppose themselves able to see that b is P (gray). They both satisfy conditions (i), (ii), and (iv). They differ with respect to their satisfaction of (iii). Hence, S_2's belief that the conditions are as described in (iii), as manifested by his belief that he can see that b is gray, *is false*. Despite what he thinks he can see, he cannot see that b is gray, and we would be quick to deny him this ability (under *these* conditions) when we discovered his inability to distinguish between gray and other colors on other occasions.

Notice, it does not make any difference how b looks to S_2 (for him to see that it is P) as long as the way it looks to him constitutes a satisfaction of condition (iii). If we should suppose that for some reason red objects look green to S_2 (and green objects look red), this alone is not a source of difference between S_1 and S_2 with respect to what they can see to be the case. For if there is an appropriate adjustment in S_2's background belief (as there most certainly would be if this 'inversion' was congenital and he had learned the application of the concepts 'red' and 'green' in a community of normal individuals), then S_2 would continue to see that red objects were red and green objects green. The way the object looks to him makes no difference as long as it only looks *that* way when it *is* red or green as the case may be, as long as (iii) continues to be satisfied. If the way the object looks meets the requirements of (iii), then S_2 sees red objects and green objects, and sees that they are red (the red ones) and sees that they are green (the green ones) in precisely the same way we do. Which simply means that there is no perceptual difference, either epistemic or non-epistemic, between S_2 and other individuals. He is perceptually *normal*.

A difference only emerges when S_2 cannot be brought to satisfy (iii) under roughly the same set of background conditions that are associated with the perceptual achievements of 'normal' individuals (most other individuals). When this happens, and we find no difference in proto-knowledge, and no relevant difference in the physical background conditions, then we assign the difference to *the way things look to S₂*.

The following two sections contain a discussion of the way individuals' differential ability to satisfy conditions (iii) and (iv), as I have summarized this in P-1 through P-3, reveals itself in ordinary and extraordinary ways. The second section examines the more routine cases; the last section is devoted to what I have called 'radical' relativity. This inquiry should reveal the extremes, and the limits, to which perceptual relativity is subject, and in so doing it will, I hope, further illustrate the schemata presented for epistemic seeing.

2. *Specialization*

As we move from occupation to occupation, and from avocation to avocation, we find a vast difference between what people can see to be the case. Such differences surprise no one; we expect it. Much of the difference is attributable to forms of *secondary* epistemic perception. The dentist is able to see, by the dark spots on the X-ray, if the patient has any caries and, if so, where they are located; the laundress sees, by looking at the discolored socks, that the dress has faded; the auto mechanic can see that your engine block is cracked by observing the oil in your radiator; a meteorologist can see, by the characteristic cloud formations, that a cold front is approaching; a welder can see when his torch is being fed the proper ratio of oxygen and acetylene by noting the characteristic shape and color of the flame; and the bridge player can see, by looking into his own hand, that his opponents cannot possibly make their bid of six hearts. There is nothing especially mysterious about these 'special' abilities, not unless one is puzzled by the fact that we can see that the 'e' on our typewriter is damaged by looking, not at the typewriter, but at the paper on which we have been typing. Participation in a special field of activity almost inevitably brings with it a heightened ability to see what is happening; it does so by breeding a familiarity with the sorts of regularities which obtain in that particular field, what sorts of events, situations, and states of affairs can be taken as a reliable sign that something is the case.

I have already said, however, that I shall concentrate on instances of *primary* epistemic perception, situations in which an isolated individual, or group of individuals, can see that b is P by virtue of the way *b* itself looks. And here, also, one can multiply examples almost endlessly. Despite the fact that I have watched several European football matches, I am still unable to see what the referee is paid to see and which many spectators can obviously see: *viz.* when one of the players is off-side. Some of my friends can see whether the overhead airplane is an F-87 or not, something I still cannot do. Fishermen can tell, just by looking at it, whether the fish they have caught is a Northern Pike or a Walleye Pike. Metal workers can see when the blade they wish to temper has reached the correct temperature for immersion—not by thermometers or dials but by the way the blade itself looks.

A seamstress can distinguish a hem stitch from a basting stitch; so can I (I am told), but I cannot see which is the hem stitch. Clearly this incapacity is a matter of not knowing which of the two stitches is called a hem stitch. I can see the difference, but I have not learned the nomenclature used to classify such differences. Much of the variability between what people can see is of this rather trivial linguistic sort: knowing the labels for items which are perceptually different. Not knowing the appropriate labels, I do not have, in the way the stitch looks to me (although it does look distinctive), a reason, much less a conclusive reason, to believe it is a hem stitch. Notice, I can believe that *this* is a foozit, I can even have quite good reasons for believing it is a foozit, without knowing anything about foozits. For I may have been told by an acknowledged authority on foozits that this was, indeed, a genuine foozit, and I, along with everyone else, believe him. But I cannot *see* that something is a foozit (or a hem stitch) in this same state of ignorance. To see that something *is* a hem stitch (in addition to seeing that the hem stitch differs from the basting stitch), I must have, in the way the stitch itself looks to me, a conclusive reason to believe it is a hem stitch. And this I cannot have without (see condition (iv)) a belief to the effect that the stitch would not look the way it does to me unless it was a hem stitch. And to this extent, at least, I must know something about the way hem stitches look.

Specialization, then, often generates a difference in what people see to be the case because the specialization involves, among other things, learning a technical nomenclature for the linguistic classification of differences which, before one learned the jargon, one could already appreciate. This is merely an extension, into specialized areas, of the same phenomenon which occurs as we learn language. We learn some concepts by learning how to use them, how to apply them correctly to the things which we see. And in relation to such concepts, this means that by the time we have reached the stage where we can be said to know what a term means, we have also reached the stage where we can see that something possesses the characteristic expressed by that term. In such cases a differential ability to see that b is P is hardly to be distinguished from a differential understanding of what the term 'P' means.

Occasionally, however, our ability to apply a term is (whether we know it or not) restricted to specialized contexts. Consider an assembly-line worker whose task it is to take the resistors from the conveyor belt and to solder them in a specific manner to a piece of electrical apparatus. Assorted items are to be found on the conveyor belt, but the resistors are easily distinguished from the other items. Being an attentive worker, he infallibly selects the resistors, not the transformers, the vacuum tubes, or the coils, for his task. Yet, although he performs well enough in this specialized setting, our worker does not know the difference between a resistor and a capacitor; he would most likely confuse the resistors with which he is accustomed to working with the many small capacitors which resemble them. His success on the asembly line in choosing only resistors is to be attributed, in part at least, to the fact that capacitors *never* appear on the conveyor belt.

Shall we say of this person that he can see which electrical components are the resistors? Shall we say this even though there are electrical components which, were they to appear on the conveyor belt, he would confuse with the resistors? Yes and no. Yes, inside the factory, on *this* conveyor belt, he can see which components are the resistors. No, outside the factory, when he is looking inside a television set, say, he cannot see which components are the resistors (not even those which he correctly identifies as resistors). Such a distinction can be made for the following reason. We may suppose that *within* the factory, on *that* conveyor belt, condition (iii) is satisfied; background conditions are such that no *component on this conveyor belt* would look this way unless it were a resistor. Regularities prevail within the factory that do not prevail outside it, and to the extent that we feel such regularities do prevail in restricted domains, we may concede that a person can see that something is the case *within* that domain that he cannot, generally speaking, see outside of it.

Of course, if the man fails to appreciate the fact that his powers of identification are greeted with continued success only because they are exercised within a special setting (in this factory, on that assembly line), then he is likely to make mistakes when he operates outside this special setting. Depending on just how we describe this situation, it is either a case of under-specification of the way the component looks (he is taking the fact that it is cylindrical with wires protruding from each end as distinctive) or under-specification (over-generalization) of what looks that way to him—i.e. he is mistakenly assuming that *any* electrical component which looks this way is a resistor when, in fact, it is only the electrical components on this assembly line. If, however, we suppose that the background belief which the man manifests in seeing which components are the resistors (inside the factory) does not depend on his over-generalized version of it (but, rather, his over-generalization occurred as a result of what he learned specifically about the resistors in the factory), then we may wish to say that within the factory, in so far as no component on the assembly line would look that way to him unless it was a resistor, our worker could see which components were the resistors. One's reluctance to admit that he could see this would stem, of course, from one's conviction that there is no irrevocable regularity preventing capacitors from appearing on the assembly line—hence, that (iii) is simply not true.

Although I have selected a somewhat unusual example to illustrate this point, it is a common phenomenon. I can see, at home alone with my wife, that those are my cigarettes on the table. At a large party, where several people happen to be smoking my brand of cigarettes, I cannot see whether they are my cigarettes on the table—not at least in the minimal sort of background conditions which prevailed on the first occasion.

There are a number of different situations which might be used to illustrate divergences with respect to P-1 and P-2, but I would like to mention just one further area in which specialization, if I may use this word in this connection, is even more pronounced and reflects elements of both P-1 and P-2: *viz.* the differential familiarity which individuals have with other individuals. In a certain sense most people are specialists, to some degree, on other people. They have known them longer, have been associated with them more frequently, and have observed them in many more situations than has the rest of mankind. We would expect, then, that this wide variability in first-hand acquaintance would reflect itself in a differential ability to see, epistemically, the condition in which these acquaintances are. And, of course, this is precisely what we do find, or would find if we were prepared to accept what people *say* they see. The difficulty, however, is that some people, philosophers included, tend to dismiss what people say they see in this regard as so much loose talk, not worthy of being taken literally as a description of what they really see. I would, therefore, like to pause just long enough to remark on some of the relevant facets of this situation.

It is not uncommon to hear statements of the following sort: 'I saw that she was embarrassed, so I changed the subject', 'He was visibly unimpressed', 'He could not conceal his anger any longer', 'I could see that she wanted to go', 'One could see that his thoughts were elsewhere', and 'He was afraid all right; you could see it'. I do not think there is much dispute about the fact that people say this sort of thing; rather, the question is, as some philosophers prefer to put it, how to *interpret* these expressions. What 'interpretation' usually means is 'how to bring the expressions into line with some preconceived view'. Very well, let us interpret these expressions.

It should be noticed at the outset that there is very little basis for saying that *all* of these instances are cases of seeing that someone is in a certain psychological state *in a secondary fashion*. There is very little basis for this unless, of course, one supposes that it is the *mind* which is angry, embarrassed, unimpressed, thinking, wanting, and so on, and that we only see the body or portions of it (the face). With this kind of approach we could never have a case of seeing that b was P (his mind was angry) which satisfied our schema for *primary* seeing; for presumably we could never see$_n$ his mind. It is apparent, though, that no one is claiming to see that another person's mind is embarrassed, angry, or thinking; the examples given above are examples of seeing that *he* or *she* is embarrassed, distracted, or angry. And since there is nothing preventing us from seeing him or her, there is nothing to suggest that these examples are cases of seeing something in a secondary fashion.

I am not, let me emphasize, denying mind–body dualism, whatever may be involved in that position. All I am concerned to maintain is that when we see that a person wants to go, or when we see that a person is afraid to speak, condition (ii) of our schema for *primary* epistemic seeing is satisfied if we see *the person*.

There is an alternative way in which one might construe these examples as examples of secondary seeing. One might suppose that if S sees that he is angry, what S sees is most plausibly interpreted as something relational in nature. That is, S sees that he *has* a feeling of anger (b is R to c), and since S only sees *one* term of the relation (b), this must be understood as a case of seeing that some relationship holds in a secondary fashion. Under this interpretation, seeing that he is angry is like seeing that he has something in his pocket by the revealing bulge in his trousers. And since feelings are necessarily unobservable by other people, we are necessarily restricted to seeing such things in a secondary fashion.

This view raises issues which go far beyond the scope of this brief discussion. One could point out that 'feelings', at least as these are ordinarily understood, are not as unobservable as some people are inclined to think. There is nothing unusual about seeing (or, at least, saying we see) *how* another person feels, that he feels uncomfortable, ill at ease, intimidated, and so on. But the crucial point is whether being angry, embarrassed, or ill at ease is constituted by the having of a characteristic private (unobservable by others) feeling such that without that subjective feeling one is not angry, embarrassed, or ill at ease *no matter what else is the case*. Is a person's being angry like a person's having a wallet in his pocket in that no matter what else may be the case (e.g. bulgy trousers) the only decisive question is whether the wallet is *in* the pocket. If one is inclined to answer this question in the affirmative, one should not do so because of the conviction that people *do* feel a certain way when they are angry or embarrassed, and are, thus, in a privileged position for reporting on their own psychological states. For the fact that people do feel a certain characteristic way when they are angry is quite adequately accounted for on other grounds than by saying that what it *means* to be angry is to have just *that* (or any) characteristic feeling; one can account for it by saying that when people are angry they generally have, as a matter of empirical fact, a certain tightening in the chest, flutter in the stomach, or whatever feeling it is that people usually have when they are angry. One needn't go on to say that what it means to be angry is to have this tight feeling in the chest or flutter in the stomach.

Furthermore, to treat 'being angry' as a relational state of affairs, on the model of a house's being occupied, is to commit oneself to certain misleading implications. For the occupants of a house can leave the house. The state of affairs which we describe by saying that the house is occupied can vanish without either term of the relation (whose exemplification constituted the state of affairs) vanishing. Both the house and the former occupants still exist. They have simply ceased to stand in that particular relation which constituted the house's being occupied (by them). If we use this model to understand what it means to be angry, the impression is conveyed that a person can cease being angry without in the least affecting his feeling of anger. He and his feeling of anger might part company, so to speak, without the feeling of anger becoming any the less a feeling of anger; he has just ceased to *have* it. Now, I know what it means for a person to lose his wallet; the wallet is somewhere else than in his pocket. But is there anything comparable to this when he 'loses' his feeling of anger? Might someone else have what was formerly his feeling of anger? Might the feeling of anger, the feeling which was formerly *his* feeling of anger (when he *had* it), have gone underground somewhere? Why, then, call it a feeling of anger? Or even a feeling?

I have scarcely said enough to warrant any definite conclusions on this matter. Suffice it to say that in either case there is nothing preventing us from seeing that someone else is angry, embarrassed, uncomfortable, afraid, etc. Whether we treat this a secondary or a primary visual achievement will depend on how we propose to interpret the psychological predicate involved, whether we propose to treat it as of the form 'b is P' or of the form 'b is R to c' where 'c' is always some term which refers to a private (unable to be seen$_n$ by others) feeling which the person (b) has (R).

Still, even with this issue out of the way, there seems to be other difficulties which I have passed by. The way a person looks might be a good reason to think he is angry, but is it ever a conclusive reason? I can see that he is frowning, but I cannot, not in the same sense, see that he is worried. The symptoms are never conclusive—or so we keep being told. This view, a rather widespread view, I believe, sounds much better on paper than it does in practice, and in this respect it is similar to many other sceptical doctrines. It is one of those interesting pieces of philosophical apparatus which, like the scopes and instruments in the physics laboratory, are NOT TO BE REMOVED FROM THE CLASSROOM. Let me mention, very briefly, some of the reasons it seldom, if ever, gets removed.

Some people are inclined to suppose that if we can see that our wife is moody (bored, nervous, etc.), then we should always be able to tell, from the way she looks, under any conditions, whether or not she is moody (bored, nervous, etc.). Or, worse yet, that we should be able to tell when *anyone* is moody. What may perhaps foster this confusion is a tendency on the part of philosophers, once we allow that one person can see that another is moody, to start speaking of 'moodiness' as an observable or an observation term. This, of course, puts it in the same class with such terms as 'has red hair'. Recognizing that this constitutes a rather strange assimilation, the philosopher then removes 'is moody' from the class of observables and consequently denies that anyone can see that anyone else is moody. It must be an inference from facial expression, etc. I shall take up the notion of 'observables' in the next chapter, but for the moment we can answer this sort of nonsense by simply pointing out that to see that your wife is moody, on a given occasion, is *not* to imply that whenever she is moody you can see it; it is *not* to imply that whenever anyone is moody you can see it; it is *not* to imply that whenever your wife looks *this* way she is moody or *whenever* she is moody she looks this way. What is implied is that under these (background) conditions (not just *any* conditions) your wife (not just anyone) would not look this way unless she was moody. If *this* state of affairs is never realized, then one cannot see that she is moody—although one might suspect or infer that she was moody from the way she was behaving. But whether this state of affairs, or a comparable state of affairs with respect to other psychological predicates, is *ever* realized, for *any* person, seems to me to be a question which cannot possibly be answered by philosophical analysis. We have to know *who* we are talking about, what sorts of regularities, if any, dominate *this* or *that* individual's appearance and behavior in various conditions. And this involves doing what we knew we had to do all along—get to know the person.

Certainly the situation becomes more complex when we are dealing with human beings. Unlike inanimate objects, they are, within certain limits, capable of controlling the way they look; they may express their anger differently among a group of friends than they do among strangers. A piece of hot metal does not look any different simply because it is brought into the presence of a distinguished person, but an angry individual may alter his appearance (without becoming any the less angry) when transported into such company.[1] And this should indicate, what should be obvious on other grounds anyway, that condition (iii) of our schema for, say, seeing that Jonathan is angry is not satisfied, if it is satisfied at all, in any simple way. If the behavior is extreme enough (for Jonathan), we may be able to say that (iii) is satisfied in a fairly straightforward way: in these background conditions Jonathan simply would not look this way unless he was really angry. He couldn't fake it (whatever may be true of *other* people). At other times the regularity on which we rely in seeing that he is angry, the regularity which is expressed in condition (iii), may be much more restricted in scope, and a commensurately greater degree of proto-knowledge is required. For example, I think it is plausible to say that we are capable of expressing ourselves in *some* circumstances in a way which, in altered circumstances, we would find impossible. Where is Jonathan? Is he in church with his mother or at a midnight brawl with his mistress? It may turn out that Jonathan can do things (hence: look a certain way) in one setting which he cannot bring himself to do in the other (not, at least, without a noticeable difference in the way he does it). If this is true, then perhaps in one setting, but not the other, one could (if one knew Jonathan well enough) see that he was bored, interested, or pleased. Whether one *did* see this or not would still depend, of course, on the satisfaction of condition (iv), and it is important to remember in this connection that (iv) embodies two essential restrictions. The qualification which is important for the present purpose is the one which requires that S (the percipient)

---

[1] It should be pointed out that the social setting, although it may affect the way b looks to S (when b is a person), is *not* a background condition as I have defined this term. A background condition must not only be capable of affecting the way b looks to S, but it must do so in such a way as to leave unaltered the state, condition, or character of b itself. The background condition must be causally independent of the particular character or condition of b itself. In the case of persons, the social setting affects the way b looks to S by affecting b itself (causing b to alter his behaviour), and in so far as this is the case, the social setting is not a background condition.

not possess an over-generalized background belief with respect to the relevant character of b (Jonathan) in virtue of which (iii) holds. That is, if S purports to see that Jonathan is bored, and he purports to see this by virtue of the (false) background belief that Jonathan (generally) would not look this way unless he was bored, then S does *not* see that Jonathan is bored. The character which is relevant to the satisfaction of (iii) is, so to speak, *Jonathan at a midnight brawl with his mistress*, and unless the percipient appreciates the fact that the regularity between the way Jonathan looks and his being bored has its scope restricted in this fundamental way, he will operate with what I have referred to as an 'under-specified' background belief. With a properly specified background belief, a belief which might be more fully articulated in this example as 'In these conditions Jonathan at a brawl with his mistress would not look the way he now does (to me) unless he was bored', S will not purport to see that Jonathan is bored unless his proto-knowledge includes not only the fact that this is Jonathan but that it is Jonathan at a brawl with his mistress. For it is only *from* this level of proto-knowledge that the available regularities are capable of bridging the remaining increment *to* 'Jonathan is bored'. There are no regularities which can bridge the larger increment from 'This is Jonathan (unspecified environment)' to 'Jonathan is bored'— i.e. no regularity of the form 'In these background conditions Jonathan (in general) would not look this way unless he was bored'.

Perhaps I have said enough to indicate some of the complexities that occur in this area. The last paragraph has brought into the open something that should have been more or less apparent from almost the beginning of my discussion of epistemic seeing. The actual subject term used to refer to what S sees to be P may not be a faithful reflection of the level of specificity with regard to b which is required of S to see that it is P. In saying that S could see that the b was P, it may not be true that b's, in general, would not look the way this b now looks to S unless they were P. This may be true for only a special class of b's, or for only *this b*, or for only *this b* under *special* circumstances. In such cases the actual increment which S has acquired by visual means may be considerably smaller than might be supposed by a simple inspection of the perceptual claim itself. In saying that I can see that this piece of fruit is ripe, it may turn out that I can see this only because I already know it is a banana and believe (correctly) that no banana would look this way unless it was ripe. Similarly, when I see that Jonathan is bored, it may turn out that I can see this only because I already know (proto-knowledge) that Jonathan is in the midst of a wild brawl and (correctly) believe that Jonathan would not look this way in the midst of a wild brawl unless he was bored. I may simply say, however, that I can see that Jonathan is bored without revealing, thereby, my application of specialized proto-knowledge.

Once again, the question of how completely one can justify one's background belief is irrelevant to whether one can see that something is the case by means of it. The questions to ask are: Is this background belief true? Is it under specified with respect to L? That is, is there a reliance on some sub-aspect of the way b looks which is not distinctive? Is it under-specified (over-generalized) with respect to the pertinent character of b in virtue of which it would not look that way unless it were P? In other words, the questions to ask are whether conditions (i)–(iv) are satisfied in the way they have already been qualified. *If* they are satisfied, then, whether or not S knows it, whether or not he can prove they are satisfied, S sees that b is P, and, in the case in which 'P' is some psychological predicate, S sees that some person is angry, frightened, embarrassed, nervous, or whatever. Hence, *he knows*—and he knows whether or not he knows or we know that he knows.

In a sense, then, I think that the philosophical question of other minds is no more a problem than the question, presumably non-philosophical, of other grimaces. How do we know that other bodies possess minds like our own? If we can take this question to mean: 'How can we know that they are people—creatures who think, fear, hate, love, become depressed, feel pain, are nervous, self-conscious, annoyed, and confused?', then the answer seems obvious. We can see that it is so. We can see that he is afraid, she is depressed, and they hate each other. We can see that the speaker is nervous, that the strange creature is watching us, and that the poor thing is suffering.[1] We can see these things,

[1] Of course, in the vast majority of cases the fact that it is *a person* we see is a piece of information which is comprehended within our proto-knowledge. In saying 'I can see that your wife is getting sleepy', 'I can see that you are embarrassed by this topic', and 'Everyone could see that he was afraid', we are not describing the acquisition of an increment of information which includes the fact that what we see to be sleepy, embarrassed, or afraid *is a*

and hence know that they are so, in the same fashion as we see (epistemically) a great many non-psychological features of our environment, the same way we see that he is grimacing or she is pulling a long face (if we treat the psychological features as non-relational), or in the same way as we can see that he is eating something (if we treat the psychological features as implicitly relational).

3. *Radical Relativity*

By 'radical relativity' I mean a form of perceptual disparity that cuts directly across our habitual forms of visual classification, that ignores the routine category boundaries, and that imposes, as it were, an altogether different set of coordinates on the spectrum of visual phenomena. Radical relativity represents, not, as in the last section, the development of some exclusive suburbs on the periphery, but the complete remodeling of our home town. Not only are there new and different things to behold, but they are there *in place* of the old and familiar.

Extreme perceptual divergence defies illustration; anything familiar enough to serve as an example lacks, thereby, the very feature which would make it a suitable exemplification of *radical* relativity. We cannot exchange our background beliefs as easily as we can our eyeglasses; and since it is a divergence in background beliefs which constitutes the heart of perceptual relativity, a discussion of radical relativity, almost inevitably, takes place in an atmosphere of unreality. This aura of artificiality and abstractness, the very antithesis of what we expect to hear about the *visual* aspects of our environment, is largely unavoidable; for we cannot suspend or drastically alter, for the space of a few pages, the habits of a lifetime. Hence, we cannot bring ourselves to see what, within an altered framework of background beliefs, it is possible to see. And if *we* cannot see it, the suspicion remains that it is not there to be seen—not really.

There is another factor which might complicate the discussion although by this time it should not. Common sense is committed, I believe, to some form of visual democracy. Whatever aristocracy might exist on the conceptual level, everyone is supposed to have the same opportunities and privileges visually. The real

person (with all that this implies about feelings, dispositions, capacities, etc.). We are telling how we discovered that *this person* (your wife, you, he) is such-and-such, not *how* we discovered that it (what we see) is a person.

world is there to be seen; those that are physiologically equipped to see it, whatever differences in what they say, believe, or think, see the same thing. This attitude, of course, reflects a large portion of the truth, and I have spent the greater part of Chapter II trying to illustrate which portion of the truth it represents. Non-epistemically, there is a common world to be seen, and, for those who bring to it a comparable acuteness of vision, a common world is seen. The Strano native and the daily commuter both see the *same* event when they witness the arrival of the 3.44 express however frightening and incomprehensible it may appear to the one. But when it comes to man's visual abilities, this is only half the story, and we are now engaged in examining the other half. If we are going to appreciate the nature of radical relativity we must keep these two halves of the story separate.

Let me, then, despite the difficulties of illustration already mentioned, try to clarify this extreme form of relativity by means of an example. I have, for this purpose, chosen to gerrymander certain kinematic and dynamic concepts—including the concept 'movement'. Perhaps movement, as much as any other feature of our visible environment, represents 'home-town' to anyone capable of reading this book.

Let us imagine Tobakee to be a stranger to such familiar concepts as weight, mass, velocity (or speed), motion, acceleration (speeding up or slowing down), and so on. He is a stranger to these concepts in the sense that he does not understand what these terms mean, nor does he have any synonomous terms to replace them. Hence, they do not form part of his classificatory apparatus for describing what goes on around him. He is a stranger to them in the way that many of us are strangers to the concepts momentum, action, impulse, as these are technically defined in our physics books. Rather, he classifies the behavior of objects, in so far as these particular features are involved in the following way: (1) an object is *stationing* if the product of its mass and its acceleration is zero; (2) an object is *mosing* if this product is greater than zero, and object A is mosing more than (faster than, at a greater rate than) object B if they are both mosing and the product of A's acceleration and mass is greater than that of B; and (3) an object is *demosing* if this product (mass times acceleration) is less than zero (deceleration being taken as negative acceleration), and object A is demosing more than B if the absolute value of this product is greater than that of B (that is, masses being equal, object A is decelerating at a greater rate than B).[1] I have explained these notions by utilizing the familiar terms 'mass' and 'acceleration'; but, of course, Tobakee does not view them this way. They are, for him, fundamental and undefined.

An object at rest is stationing; any object that happens to be moving with a uniform velocity is also stationing (since its acceleration is zero). A heavy man would be mosing more than a small child if they both fell from an equal height; even if their downward acceleration was equal, the greater mass of the man would be responsible for his greater rate of mosing. Again, this is how *we* construe Tobakee's concepts; it is an explanation of his conceptual system in terms of our own.

Ignoring for the moment the visual status of these notions, let us note the category modifications embodied in this altered system. Lacking the concept 'mass', Tobakee does not ascribe a differential mosing rate (when, as *we* would say, the differential mosing rate is exclusively a function of the differential mass of the two objects) to any permanent difference in the two objects which are mosing. Since 'mosing' is, for Tobakee, a fundamental concept (not defined in terms of other magnitudes), a differential mosing rate between, say, the man and the child is exclusively a difference in *what they are doing*; it does not depend (as it does for us) on a difference between *the things* that are doing something. The difference which Tobakee ascribes to the falling man and child is not a difference, nor is it explicable in terms of a difference, which persists beyond the activity in which they are engaged. For us, they still differ in mass even when they have stopped mosing; for Tobakee, once they have stopped mosing (and are stationing on the ground), the only relevant difference between them has vanished; for the only relevant difference between them was in what they were doing—mosing at a different rate, and they are no longer doing that.

There is, however, a complementary difference. Uniform motion is, for Tobakee, a *property* or *disposition* of certain objects

---

[1] Throughout this section I will assume that all motion, and all mosing and demosing, is referred to a permanent system of reference: the earth with its familiar system of landmarks (trees, buildings, etc.) or, when the motion is non-terrestial, to the fixed stars. I shall also be assuming that the mass of an object remains constant.

which are stationing; it is not something which the objects are *doing*. If Tobakee studied his physics books, he would discover a technical definition of those concepts which *we* call 'rest' and 'uniform motion', definitions which are framed in terms which Tobakee already understands. Objects at rest are those which are stationing and which cannot demose (in *our* terms: they cannot demose because, being at rest, they cannot decelerate). Uniformly moving objects, on the other hand, are those which are stationing and which *can* either mose or demose. A moving object, then, is an object that is not at rest (i.e. it is either mosing, demosing, or stationing with the potential for demosing). Hence, for Tobakee, there is, in his physics books, a defined distinction within the class of stationing objects; some of these stationing objects possess the same disposition as objects which are mosing or demosing: *viz*. the potential for demosing. When a stationing object possesses this disposition, *we* say it is moving uniformly, but for Tobakee the object which possesses this disposition is not *doing anything* different than other stationing objects. It is simply a difference in its disposition to behave, a difference in how it *would* behave in altered circumstances.

So much for the explanation of Tobakee's novel conceptualization. Granted that such a system is possible, what does it have to do with perceptual differences? Does it really make any difference in what Tobakee can see? Indeed, it makes a great deal of difference, although it should be understood at the outset that Tobakee still sees (see$_n$) moving objects, objects at rest, objects with mass, and objects which are accelerating and decelerating. He does not need the concepts to see the objects which exemplify the attributes corresponding to these concepts. But we are in no different position with respect to his novel categories; we see objects which are mosing, objects which are stationing, and objects which are demosing. Neither system occupies a privileged position when it is a question of seeing something non-epistemically; for the conceptual organization of what we see has nothing to do with what we see in this fashion.

Let us suppose that Tobakee has not studied physics and is ignorant of the technical definitions ('technical definitions' for *him*, not us) of 'motion' and 'rest' as these were sketched above. Given this state of affairs, let us suppose that Tobakee sees two objects, *A* and *B*; *A* is at rest and *B* is moving uniformly. From

our point of view the difference between A and B is obvious, sufficiently obvious to prompt any one of us to say that we could see
that B was moving and A was not. Tobakee, however, insists that
he fails to see a difference between what A and B are doing. It is
not simply that he fails to see that B is moving and that A is at
rest; he fails to see that there is any difference between what A
and B are doing.

In order to make a direct comparison, let us imagine a hypo-
thetical counterpart to Tobakee in our conceptual system; Harold
is watching two objects, C and D, both mosing from the same
height. C is much heavier than D, but they are falling at the same
rate of acceleration.[1] Tabokee takes the difference between what
they are doing as obvious; he can (or so he says) see that C is
mosing more rapidly than D. What does Harold see? Does he see
that one is mosing more than the other? Does he see that C is
doing something to a greater degree, or at a greater rate, than D?
Apparently not, for he insists that they are doing the same thing.
Even if we told Harold what the mosing rate of an object was,
how to calculate it in terms of the mass and acceleration of an
object, he would, no doubt, demur at Tobakee's claim to be able
to see that C and D were mosing at different rates. In *this* situation C is mosing more than D *only because* it has a greater mass,
but *mass*, or *relative mass*, is not a visible feature of things. One
cannot see what the mass of something is or that the mass of one
thing is greater than that of the other. Tobakee does not *see* that
C is mosing more than D (this is not *how* he knows); rather, he
infers it on the basis of their identical acceleration (which, we
may grant, he does see) and their assumed difference in mass—a
fairly safe assumption since C is, let us say, a much *larger* object
than D.

I think this is the sort of objection Harold might be tempted to
lodge against Tobakee's claim. Notice, however, that Tobakee is
not claiming to see the mass of anything; nor is he claiming to see
that two things differ in mass nor that they have the same accelera-

[1] For the purposes of the illustration I shall have to assume something
which is not altogether plausible: *viz.* that the difference between accelerated
(or decelerated) motion and uniform motion is generally distinguishable. It
is, of course, sometimes a simple matter to see that something is accelerating
(when the *rate* of accceleration is great enough), but to see that something is
moving uniformly is not such a simple matter (might it not be accelerating
very slowly?).

tion. What Tobakee is claiming to see is a difference in what C and D are doing, and once they cease mosing (come to rest on the ground) he sees no relevant difference between them any more—at least none that accounts for their former difference in mosing rate. It is, in fact, unfair to criticize Tobakee from the standpoint of *our* conceptual system. This begs all the questions since, if this is permitted, Tobakee can reciprocate with an identical objection; Harold cannot see that A and B are doing anything different because these two objects are doing precisely the same thing—*stationing*. The only relevant difference between them is a dispositional difference, a difference in their *potential* for demosing, but this is not a visible feature of things. *If A and B were allowed to interact*, to collide, say, or if they were both brought into some other specifiable environment, B would demose while A never would. But this difference, Tobakee insists, is not a visible feature of A and B; they are not manifesting this dispositional difference *now*. Apparently Harold is inferring that A and B differ with respect to this disposition, and he is using this inferred difference as his basis for ascribing a difference in *current activity* to A and B.

Tobakee will, of course, concede that A and B look different relative to one another (A *looks like* it has no potential for demosing while B does), but he does not regard their looking this way as a conclusive reason for believing that the one has a potential for demosing and the other not. Hence, he does not *see* any difference (where this is understood to mean: 'see *that* they differ in some respect'). Analogously, Harold will concede that C and D look different relative to one another (C *looks as though* it is heavier than D), but Harold does not regard their looking this way as a conclusive reason for believing that C is heavier than D. Hence, he *sees* no difference in their mass, and, consequently, no difference in their mosing rate. Both mass (from Harold's point of view) and demosing potential (from Tobakee's point of view) are dispositions of an object which are not infallibly identifiable on the basis of the way the objects *look* at the moment. There is no difference between Tobakee and Harold in this respect.

Still, the feeling persists that Tobakee is 'getting away with something'. Really (one is inclined to say), he must see that A is doing something different than B; how can he possibly miss it? This attitude reflects a mistaken conception of Tobakee's position. Of course A and B look different to him, but so do C and D look different to Harold. Harold and Tobakee are simply exploiting the way these objects look to them in different ways. Tobakee does not see that A and B are *doing* anything different because, for him, they are doing the same thing (stationing). He does not see that they have a different dispositional property (potential for demosing) because he does not regard the way they look as a conclusive reason for believing they *will* demose differently (after all, he might say, it must be an extended use of the verb 'to see' to say that one sees that something *will* behave in a certain way). Harold, on the other hand, does not see that C and D are doing anything different because, for him, they are doing the same thing (accelerating downward at the same rate). Nor does he see that they differ in their dispositional properties (mass) since he does not regard the way they look as a conclusive reason, by itself, for believing that they differ in mass.

Certainly Tobakee can make mistakes; everyone, including Harold, can. Suppose C and D look identical (both rocks of the same size). Can Tobakee now see that they are mosing differently, or can he detect a slight difference in their mosing rate. Of course not. But can Harold detect the difference between the velocities of A and B when their velocities are almost identical? Some differences are just too small to be seen, and this is true for Tobakee as well as Harold. Suppose, however, that we dropped two objects, identical in appearance and size, *one* of which had a much greater mass (a real rock and a paper imitation). Wouldn't Tobakee be unable to detect (see) the difference in their rate of mosing even though this difference was quite large? Certainly he would. Suppose we arranged a situation in which A and B were located at different distances from Harold and had them move in such a way that they looked like they were at the same distance moving with the same speed. Would Harold be able to detect (see) the difference in their motion? The difference could be made quite large. No, he might easily be misled. What do such examples show? Nothing but that both Tobakee and Harold can be mistaken in the application of their respective concepts.

Nevertheless (our challenger persists), there is a basic difference between velocity and mass. Tobakee is clearly relying on the *size* of something to discover a differential mosing rate; this can easily be shown by such experiments as the one mentioned above. Once again, this misrepresents the actual state of affairs. If we asked

Tobakee about it, there is no reason why he should not tell us that size was, strictly speaking, irrelevant. Small objects can mose at a much more rapid rate than large objects; for instance, bowling balls mose at a visibly greater rate than do basketballs (when dropped from the same height). Besides, the two balls differ in size whether they are mosing or not. The difference which Tobakee sees *ceases* to exist when the two objects cease mosing.

It is certainly the case that when C and D are (as we say) accelerating at the same rate, and when C and D are similar in all other respects, Tobakee must *know* something about C and D in order to see that they are mosing differently. If he knows, for example, that C is a rock and D is a paper imitation, then there is nothing preventing him from seeing (given the above similarities of acceleration and size) that they are mosing differently. For with this proto-knowledge condition (iii) is, under some conditions, quite routinely satisfied: in these background conditions *the rock* and the *paper imitation* would not look the way they do (relative to one another) unless the former was mosing faster than the latter. The role which Tobakee's proto-knowledge plays in this visual achievement is not a unique phenomenon, nor does it mean that he did not discover something (a differential mosing rate) by *seeing* that it was so. The fact that C is a rock and D a paper imitation does not imply that C is mosing more than D; Tobakee has to use his eyes to discover whether this is so or not. There is still an *increment* that he is bridging by purely visual means.

The same is true of Harold. Generally speaking, it is not the case that *any* two things which look the way A and B now look (relative to one another) are such that the latter (B) is moving and the former standing still. The moon and the clouds look this way relative to one another, and it is the moon, not the clouds, which are standing still in this case. And this is simply another way of indicating that Harold, also, must begin with some preliminary information about the general character of A and B if he is to see that one is moving and the other not. He sees that one airplane is moving, the other not; that one automobile (person, animal, etc.) is moving faster than the other, and so on. And what is true for two automobiles (airplanes, persons, etc.) may not be true for just *any* two objects; condition (iii) also has its restrictions in Harold's case.

Tobakee and Harold need different proto-knowledge; or, better, they *exploit* different portions of their proto-knowledge. But they both require some degree of proto-knowledge to see what they allege themselves to see. Tobakee's visual achievements strike us as suspicious, not because his proto-knowledge includes suspicious elements; for we often know, or it is often quite obvious, which of two objects is the heaviest. His achievement strikes us as suspicious because we are not accustomed to letting this particular piece of information, obvious though it may be on many occasions, get absorbed, so to speak, in what we see to be the case. And, conversely, Harold's visual achievement may strike Tobakee as suspicious because he is not accustomed to letting certain obvious differences (what Harold would describe as the obvious difference in the way two objects look which are moving at considerably different uniform velocities) get absorbed into his final observation. He treats this 'obvious' difference between stationing objects as a symptom (sign?) of a non-visible (unobservable?) difference in demosing potential. And Harold treats the 'obvious' difference between a full-grown man and a small child as a symptom (sign?) of a non-visible (unobservable?) difference in mass. They both know that this is a man and that is a boy, but they exploit different portions of this knowledge in reporting what they have discovered—what they can see. Harold depends on the constancy in size (texture, degree of differentiation, etc.) of objects to detect a different angle of movement, or an appreciable difference in distance (from him), and, hence, a different rate of uniform motion. Tobakee also relies on these features to some extent (to detect accelerated movement and differences in acceleration), but he also relies on the acknowledged differences in mass between such objects (proto-knowledge) or the regular connection between *people* of different mass and their consequent differences in appearance (background belief). By virtue, then, of systematically different background beliefs, or a different exploitation of their proto-knowledge, the way two objects look to Tobakee and Harold become conclusive reasons to believe different things, although the way the objects look to each of them is, in one sense, the same.

The difference between Harold and Tobakee could be put in terms of condition (iii) in the following way. There are occasions on which Harold and Tobakee see a pair of airplanes and one or more of the following circumstances prevail:

(1) In these (background) conditions the two airplanes would not look the way they do (relative to one another) unless the first, *A*, was moving faster than the second, *B* (both moving uniformly).

(2) In these (background) conditions *A* and *B* would not look the way they do (relative to one another) unless *A* was accelerating at a more rapid rate than *B*.

(3) In these (background) conditions *A* and *B* would not look the way they do (relative to one another) unless *A* was of greater mass than *B*.[1]

(4) In these (background) conditions *A* and *B* would not look the way they do (relative to one another) unless *A* was mosing faster than *B*.

Tobakee sees that one plane is mosing faster than the other because, in circumstances such as (4), he is willing to assume that conditions are as described in (4). Even when conditions are as described in (1), Tobakee does not customarily assume that conditions are as so described, and, hence, prefers to say that, although *A* certainly looks as though it has a greater potential for demosing than *B*, looks can be deceiving. Harold, on the other hand, does frequently manifest the appropriate background belief. However, he does not customarily assume that conditions are as described in (3); he prefers to say that although *A* certainly looks as though it is heavier than *B*, looks can be deceiving. And since the conditions described in (3) are intimately connected with those described in (4), Harold prefers not to say that anyone can see that one thing is mosing faster than another.

Both Harold and Tobakee can cite reasons why the other should be cautious in assuming conditions are as described in (1) or (4). After all, there are *some* conditions which do not conform to (1) and (4) and both Harold and Tobakee will be quick to point out to the other the possible failures in the other's background beliefs. But none of this implies that when conditions are as described in (1), and Harold assumes that they are, he does not thereby see that one plane is moving faster than the other. And, likewise, none of this implies that when conditions are as described in (4), and Tobakee assumes they are, he does not see that one plane is mosing faster than the other.

One can even envision situations in which Tobakee's system

[1] I hope I will not bore the reader by emphasizing, once again, that the regularity expressed by this condition is a regularity concerning *airplanes*, between the way *airplanes look* and the airplanes' *difference in mass*.

would be more convenient to apply. An astronaut drifting through inter-stellar space would find Tobakee's system more useful. If he was approaching an object at a uniform velocity, for instance, he could hardly tell whether it was he or the object (or both) which was moving with uniform velocity. He might say, with Tobakee, that although it looked like the object had a potential for demosing, one could not be certain of this. Any object which was mosing or demosing, however, would be more quickly identified; for presumably he could tell whether he was mosing or demosing (by the force of acceleration affecting his body), and, hence, he could begin to sort out those other objects which were stationing, mosing, and demosing. He would be like a sailor who (without seeing the water) could tell whether a nearby ship was accelerating or not, but could not tell whether it was moving uniformly or not (since he could not be sure the apparent motion was not due to a movement of his own ship).

The reader will have noticed by this time that Tobakee's concept of mosing is simply, as it were, the activization of our concept of 'impressed force'. Tobakee's claim to see a differential mosing rate is, in our terms, the claim to see a difference in the (net) impressed forces on two objects. I didn't mention this earlier since Tobakee had enough conceptual prejudice operating against him without introducing what, so some people, would be another red flag. We are too accustomed to hearing that *force* is not an observational concept; rather, it is supposed to be 'theoretical' in nature. These matters will be taken up in the following chapter; I don't wish to digress now. I simply mention it for the sake of those, if there are any, who happened to be persuaded by this rather lengthy example. For one should be aware of the consequences, and one of them is that 'force' is as much of an observ*able* (which is not to say it is as observed as much) as is 'motion'.

Radical relativity, then, can be bred by a radically different conceptual framework. A significantly different systematization can lead to a significantly different set of habitual assumptions, asumptions that are deployed in assessing, for descriptive purposes, the way things are on the basis of the way they look. I do not know whether any individual, or group of individuals, exemplify such a radical departure from what we are accustomed. I suspect not, but this seems to be a matter which is irrelevant to the point of the illustration. We have heard it alleged that certain cultures possess a radically different conceptual orientation. If I am right, this difference could issue in perceptual differences of the kind I have just described. It could result in their not seeing the kinds of things we find it common to see, and vice versa. And I hope to have shown that this is a difference, or could easily be a difference, in what they see in the most direct and primary way of seeing something epistemically. Radical conceptual disparity can issue in radical perceptual disparity in the same way that the acquisition of a new job can alter one's ability to see what is the case. It is a difference of degree, but the extremes of this scale appear to be differences in kind. For extreme relativity of this sort impinges on our most fundamental and unquestioned beliefs: those that transform the way something looks into a reason for believing it to be of a special character. And although it is difficult to imagine extreme alteration in these background beliefs, they are the chief source of whatever divergence exists in individuals' ability to see something epistemically. Alter these and the world stays the same, but what we see of it changes; it changes to just that extent in which seeing is understood as a way of finding out about that world. We still see (see$_n$) the same things, but our ability to see what they are and how they are behaving is commensurately altered.

VI

OBSERVATION AND SCIENTIFIC

PRACTICE

One hears a good deal about the importance of observation to scientific practice. No doubt it is important. Nonetheless, there seems to be a tendency on the part of philosophers to neglect it. Afraid, perhaps, that anything more than a cursory treatment of observation would embroil him in traditional epistemological disputes, disputes in which he has little interest, the philosopher of science has confined his attention to such topics as the nature of theories, the contrast between theories and laws, the role of explanation and the differences between it and prediction, the paradoxes of confirmation, the nature of the causal relation, the status of probabilistic hypotheses, and so on. I do not wish to deny the importance of these matters, but I do want to suggest that such discussions are frequently vitiated by a perfunctory characterization of what constitutes an observation and the relationship, the reciprocal influences that exist, between observation and these other facets of scientific practice. This chapter, then, is an attempt to show how a deeper appreciation of observation itself can provide us with a new base from which to attack some of the traditional issues in the philosophy of science.

1. *Observation*

The noun 'observation' seems to be in current use both within science and the philosophy of science, and the adjective 'observable' appears to be the favored terminology of those who have a philosophical interest in the sorts of entities and processes with which scientists deal. Since the usuage is already well established, I shall adopt it, to an extent, in the following discussion. For the purpose of emphasizing the continuity between this chapter and the preceding chapters I would prefer to continue using constructions involving the verb 'to see', but I shall compromise by constructing a terminological bridge, so to speak, between the (partially) corresponding set of terms.

When we say that something is observable, we mean that it *can* be observed. What, then, can be observed? Although the equation is by no means entirely satisfactory (see below), I think for the purposes at hand we can say that anything which can be seen can be observed and vice versa. Or more precisely: X is observable if and only if X can be seen in a non-epistemic way (see$_n$), X is a state of affairs, condition, or situation which can be seen to obtain in a primary epistemic way, or, finally, a state of affairs, condition, or situation which can be seen to obtain in a secondary epistemic fashion. Once this equation is made, of course, we have within the idea of 'the observable' the same distinctions that apply to seeing something. Something may be observable in a secondary epistemic way but not in a primary way: e.g. if a pi-meson is not observable (if we cannot see$_n$ a pi-meson), then the state, condition, or behavior of such a particle is not observable in any primary epistemic way. There may, however, be ways of observing what such a particle is doing, or what properties it has, in a secondary way. Notice, this proposal says nothing about the observability of properties or relations. This is intentional. I shall go into this matter later, but I do not think it makes sense to speak of a property, feature, attribute, or relation as being observable except in the *derivative* sense that a state of affairs, event, situation, or condition that is (in some sense) constituted by the exemplification of that property or relation is itself observable in one of the above senses.

There may be some who consider the above proposal too liberal. It may be thought that those states of affairs which can only be seen (to obtain) in a secondary way should not be dignified by being called observable. It is the primary mode of seeing which alone represents the fundamental epistemological mode of perception and, hence, 'the observable' should be restricted to what can be seen in this way. In answer to such a challenge I can only admit that my proposed use of the term 'observable' is too liberal to reflect the narrower interests of some epistemologists;

but that it is too liberal in any other sense I would deny. It is *not* too liberal if one is interested in what passes as observable within the context of a scientific investigation; on the contrary, for this purpose it may even be too restrictive (see Section 4 of this chapter). The attention of the epistemologist will, no doubt, center on what can be seen in a primary epistemic way since, as I have already admitted, there is a sense (although not a very significant sense) in which this is fundamental. But we can admit the epistemological significance of this form of observability without converting our entire terminology to suit this single interest. Such shifts in terminology have the inevitable effect of leading one to deny that any other use of the words is appropriate or legitimate. One begins, that is, to regard every *other* use of the words as incorrect, a move that is often heralded by such pronouncements as 'The only thing that is *really* observable is . . .' The reports of scientists, then, are disparaged (or ignored) as 'loose talk' or 'language lacking philosophical rigor'. We needn't go this far. We have already baptized the distinctions in which the epistemologist might be interested; let us, therefore, simply acknowledge that the observable is what can be seen. We can always ask: 'In what way is it seen?' I shall return (in the following section) to the discussion of those things which can *only* be seen in a secondary epistemic way, and I shall urge (again) that this distinction is not as significant as one might suppose.

It should be understood that my equation of '—— is observable' with '—— can be seen' does not provide us with any quick analysis of what it means to observe something. I do not wish to equate the meaning of the verbs 'to observe' and 'to see', I think, on the contrary, that such an equation would be a positive mistake. To observe something (a man, a dog, a strange phenomenon) implies a degree of attentiveness on the part of the observer that is not suggested by the verb 'to see'; it suggests that one is *watching* it or *keeping* it under surveillance. 'I observed the mixture' and 'I saw the mixture' are two different things. In a sense, one can only *begin* observing something *after* one has seen it, and one does not observe everything one sees. I do not wish to deny these differences, but neither do I intend to get sidetracked in an attempt to pin down all the distinctions. For I am not particularly interested in what it means to observe something. Rather, I am concerned with *what can be observed* (what is observable). And although what *is* seen (by S at t_1) and what *is* observed (by S at t_1) may differ considerably by virtue of the fact that of all those things which one sees, only those are observed towards which one exhibits the requisite attentiveness or interest (if, indeed, this is the difference), I do not believe that what *can* be seen and what *can* be observed differ to the same extent.[1] Hence, within certain loose tolerances, I think the equation between what can be seen and what is observable can be sustained despite the differences between observing something and seeing it.

Given this notion of observability, what is to be understood by an *observation*? Is an observation something we do? No.[2] Although we can *make* an observation at 3.45 p.m. or have someone *under* observation during the morning, our observations are not located at these times. Observations are the sort of thing that can be recorded, tabulated, or summarized on a graph; they may be accurate or inaccurate, precise or imprecise, in agreement or disagreement with what is expected. Our observations agree if *what we have observed* (to be the case) is the same, if the data or information that we have accumulated is the same. This suggests that observations are expressible in *sentential* form. It also suggests that not every object of the verb 'to observe' counts as an observation. To pull these assorted hints together, let us say that an observation (for S) will be anything which S sees to be the case which is relevant, or thought to be relevant, to his inquiry. To put it a bit more pretentiously: S's observations are those pieces of information, P_1, P_2, . . . , which (i) are relevant, or thought to be relevant, to his inquiry, and for which (ii) the statement

---

[1] But they still differ. One might wish to say that some things (that we see) happen too quickly to be observed, that we can observe the rules without seeing the rules, and that (perhaps) we can observe the growth of a plant without seeing the growth of a plant. Furthermore, there seems to be many noun phrases which fit into one context but not the other, or, if they do, significantly alter the meaning of the verb—e.g. 'He saw that it meant war' and 'He observed (remarked?) that it meant war'. My only excuse for ignoring such differences is my belief (possibly mistaken) that the important element which the somewhat technical notion of an 'observable' is supposed to capture is that element which is associated with what we can see or can see to be the case.

[2] Once again this blunt answer must be understood as partially stipulative. I am choosing to ignore what I take to be a process–product ambiguity in the notion of an observation in order to clarify one of its important uses (product sense).

that S saw that P_i is true.[1] The first clause is intended to be as vague as is the notion of 'an observation' itself. Its function is to exclude those things which S saw to be the case, but which would not be included in, say, a complete record of his observations. For example, one might notice, during the course of an experiment on nuclear decay processes, that one's fingers were badly stained with nicotine. One does see that one's fingers are stained with nicotine, but is this to be included in one's observations? Most likely not: the state of one's fingers is simply not pertinent. On the other hand, the investigation might be such as to make this a relevant consideration. When one is urged to record *all* of one's observations, one is not being asked to record *everything* that one sees to be the case. One is being asked to record *everything* that one sees to be the case that one considers relevant to the purposes of the inquiry. The first clause, then, is meant to capture this more or less vague connotation of the term 'observation'.

The 'P_i' in the second clause is not meant to be the *name* of anything; it is not, for instance, the name of any *sentence* which expresses what S saw. I have not overlooked any quotation marks; their avoidance was intentional. 'P_i' may be thought of of as a variable which takes sentences as values, and any sentence which, when inserted for 'P_i', makes the statement form 'S saw that P_i' true is thereby an expression of one of S's observations (assuming (i) satisfied). Such a sentence is *not* his observation. Furthermore, the verb 'to see' is to be understood in either a primary or secondary epistemic way. The justification for including secondary seeing is the same as was given for its inclusion in the notion of observability.

It should be clear that not everything that we can observe counts as an observation when we observe it. We can see the man who is blinking, the needle on the meter which registers 5·4, and the rust on the metal, but none of these things, the man, the rust, or the needle, are observations. It is only when we see these things epistemically, when we see *that* the man is blinking, *that* the needle registers 5·4, and *that* there is rust on the metal, that what we see qualifies as an observation. A lightning flash is

---

[1] This clause renders inconsistent the idea of a *false* observation. I am not altogether certain that usage supports this stipulation, but whether it does or not, it should at least be clear what *I* mean by an observation.

observable but never an observation—although one of our observations might be that *there was a lightning flash*. Non-epistemic seeing, taken in isolation, does not provide us with any observations. Neither does every form of epistemic seeing. I can see *what* a man is doing, *where* he is going, and *how* he is traveling, but what he is doing, where he is going, and how he is traveling are not observations of mine. My observations will be that he is combing his hair, that he is going to a party, and that he is traveling by taxi. Clause (ii) in the above equation automatically imposes these distinctions by its requirement that the object of the verb 'to see' be a factive nominal; hence, the observation will always be something that can be appraised in terms of its correctness, accuracy, relevance, and so on.

Since I am primarily interested in man's *visual* abilities, and the conditions under which they can be successfully exercised, I have restricted the application of the noun 'observation', by means of my interpretation of the verb 'to see' in clause (ii) as either primary or secondary epistemic seeing, to that information which is acquired in some visual manner. I have, in other words, excluded what might be discovered by *hearing* the stutter of a geiger counter, *smelling* the presence of hydrogen sulfide, of *feeling* a difference in temperature. Since I have not undertaken an analysis of these other sense modalities, I wish to confine my attention to those observations which a man lacking the sense of sight could not have achieved—at least not in the same way in which they were achieved. If observation is to include, beside what we see, what we smell, feel, hear, and taste, then I am confining this discussion to only *one sort* of observation.

I shall occasionally use the phrases 'primary observation' and 'secondary observation'. A *primary* observation is an observation in which the verb 'to see' in clause (ii) is an instance of seeing something in a primary epistemic way; a *secondary* observation is when this verb is understood in a secondary way. There are, of course, no non-epistemic observations. Consequently, what we see in a non-epistemic way is not extremely important when one is discussing the 'data', so to speak, which scientists attempt to explain and on which their theoretical speculations are based. For the 'data' often comprehends just the available *observations*. Nevertheless, it is important to be clear about what is seen non-epistemically since it is this feature which distinguishes between primary and secondary observations. In primary, but not in secondary, cases of seeing that b is P one must see b non-epistemically. Hence, when epistemological issues predominate, and the pressure builds up to distinguish between direct (primary) and indirect (secondary) observation, it is important to be clear about what can, and what cannot, be seen non-epistemically. If we cannot see (see_n) a molecule, then anything which counts as an observation on the state, condition, or behavior of a molecule must, of necessity, be of a secondary sort. Such distinctions are certainly relevant to an epistemological analysis of scientific theories. Therefore, although our ability to see something non-epistemically is not of direct epistemological significance, being, on the contrary, positively devoid of such significance, it acquires a special status as the basis by which we differentiate between the sorts of observations that are made.

2. Laws and Observation

Scientific laws are instrumental in vastly enlarging the scope of secondary and, to a lesser extent, primary observation. 'Law' is, perhaps, not quite the right word, since I wish to include in this category not only those regularities which are commonly designated 'laws' but also those principles, rules, effects, and even theoretical considerations which serve as a bridge between logically distinct states of affairs, conditions, and events—which serve, in other words, to relate disparate features of our environment by virtue of their regular pattern of occurrence. The process is, of course, a familiar one; we find it embodied in such everyday phenomena as: a carpenter who sees (by the position of the bubble in his level) that the beam is level, the housewife who sees for herself (by consulting the butcher's scale) that her roast is over four pounds, the mechanic who sees (by the compression gauge) that your piston rings are badly worn, the man who sees (by the photographs) that his niece is now a young lady, and the hunter who sees (by the tracks) that some animal has passed this way. Each of these cases, it seems clear, presuppose a degree of familiarity with certain regularities which obtain in our routine environment. Each of them illustrate the pattern associated with seeing something in an epistemically secondary fashion. One sees that b is P (or that b_1 is R to b_2) by seeing$_n$ c (or c_1 and c_2); it is not the way b looks that leads (via clause (iii) in our various schemata) the percipient to believe that b is P. Rather, it is the way c is, or the way c_1 is related to c_2, that serves in this capacity. On the presumption of a uniform association, in these conditions, between c's being in the condition it is and b's being P, one sees that b is P. To put it somewhat picturesquely, one sees through one state of affairs to another. Such visual achievements are quite frequently reported without any qualifier on the verb 'to see' (i.e. 'by the level', 'by the tracks', etc.); generally speaking, this omission is possible because the qualifications are understood. It becomes imperative to make them explicit only when justificatory considerations arise ('How could you have seen . . . ?') or when such considerations may be expected to arise. Let us look, then, at the way this common practice is extended, sometimes to an almost paradoxical degree, in science.

Laws (principles, rules, effects, theories) provide the scientist with a huge body of regularities or uniformities which he can, subsequent to their establishment and routine acceptance, utilize to extend the scope of his secondary and, sometimes, primary observations. Such regularities provide us with fresh cases of circumstances in which c would not be Q unless b were P—the state of affairs which is imposed by the third condition in secondary epistemic seeing; and our familiarity with these regularities permits us to *have* in c's being Q a conclusive reason for believing b to be P. The most notable illustration of this practice is in the scientist's use of meters, counters, analyzers, and other detection devices. Judging from modern physics, one might almost draw the conclusion that the information supplied by such instruments exhausted the class of observations. There are, of course, reasons why this should occur in such a theoretically advanced field as modern micro-physics, and one of the reasons, the one with which we are presently concerned, is the vast corpus of knowledge, knowledge of general uniformities, which has achieved a sufficient level of routine acceptance to permit its absorption into secondary observation.[1] One needn't be a physicist to see, by the sudden swing of a galvanometer needle, that there has been a sudden increase in current intensity. Presumably, one need only be acquainted with the function of a galvanometer to make such

---

[1] Another reason is the need for relatively precise numerical observations. The relation of observation to precise numerical measurements will be discussed in Section 4 of this chapter.

an observation. Somewhat greater technical background is presupposed, however, in seeing, by the same sequence of events, that the capacitor has discharged. The differences between what people see to be the case are generated by the differences in what they (truly) take for granted when they watch the galvanometer, by a difference in their background beliefs. There may be a variety of different events or states of affairs about which it would be true to say that, under these (background) circumstances, the galvanometer would not have behaved the way it did unless this other state of affairs obtained or unless this other event occurred. And each of these other states of affairs or events *can* be observed in a secondary way. Whether they are observed or not will depend on what the observer is (truly) taking for granted about the connection between the galvanometer's behaviour and this other state of affairs. And this, in turn, will depend on who the observer is, what his technical background happens to be, and the extent of his familiarity with situations of this sort.

Some philosophers take it as axiomatic that everyone sees *only* what the needle on the galvanometer is doing; anything beyond this is a theoretical inference or interpretation. If what this means is that, in the circumstances I have depicted, only the galvanometer's needle is seen (seen$_n$), not the current intensity or the discharge from the capacitor, and that consequently only the behavior of the needle is seen in an epistemically *primary* way, I would tend to agree. But if it means that the observer, in every such case, engages in some discursive process beginning with a premise about the behavior of the galvanometer needle and, via certain acknowledged theoretical principles, arrives at a conclusion describing what he purports to see, then I would flatly disagree. I would disagree because I think this is a misdescription of what occurs in *every* such case, not because I think that this is never an accurate portrayal of what happens when instruments are used. If the connecting generalities (the laws and principles which relate the behavior of the instrument to the processes which the observer alleges himself to see) are not well established, or if, being well established, they are not taken for granted in *this* context, or if, being taken for granted, they are simply not true, then it becomes plausible to suppose that the observer does not see what he claims to see. Perhaps, in such circumstances, he *is* interpreting, concluding, or tentatively supposing, on the basis of the instrument's behavior, that certain other processes are occurring. But this is rarely the case when instruments are involved, unless, of course, one has some reason for supposing the instrument to be functioning abnormally or for supposing that it is connected improperly. Commercial enterprises do not invest a fortune in the manufacture of devices which are constructed on principles to which only reluctant acknowledgment is given by the scientific community which uses them. The principles employed in the construction of such devices are not just probably true; at least the specialist who uses the instrument does not regard them as such when he uses it. Such instruments are manufactured because *there are conditions* in which c is Q only when b is P; that is, they are produced because condition (iii) of our schema for secondary epistemic seeing can be realized and, hence, we can, by the use of such instruments, see that b is P. Seeing that b is P, whether this is done with instruments specially designed for the purpose, or simply on the assumption of the pertinent regularities which such instruments exploit, is the very antithesis of reasoning, concluding, or inferring, that b is P on the basis of the way something else behaves or looks. On the contrary, the assumption of these general truths transforms the way the device behaves into a conclusive reason, by itself, for believing that b is P. One doesn't need to reason about it, or make inferences; this would only be necessary if one could not already see that it was so.

Secondary observations are not observations by virtue of any special indulgences, any wink of the eye at extended uses of the term, or any extraordinary dispensation to use words in a 'loose' and 'imprecise' way. They are observations because they share with primary observations a crucial characteristic: they manifest the direct, non-mediated, attainment of knowledge by the possession of visually conclusive reasons to believe. Admittedly, a requisite system of background beliefs is involved in secondary observation, but this does not make it distinctive. Such a system of beliefs is required in *any* form of epistemic seeing, They do not alter the character of secondary observation, they do not make it any the less a visual epistemic achievement. Secondary observation, as well as primary observation, permits us to know what is the case by seeing what is the case.

Philosophers of science have a habit of talking about observation in a meta-linguistic way; i.e. one asks 'Is this term an observation term or not?' or 'What sentences are observation sentences?' The result of such a procedure is the suppression of all the important distinctions. In my discussion of radical relativity in the previous chapter I suggested that the observational status of 'movement' and 'force' had no absolute significance. Is 'movement' an observable? The movement of what? For whom? When? Can we observe the movement of the moon or the stars? Is 'force' to be taken as a non-observational term? Why? Is it really impossible to see which of two teams in a tug-of-war match is exerting the greater force (and I mean by 'force' here exactly what is meant in the physics class)? Is 'mass' an observation term? Is the statement 'Mass A is greater than mass B' an obser-vation statement or not?[1] I suppose it would be urged that when 'A' and 'B' are terms which designate a proton and an electron the statement is not an observation statement. At least it seems as though we are committed to something of this sort if we regard 'electron' and 'proton' as theoretical (non-observational) terms. I should be inclined to say, however, that in this case although the statement could not be an expression of a primary observa-tion (unless, of course, we could see$_n$ electrons and protons), there is no reason why it could not be a secondary observation. One need only compare the trajectories of the two particles in a cloud chamber on which is imposed an appropriate magnetic field (the mass spectrograph). But how do we know that the one is a proton and the other an electron? There are well-known procedures for producing and identifying these particles, but, more to the point, the above observation does not imply that the observer could *see* that one particle was a proton, the other an electron. These identifications are a reflection of the observer's proto-knowledge. I do not have to be able to *see that* the two trees are, respectively, a spruce and an oak in order to see that the oak is taller than the spruce; I may know this, of course, and my perceptual claim implies or suggests that I do know it, but I need not have acquired this information by any distinctively visual means.

Even if we confine ourselves to primary observations, how-ever, the situation is still not clear. It is trivial, a consequence of

---

[1] I regard the locution 'seeing the mass of A' to be tantamount to seeing what the mass of A is, and I shall discuss this matter in Section 4 of this chapter.

our definitions, that if neither A nor B can be seen$_n$, then one cannot see that they are related in a particular fashion in any *primary* way. But surely this, alone, is no reason to think that the relations which A and B exemplify are themselves unobservable. I may be unable to see whether one flea is on another flea's back (if they have backs), but I certainly would not want to count the relation 'being on something's back' a theoretical (non-observation) term on this account. And neither is the fact that an electron or a proton cannot be seen$_n$ an overwhelming reason to classify the terms 'electron' and 'proton' as non-observation terms; for, as we have just seen, these terms can occur in observation statements (secondary). And we might even find them, or their derivatives, popping up in primary observations: e.g. this is an electron track (trail, etc.).

We are still left, therefore, with our original question: Is 'mass' an observation term or not? We have just seen that we cannot (plausibly) interpret this to mean: Can we, for *every* pair of objects A and B, see which (if either) has the greater mass? For if we interpreted it this way, we would be left with virtually nothing as an observation term. Suppose it meant: Are there some objects A and B, in regard to which we can see which (if either) has the greater mass? Consider two ordinary-sized stones. When they are lying together on the ground, there doesn't appear to be much we can say about their difference in mass; we cannot, in *this* set of circumstances, see that one has a greater mass than the other. Suppose, however, that they are resting in opposite pans of a calibrated balance, one side of which is down, rather securely down, and the other up. Can we now see that one is of greater mass than the other. Someone might tell us that we still cannot see it; the most that is visible (and at this point one must listen for the parenthetical 'technically speaking') is a difference in weight (weight being a function of the mass: $W = Mg$). Perhaps the challenger will go even further (mistrustful of the term 'weight') and maintain that we do not even see a difference in weight; all we can see, technically speaking, is the behavior of the balance: one side went up, the other down. There are still greater extremes: *viz.* we infer, or somehow more or less automatically arrive at the conclusion, that the balance is off-set on the basis of what we directly sense—the appearance of the balance. I think every step of this retreat (the last represents a complete rout) *could* be an accurate description of what one sees epistemically. One may not have calibrated the balance before placing the stones on it; in such a case one may see *only* what the balance is doing, the difference in mass remaining a matter of speculation. But that each stage can, and sometimes is, an accurate description of what we see does not mean that it is *always* a more accurate description. Certain things can be, and habitually are, correctly assumed about the condition of the balance, the variation in '*g*', and the principles incorporated into the construction of such an instrument. And when these things are correctly assumed (calibration of an instrument is one of the procedures whereby we assure ourselves that some of these assumptions are correct), the behavior of the stones on the balance is a conclusive reason, by itself, for believing that one has a greater mass than the other. In such circumstances one sees that one has a greater mass than the other.

It still may be doubted, however, whether this is an instance of *primary* observation. Are we not still relying on the way the *balance* looks (how it is behaving) to ascertain the difference in question? Seeing the stones themselves is quite incidental. The point of this objection is well taken, but I think the answer to it depends a great deal on the actual physical arrangement of the instrument. If we observe the movement of an indicator (attached to the arm of the balance), then it seems to be a case of secondary observation. If, however, we utilize an apparatus in the form of an Atwood Machine (a cord over a simple pulley with the weights attached to either end), then it is the behavior of the stones themselves (relative to one another, of course, since we are concerned with a *relationship* between the two) that becomes essential or, if not essential, at least what, in point of fact, we exploit to determine the difference in mass.

There are many detection devices which straddle this borderline separating primary and secondary observation. To cite only a few examples, consider the optical pyrometer which allows one to determine the temperature of certain materials by a direct comparison of their brightness with the brightness of certain standard materials. This procedure, I think, contains elements of primary and secondary observation. It embodies some of the same features to be found in our seeing that the filament (burner, coal, etc.) is hot; these things look a certain characteristic way ('red hot', 'white hot') when their temperature rises beyond

certain levels. This is primary observation. Still, the optical pyrometer necessitates a *comparison* between these materials and other
standard materials; it allows us to see not only *that* it is hot but
(approximately) how hot it is. And this latter information embodies elements of secondary observation. Another, less familiar,
example on this 'borderline' is the commercial use of Magnaflux
in detecting fatigue cracks, weld defects, stress-corrosion cracks,
and so on in steel and other magnetic alloys. A piece is magnetized
and:

> At cracks or other discontinuities, local flux-leakage fields are formed.
> A magnetic powder applied to the magnetized piece will be attracted
> strongly to the areas of flux leakage, forming a pattern which reveals
> the location and extent of the defects.[1]

Here, I believe, it is almost an arbitrary matter whether one calls
this primary or secondary observation; is it the way the magnetized piece looks that allows us to see that it has defects, or shall
we say that it is the way the powder looks; or the way the powder
on the magnetized piece looks? I see no point in trying to decide
this matter since the observations that result from this technique
are unaffected by how we classify it. The question is, not whether a
piece of metal can be seen to have cracks in this way, but exactly
what epistemological category the resultant observation is to be
placed. This is somewhat like asking whether we see, primarily or
secondarily, what the grain pattern of a piece of wood is *after*
we apply the stain. Does the stain bring out the pattern (so we
see it in a primary fashion) or does the pattern remain invisible
and what we see is the relative concentration of stain (seeing the
grain pattern only secondarily)? Do we see (primarily) that our
record turntable is revolving at the correct number of revolutions
per minute when we use one of the specially designed strobo-
scopic discs (under appropriate lighting)? If this is a secondary
observation (since we are relying on the way the disc, not the
turntable, looks) does it become primary observation if we
place the appropriate pattern of marks on the turntable itself?
Do we see primarily or secondarily that the telescopic mirror we
are grinding is not yet parabolic when we observe the characteristic shadows that it displays under the standard test procedures?
 Despite the vague boundary between primary and secondary

---

[1] Taken from Van Nostrand's *Scientific Encyclopedia,* third edition, p. 1012.

observation, there are hundreds of clear cases on each side. It is a simple matter to cite cases of secondary observation in science; for, in its continuing quest for greater and more comprehensive theoretical systems, more and more of what is already well established is absorbed into the devices which aid in the exploration of what is not known. And these devices are a steady source of observations. Some of these devices have found their way into our everyday affairs: barometers, thermometers, gauges, watt-hour meters, and so on. The watt-hour meter, for instance, utilizes, among other things, general principles relating induced electromotive forces and magnetic forces. As a result, even without being aware of these principles, but simply taking the meter's function and reliability for granted, we can see whether we are still consuming electrical power. Instances of primary observation in the theoretically more advanced scientific fields are more difficult to find; and one of the reasons for this is the demand for quantitative observations. Hence, the use of specially designed instruments which allow us, within the required limits of accuracy, to see what the value of a given magnitude is and the consequent conversion to secondary observation. Nevertheless, primary observation does become somewhat more common in the technological applications of these fields, within certain engineering contexts, within theoretically less well-developed areas (and here we may include the earlier, qualitative, phases of those fields which are now more sophisticated), and within such admittedly descriptive enterprises as geography, plant classification, etc.

I think, then, that a meta-linguistic approach to observation is fruitless. One must ask about specific information whether it was seen to be the case or not, and if it was, whether this was in a primary or secondary fashion. The answer to these questions will depend on who acquired the information, what he was assuming when he acquired it, what he saw (non-epistemically) in the process, and the conditions under which he saw it. These questions, the crucial ones, are ignored by making observation a question of the linguistic formulation in which such observations can be expressed.

Before leaving the discussion of laws and observations I would like to make one final point about the nature of secondary observation when it relies on certain principles that are theoretical in nature. Some philosophers of science take considerable pains to distinguish between a law and a theory. My discussion up to this point, and the examples I have used, exhibit a neglect of such distinctions. I have spoken of secondary observations with a total disregard to whether such observations embody (in clause (iii) of our schemata) principles which some might wish to call laws or whether these principles were what they might prefer to call theories (or parts of theories). The neglect was intentional since, for the purposes of clarifying what can be seen in a secondary way, the distinction between laws and theories is, I believe, largely irrelevant. Let me indicate why this is so.

It may be said that I have ignored a vast and significant difference between the things which scientists treat as observable (the things they call 'observations') and what we commonly say we see, even when both are admittedly secondary. Spectroscopic observations concerning the orbital arrangement of electrons in an atom exhibit some similarities to the case of a person who sees that his gas tank is almost empty by glancing at his fuel gauge, but the differences are more important than the similarities. Whereas we *can* see (primarily) what, in glancing at the fuel gauge, we see secondarily, this is not (always) the case with the scientist. He cannot 'open up' the atom, look directly inside it, and see that the electrons are arranged in the way his spectroscopic observations would imply. Scientists are, in many areas, *restricted* to secondary observation since what is seen in this secondary way *cannot* be seen in a primary fashion.

This is most certainly true, but the objection shows only two things, neither of which affects what I have already said about secondary observation. It shows, first, that some of the things scientists talk about, and some of the things they say they observe, cannot be seen in a primary fashion. This I have already admitted. Secondly, the objection shows that the regularities on which the scientist relies in seeing something secondarily *must be established in a different way* than the way in which many of the regularities on which we commonly depend are established. Although we (commonly) *can* acquire a confidence (sufficient to routine assumption) in the fuel gauge by repeatedly checking its indication against the gas level in the tank itself (although I doubt whether people acquire their confidence in it in this way), the scientist is often precluded from establishing the reliability of his assumptions in a similar manner. He cannot make a direct (primary) comparison between the spectrograph and the electronic orbits themselves he has only the spectrograph (and, of course, other similar data which he sees in a primary epistemic way) and the theory which relates the spectrographic pattern to the state of affairs described by his observation. But this difference in justificatory techniques, and the consequent difference in the manner in which the scientist acquires his confidence in these matters (sufficient to their routine assumption), does not in the least alter his ability to see something on the assumption that these regularities obtain. It affects the manner in which they acquire the status of assumptions, not what can be achieved with them *as* assumptions. What affects our ability to see something, in relation to these connecting regularities, is the *truth* of these regularities (condition (iii)) and, so to speak, their assumability (condition (iv)). If the differences between the justification of a theory and the justification of other, non-theoretical, regularities is sufficient to deter *anyone* from *ever* assuming the truth of the theory, or *any* part of the theory, in *any* research context, then, of course, the theory will not be responsible for a broadened system of secondary observation. Or if the differences in justification imply that *no* theory, or *no* part of a theory, within *any* degree of tolerance, is true, then, in point of fact, we will not be able to see (secondarily) what we suppose ourselves to see on the assumption of that theory. But I see no reason to think that either of these things are the case. Whether a theory, or parts of a theory, are true or not seems to me to be a matter for the scientist to determine. The claim that no theory is true, no matter how restricted in accuracy or scope it may be, not even those theoretical principles on which various instruments are designed, strikes me as a position that only a person with a peculiar conception of truth could maintain. And on the question of what can be, and actually is, assumed by practising scientists, I think there is little question but that in specific research contexts a good deal is taken for granted. Therefore, whatever differences there are between the justificatory procedures for theories and those for other, non-theoretical, regularities, these differences do not affect what can be seen in a secondary fashion. For it does not affect what is true (as distinct from what is known to be true, or how it is known to be true); nor does it affect what is in fact taken for granted in various areas of investigation; and these are the only two factors in relation to such principles which could affect the successful realization of those secondary observations which depend on them.

There are, of course, theories which do not provide any specific correlations between the state or behavior of the theoretical items (those elements which cannot be seen$_n$) and the things which the observer can see in a primary epistemic way; that is, the theory does not make the way c looks, for *any* c which we can see$_n$, a conclusive reason, ever, for believing that the theoretical item, b, is in any specific state, P. In such a case one cannot see, even secondarily, the state or condition of the theoretical item. Even given the truth of the theory, and given the fact that its truth is being taken for granted, it still does not transform the way anything (that the observer can see$_n$) looks into a conclusive reason for believing something about the specific state of the theoretical entities. One of the most obvious instances of this condition occurs in relation to theories which are statistical or probabilistic in nature: e.g. we cannot see that the molecules have a certain specific velocity (in contrast to a certain mean velocity) even though the kinetic theory of gases does relate this sort of thing to the temperature and pressure of the gas. This theory allows us to see that the *mean kinetic energy* of the molecules is increasing, by glancing at a thermometer, but not that any given molecule, or that all molecules, are increasing their kinetic energy. *Relative* to this theory, then, the specific state of a specific molecule cannot even be observed in a secondary epistemic fashion. There may, however, be other theoretical systems, or more elaborate circumstances (more elaborate, that is, than the simple thermometric situation mentioned above), which would allow such an observation, which would correlate a *specific* state of the molecule to something we could see to be the case in a primary epistemic way.

To sum up, then, we may say that a given piece of information could not represent an observation relative to prevailing theories if it could be neither a primary or a secondary observation. It could not be a primary observation if the state of affairs which it described did not have its constituents, the elements which were in that state, themselves observable (able to be seen$_n$). It could not be a secondary observation if (*a*) the state of affairs it described was not correlated, by any prevailing theory, to a state or condition which we could see to be the case in a primary way; or (*b*) no theory which embodied the appropriate correlation (i.e. clause (iii)) was, with respect to this particular correlation, true; or (*c*) the theory, whose presupposition was essential to seeing (secondarily) that this state of affairs obtained, could not, for some reason, be taken for granted in any particular research context. The latter circumstance might arise if, for example, the theory was itself in the process of being tested. In such a case the scientist should not (and, presumably, would not) assume the theory to be true in his attempt to test it. Notice, however, that if he *did* assume it true (and it was true), his resultant observations would not be any the less observations (as I have defined this term); but, of course, they would be valueless as a means of *convincing* anyone that the theory was true and, therefore, valueless, as a test of the theory. Once a theory has passed the 'test' stage, though, there seems to be nothing to prevent it from being absorbed into the background beliefs which structure the observations involved in the testing of *other* theories.

3. *Generalization and Causality*

Suppose we have a law which asserts that, certain specifiable things being held constant, the two magnitudes M and N are proportional to each other for various substances. Since the constant of proportionality, '*k*' in '$M = kN$', is generally different for different types of material, it may be a useful device for classifying and distinguishing between such material. Suppose, then, that we call it *the M & N index*. That is to say, *because* $M/N = k$ (a constant) for a given material, we let the M & N index equal this constant of proportionality. Our newly defined 'quantity' then derives its significance from the validity of this law; for it was on the assumption of this law's validity that the definition of the M & N index was framed. The law assures us that the M & N index will, for a given material, other things being held constant, *have a value*. If the law does not hold, the M & N index will have as many different values for a given material as there are different ratios between M & N. And this is simply another way of saying that for that material there is no such thing as *the M & N* index. The index remains *undefined* in relation to those items for which the law does not hold.

Since the M & N index is to be understood in terms of magnitudes which are interrelated, which bear some kind of functional relationship to each other, let us call it, and any other concept which displays the same feature, a systemically loaded concept:[1]

C is a systemically loaded concept $= df$

  (i) Two or more of the magnitudes in terms of which C is defined are such that there exists a lawful or theoretical relation between them.

  (ii) The application of C is restricted to those cases in which this lawful or theoretical relation holds.

For example, 'velocity' is not, according to this definition, a systemically loaded concept. Although average velocity (I neglect the vectorial feature) may be defined as the ratio d/t, of the distance travelled, d, to the time taken to travel it, t, there is, generally speaking, no lawful relation which exists between d and t; for a given object or class of objects, these magnitudes vary independently of one another. Even when, in particular circumstances, these two variables do happen to be connected, when the velocity happens to be rigidly controlled by external factors, the concept 'velocity' is not restricted to the occasions in which this connection between 't' and 'd' obtains. In contrast, consider the systemically loaded idea of electrical resistance.[2] This is usually understood as the ratio of the applied electromotive force (E) and the current intensity (I): i.e. the resistance, R, is E/I. But, and this is the important qualification, the resistance is defined only for those materials, and only within those limits, in which Ohm's Law applies. Since Ohm's Law states that the current intensity is proportional to the applied electromotive force ($E = kI$), R turns out to be the constant of proportionality, and this has the effect of making resistance a systemically loaded concept according to the above definition. Hence, when we ascribe a particular resistance to a circuit or to a specific piece of material, say, $R = 9$ ohms, the implication is that throughout a certain range the electromotive force and the current intensity are

[2] Compare N. R. Campbell's definition of a 'concept': '. . . many of the words used in expressing scientific laws denote ideas which depend for their significance on the truth of certain other laws and would lose all meaning if those laws were not true . . . they will in future be called "concepts".' (*Foundations of Science* (New York, 1957), p. 45).

[1] For certain purposes what I have to say could more accurately be said about the concept 'resistivity', but since this would only complicate the discussion without adding anything essentially new, I shall work exclusively with the idea of electrical resistance. I neglect reactance and capacitance.

related in the ratio 9 for that circuit or that piece of material. That is to say, if we determine the resistance of a circuit to be 9 ohms by means of a *selected* measurement of E and I, the statement that the resistance of that circuit is 9 *implies more than* that the *selected* values of E and I are in the ratio 9; it implies that *any* E, within a certain range, will generate the current intensity $E/9$ for that circuit. If we wish, we can make a temporal variable explicit; to say that $R = 9$ ohms at t_1 is to imply that at t_1 *any value of E* would have given the current intensity $E/9$.

Literally scores of scientific concepts are systemically loaded in this manner. Whenever one speaks about conductivity, specific heats, permittivity, dialectric constants, emissivity, magnetic reluctance, the acceleration of gravity, mass, and, in general, any 'coefficients' (e.g. coefficient of friction, expansion) or 'indices' (e.g. the index of refraction), one is talking about systemically loaded concepts. Even those notions which are regarded as fundamental and receive no explicit definition, but are introduced in terms of what has been called an 'operational definition', display this character, although it is generally more difficult to extract the regularities on which these concepts depend.[1] This procedure gives rise to a hierarchy of interdependent concepts: for concepts which are themselves systemically loaded appear in other laws, laws on which their application does not depend, and these new laws may be the origin of further systemically loaded concepts.

It is not my purpose, however, to present an extensive analysis of systemically loaded concepts or the role they play in unifying, systematizing, and integrating a body of scientific propositions. I mention them only in order to examine the connection which they have to observation. If what I have said about such concepts

[1] Even the concept 'velocity' may exhibit this character in so far as it depends on the operationally defined notions of length and time. To cite only one of the respects in which this may occur, we may note that the ascription of a velocity to something on the basis of a selected measurement of distance and time implies that the assorted ways we have of determining the distance (and time) will each, in their own way, issue in *the same ratio*. Whether we measure the distance from right to left or left to right makes no difference. Why? Because the equivalence (in result) of these two procedures is taken for granted. If such operations always gave significantly different results the concept 'velocity' would have to be drastically modified—as it was, for example, by the advent of relativity theory.

is true, then, recalling what has been said about primary and secondary observation, we arrive at the following result: observations may frequently be expressed in either a singular or a generalized sentential form. If, for example, an electronics engineer can, by the use of his ohmmeter, see *what* the resistance of a circuit is (see *that* the resistance is such-and-such), and if electrical resistance is, indeed, a systemically loaded concept, then this observation may assume either the form 'R = 9 ohms' or the form 'For *any E*, the current intensity of this circuit is *E/9*'. In both cases restrictions are understood: e.g. constant temperature and no extremes in the applied electromotive force.

Such a result will appear paradoxical only to those who suppose that observations are, to use the logical jargon, confined to that information which is expressible by *singular* statements of fact. That is, the conventional treatment goes something like this: we can see that this particular thing, call it a_1, has the property P, and we can observe that another particular thing, call it a_2, has the same property P. But to reach any kind of general truth, to arrive at a conclusion of the form '*All a*'s are *P*', where there are an indefinite number of *a*'s or, at least, some *a*'s which we have not yet checked, requires something *beyond* observation; it requires some kind of *inferential* leap or *inductive* argument. If one depends on this kind of picture to understand what we can see to be the case, I believe that confusion is inevitable. For in many cases, both within scientific practice and outside of it, one approaches a particular phenomenon with the knowledge that it *does* exhibit regular behavior in certain respects, that the uniformities to which such things are subject are, as it were, on display in this particular instance. No engineer would take the reading of his ohmmeter as one of his observations on the resistance of a circuit unless (among other things) he had reason to suppose that the circuit whose characteristics he was determining *had* a resistance, that *there was a constant ratio* between E and I. The knowledge that the circuit *has* a resistance (that there is a constant ratio between E and I) functions in these perceptual situations as *proto-knowledge*. He sees that *the resistance* is such-and-such. His increment in knowledge, the increment in knowledge which he bridges by visual means, is the increment between (1) this circuit has a resistance, and (2) the resistance is such-and-such. Seeing *what* the resistance is does not involve him in seeing *that* the circuit has a resistance. One, ten, or twenty readings with the meter do not constitute conclusive grounds for supposing that the circuit *has* a resistance (that the ratio between *all E*'s and the resultant *I*'s is constant), but one reading may be conclusive grounds for supposing that the resistance is 9 ohms. It may be conclusive for the latter because one is *only* trying to determine the numerical value for a given constant; one is not trying to determine whether there is any constant.

Although the case of electrical resistance illustrates a generalized secondary observation, the same pattern can be exhibited in primary observation. If, as I have already suggested, we can see (primarily) the difference in mass between two objects (for some objects, under some conditions), then what we see bears all the marks of an observation which can assume a generalized form. For if the concept of 'mass' is understood (it needn't be) as the constant of proportionality between the impressed (net) force on an object and the object's acceleration, then to see that mass A is greater than mass B is to acquire an observation which logically implies that for *any* given applied force F, the acceleration of A will be smaller than B.[1] Once again, however, the fact that this ratio between impressed force and acceleration is constant is a fact embodied in one's proto-knowledge that the two objects *have mass*; all one is doing when one sees that one mass is greater than the other is determining, by visual means alone, that the one constant is greater than the other. One is *not* determining, by visual means alone, that such constants exist. Or, to take another case, can one see (primarily) that the prism's index of refraction is greater than that of the surrounding air? Suppose we see a light ray enter and emerge from the prism, can even see its trajectory through the prism, and see how the angle of the ray shifts as it enters and emerges, I see nothing preventing one from seeing that the prism's index of refraction is greater than that of the air, but in saying this I certainly do not commit myself to the view that, when one sees this, one is also seeing that, for *any* angle of incidence, the sine of the angle of incidence bears a constant ratio to

[1] If 'o_1' entails 'o_2' it does not follow that 'S sees that o_1' entails 'S sees that o_2' or even 'S is *able* to see that o_2'. To appreciate this fact, consider an earlier example; although 'the water is boiling' implies that 'the liquid is boiling water', it does not follow that if S can see that the water is boiling, he can also see (in a primary epistemic way) that the liquid is boiling water.

the sine of the angle of refraction. Yet, what one has seen can be expressed as: 'For *any* angle of incidence, the ratio between the sine of this angle and the sine of the angle of refraction is greater than 1.'

I have introduced the topic of 'seeing the general in the particular' by speaking about systemically loaded concepts, and describing situations in which one's proto-knowledge ('This circuit has a resistance', 'These objects have mass', and 'This prism has an index of refraction') *already* embodied all of the *generalized* information which can ultimately be derived from one's observation. That is, one's observation assumes a generalized form only because the subject of one's observation (the '*b*' in '*S* sees that *b* is *P*') is already subsumed under a concept ('resistance', 'mass', 'index of refraction') which embodies the elements of generalization which appear in one's observation. What one finds out by observing is *not* that something is generally true; rather, what one finds out is that something which is generally true has, in this instance, a particular numerical specification. It is a bit misleading, therefore, to speak of 'seeing the general in the particular'. I have not described a perceptual situation in which the *increment in knowledge* which one bridges by visual means is itself an increment which begins, so to speak, with a particular truth and ends with a general truth. I have only described a situation in which one can arrive at a generalized observation by beginning with a piece of generalized information as proto-knowledge. The increment in knowledge which one bridges by visual means is *still* only the determination of a particular numerical value which one knows, perhaps on *other* grounds besides the visual, to be characteristic of a wide class of related examples. All I have established up to this point is that observations may entail statements of an essentially generalized form without being any the less observations; I have not shown that this can occur when one's proto-knowledge does not itself embody all of the generalized elements which appear in the observation.

Can one see that the screwdriver is magnetized by the way the tacks cling to it (but not to each other in the absence of the screwdriver)? It would certainly seem so. This may be interpreted as a form of secondary observation; one sees that *b* (the screwdriver) is *P* (magnetized) by seeing that *b* is R (attracting) to *c* (the tacks). But what is it that one has seen? Has one seen, simply, that *these* tacks are, at *this* moment, clinging to the screwdriver? Yes, of course, one has seen this, but one has seen more. One has seen that the screwdriver is magnetized, and this state of affairs (the screwdriver's being magnetized) entails much more than that the screwdriver will attract these tacks at this moment. It entails that the screwdriver will forcibly attract *any* iron object in its vicinity—tacks, paper clips, pins, iron filings, file cabinets, and so on. That is, given what it means to be magnetized, one's observation can be expressed in the form: 'For *any* iron object in the immediate neighborhood of this screwdriver, the latter will forcibly attract the former'. We have here a generalized observation for which the proto-knowledge ('This is a screwdriver' and 'These are tacks') is not responsible.

I am sure that there are some who will find in this discussion, not a reason to admit that observation can assume a generalized form, but a reason to *deny* that one can see that the screwdriver is magnetized. In the light of our previous chapters I think the only way to answer this objection is to point out that whether we can see that the screwdriver is magnetized or not depends, chiefly, on whether conditions (iii) and (iv) of our schema for secondary seeing are ever satisfied. That is to say, do we ever see a screwdriver (or any other piece of metal) and a set of tacks, and see that the latter are clinging to the former when:

(iii) Conditions are such that the tacks would not cling to the screwdriver (in the way they are now doing) unless the screwdriver was magnetized,

and

(iv) We, believing conditions are as described in (iii), take the screwdriver to be magnetized?

I do not think there is much doubt about (iv). The question really is: Are there situations in which (iii) is satisfied? This strikes me as being an empirical question, and although this is a book on philosophy, I do not feel I am over extending myself by saying that (iii) is sometimes satisfied. This is not to say that it is *always* satisfied. It is to say, simply, that under some conditions a demagnetization of the screwdriver would result in the tacks no longer clinging to it in the way they had been, that the magnetization of the screwdriver is, as a matter of fact, a causally necessary condition of the tacks behaving the way they do.

In this case one's observation can be expressed in an essentially

generalized form because one's background belief reflects a connection between a particular state of affairs (these tacks are
clinging to this screwdriver) and a type of uniformity (involved
in the concept 'magnetization'). To put it roughly, one's observations can assume an essentially generalized form (when one's
proto-knowledge is not, in the same respect, generalized) when
the particular state of affairs with which one is confronted is, as a
matter of fact, a manifestation (in these conditions) of a uniformity
or regularity of some sort, or when it is connected with the
application of a concept which itself presupposes such a uniformity.

Some people seem to be unaware of the ease with which we
'see into the future' and 'see into the past', and I do not mean to
suggest by these phrases our ability to predict what will happen
or retro-dict what has happened. Doesn't the clever spy leave a
hair attached to his door so that he can, later, see whether anyone
entered his room? Can we see, by looking at the postmark of a
letter, where it *came* from? Can one tell, by looking at two coins,
which *was* minted earlier? Does anyone ever see that a man is
old, or does he never mean by 'old', in this connection, 'born a
comparatively long time ago'? Can one see that the key will not
fit even before one tries it? Or is this impossible no matter how
large the key and how small the lock. Is there always something
that interferes with our seeing what *will* happen. Do we *predict*
or *infer* that the key will not fit? I suppose one could say this, but
I am sure that if one does say it it will not be as a psychological
description of everyone's rational deliberations when they are in
such situations. Some uniformities are so pervasive in our environment that to insist that we always infer in accordance with
them is like insisting that we always infer that the chair will
support us before we sit down.

Often, of course, the situation can more adequately be described
by a conditional clause; I can see that *if . . . then . . . .* I am not
talking about such cases. I am interested in those situations when
we see that something *will be* the case or that something *was* the
case, where the 'if' clause has been absorbed into one's background beliefs by virtue of its routine satisfaction. It is quite
true that *if* the key and the lock do not change size for the next
few minutes the key will not fit into the lock. However, I see
that the key will not fit the lock (this is *how I know* it will not fit)

by virtue of a routine assumption to the affect that neither the key nor the lock is going to change size within the next few moments (under *these* conditions). I take for granted a regularity about the invariance in size of the key and the lock over short durations under these conditions. With such routine assumptions (when they are true), seeing that the key is larger than the lock can, quite naturally, be transformed into the observation that the key *will not* fit into the lock. Condition (iii) is transformed from:

(iii) Conditions are such that the key and the lock would not look the way they do (relative to one another) unless the key was larger than the lock,

to

(iii)' Conditions are such that were the key able to fit the lock (if tried within the next few moments) they would not look the way they now do (relative to one another) to S.[1]

It is a belief that conditions are as described in (iii)' that is manifested in seeing that the key will not fit into the lock; and to ask whether one can *really* see something of this sort is to ask whether (iii)' is ever *really* true. And, once again, I think the answer to this question is 'Yes'.

'Seeing into the future' and 'seeing into the past', as these are illustrated in the above examples, do not, of course, reflect generalized observations. Nonetheless, these observations represent pieces of information which many philosophers would deny could be attained without a reliance on *general principles* relating the past and the future to the present. Up to this point, I would agree. General principles *are* involved; condition (iii)' can only be satisfied if the elements which one does see$_n$ exemplify, at the time one sees them, a certain regularity of behavior. But this is scarcely unusual. Every form of epistemic seeing depends, for the satisfaction of (iii), on some regularity of some sort. The present cases differ only in that the regularity is a dia-

[1] I have given (iii)' a somewhat altered formulation in order to overcome the obvious difficulties in expressing it in the 'standard' mode. It is obvious, of course, that the key's failure to fit the lock within the next few moments does not *cause* the key and the lock to look the way they do to S in the same way as it might be said that the key's being larger than the lock *does cause* (or is part of the cause) of the key and the lock looking the way they do to S. Nevertheless, there is a regularity (not just a coincidental association, between the way the key and the lock look to S and their subsequent failure to fit, and it is this regularity which I have tried to express by (iii)'.

chronic uniformity (a uniformity over a period of time) instead of or in addition to, a synchronic uniformity (a uniform association at a given moment of time). But this fact alone does not prevent us from seeing what we allege ourselves to see in those circumstances where we assume, and *correctly* assume, that such regularities prevail. In seeing that the key will not fit, we assume that the conditions are such that the key and the lock only look the way they do when the lock is smaller than the key (synchronic uniformity), and also that, in these conditions, keys and locks retain their relative size (diachronic uniformity). Both of these assumptions can, perhaps, be analyzed out of (iii)' above. But the presence of these assumptions does not mean that we do not see what we purport to see. To show this, one would have to show that the assumptions were, in these conditions, false. And although this might be possible in isolated cases, I doubt whether it can be done for *every* case.

Several of the selectors words discussed in Chapter IV, along with our capacity to see *what caused* certain things to happen, also testify to our ability to see the general in the particular. Can you *see why* the wheel won't turn? Yes, the sprocket is being jammed. Could you tell who was causing the disturbance? Yes, I could see that Bill was doing it. We can see what is preventing the paper from burning, what is making the smoke back up, and how the windmill works. Once again, a set of general background beliefs are operating which structure the perceptual situation, a set of beliefs about the way things regularly behave, what sorts of things are relevant to various changes, what kind of things operate as effective causes, and what actions are capable of what effects. Consider the first example. One sees a piece of wood wedged into the sprocket, and then one sees the connected wheel come to an abrupt halt. What *more* is involved in seeing that the jammed sprocket is responsible for, the cause of, the reason why, the wheel stopped turning. Obviously *something more* is involved since one could see that the wheel ceased to turn, and see that the sprocket was being jammed, without seeing that the one was the cause of the other, without one, in fact, being the cause of the other. There is a philosophical view which maintains that any statement to the effect that one event, e_1, is the cause of another, e_2, is implicitly general in nature; it must be understood within a framework in which their is a general law-like connection between events of the type e_1 and events of the type e_2. When one asserts that e_1 is the cause of e_2 one is not just asserting that the two events are simultaneous, or succeed one another rapidly, or are spatially juxtaposed; one is, in effect, saying that e_1 and e_2 exemplify a regular pattern of occurrence, a pattern which can be articulated in the form of a 'law' between events of type e_1 and events of type e_2. There are difficulties here, but I think it is fairly clear that the statement 'e_1 caused e_2' carries with it the implication that in this sort of situation, under these ambient circumstances, an event such as e_1 is (together with selected aspects of the situation) a sufficient condition for the occurrence of an event such as e_2. In other words, it seems that one's observation to the effect that the wheel stopped turning because the sprocket was being jammed implies a generalized statement to the effect that, in these particular conditions, wheels (such as this) stop turning when something is jamming the sprocket mechanism (as this piece of wood is presently jamming this mechanism).

If this is implied in seeing that the jammed sprocket caused the wheel to stop turning, some people, no doubt, would wish to deny that we see anything of the kind. How can we, so they might ask, see (just by looking at *this* wheel and *this* jammed sprocket) that wheels *in general* fail to turn in these conditions when there is something fouling up a related mechanism? The answer to this question is quite simple; seeing that e_1 is causing e_2 does not entail that one sees that all events relevantly similar to e_2 occur, in these conditions, when an event relevantly similar to e_1 occurs. This latter, general, feature is an expression of the background belief manifested in seeing that e_1 is causing e_2, but one needn't *see that* the regularity to which this belief gives expression obtains in either a primary or a secondary epistemic way. Seeing that e_1 is causing e_2 only manifests a belief (background belief) that a (causal) regularity is on display in this particular sequence of events. Analogously, one can see that an object is red in conditions such that the object only looks the way it does when it is red, but one can see that it is red (under these conditions) without *seeing* that the conditions are as so described (in either a primary or secondary epistemic way). S sees that e_1 is causing e_2 (in a primary way) if he sees$_n$ these events (or states of affairs) and

(iii) The conditions are such that e_1 and e_2 would not look the way they do (relative to one another) to S unless it were the case that e_1 was causing e_2[1].

(iv) S, believing conditions are as described in (iii), takes e_1 to be the cause of e_2.

Whether S can see that the wheel stopped turning because the sprocket was being jammed depends on whether or not (iii) is true. Notice, incidentally, that (iii) is not trivially true by virtue of any 'packing' of the notion of 'conditions' or by virtue of a *de facto* satisfaction of the consequent ('e_1 was causing e_2') of (iii). Other possible causes are not being excluded (trivially) by stretching 'the conditions' to cover the absence of any other alternative cause for the wheel's abrupt halt. Background conditions (see Section 1, Chapter III) are only those conditions which affect, or are capable of affecting, the way e_1 and e_2 *look to* S without affecting e_1's being, or not being, as the case may be, the cause of e_2. If, for example, some other event or state of affairs, e_3, might (given the type of regularities which prevail in such situations) be causally responsible for e_2 *without altering* the way e_1 and e_2 look to S, then (iii) is simply false. In such a case, even though e_1 is the cause of e_2, S cannot *see* that it is. Similarly, even though the consequent in (iii) is true, even though e_2 would not have occurred without e_1, this alone does not make (iii) true. For it may be true that e_1 and e_2 would look the *same* way to S even though something else (not e_1) was causing e_2. If this is true (and whether it is true or not is an *empirical* question), then, once again, S does not see that e_1 is causing e_2 even though e_1 is causing e_2.

The discussion is beginning to sound as though the philosophical subtleties are being by-passed. Philosophers, at least, may feel some apprehension at the thought that if our observations entail statements of a generalized form, if we can see into

---

[1] Notice the formulation of (iii) allows different people to see different things as the cause of e_2; for there may be different events or states of affairs, other than e_1, which satisfy (iii). This is, I believe, as it should be since, depending on context and interest, different elements in the situation will be designated as 'the cause' of e_2. For example, another person might see that the wheel stopped turning because of the sudden braking action of the chain connecting the wheel with the sprocket (itself caused by the piece of wood in the sprocket). There is nothing in (iii) which prohibits *both* of these perceptual statements being true.

the future, see what causes are operating, and so on, then where is the traditional problem of induction? Is there any longer a problem about how to justify general truths by multiplication of particular instances or by the elaborate inductive techniques over which empiricists have labored so long? It is beginning to sound as though the 'inductive leap', the inferential gap between the particular and the general, can be bridged by observation. But really, is this not going too far? No, as a matter of fact, it is not. It should be clear that my discussion has not disposed of the traditional puzzles about induction; for observations can assume a generalized form *only when* either (i) the proto-knowledge which they presuppose is already general in nature or (ii) the observing takes place in a context of background beliefs which themselves mediate between the particular and the general. I can see that e_1 caused e_2 only with a set of true background beliefs which already establish, to my satisfaction, the general correlation between events of the two types. I can see what the value of a systemically loaded concept is only by taking for granted the fact that it *has* a value. I can see what *will* happen, or what was the case, only within a framework of assumptions (background beliefs) about the general pattern of such events. Such visual achievements do not provide an easy solution to the traditional problem of induction, at least not to those aspects of it which have interested philosophers, because the crucial elements are being taken for granted or they are already given in one's proto-knowledge. The point I have been stressing is that this 'generalized' background context is a much more pervasive affair than one might at first suppose.

Having said this much, however, I must make a partial retraction. The discussion does bear directly on the 'problem of induction' in a particularly interesting way. As I have already argued at great length in previous chapters, the *justification* of one's background beliefs is not necessary to their effective operation in seeing (epistemically) what is the case. All that is required of these beliefs is that they be *true* and be *assumed* to be true; in so far as the antecedent justification of these beliefs is relevant, psychologically, to a person's assuming them to be true, then, to that extent, their justification is relevant to the epistemic achievements which depend on such beliefs. But aside from this psychological relevance, the justification of one's background beliefs is not a pertinent issue in the *epistemology* of perception. What is necessary, at least let us hope it is necessary, is that the psychology of observers is such that they will not assume something for which they do not have adequate justification. But this is a question of the psychology of those who do the observing, not of what they observe to be the case. Hence, it is possible to acquire information of a generalized sort without being able to justify the general background beliefs the assumption of which makes possible those observations in which this information is to be found. The information contained in these observations is itself not in question, of course; one has *seen* it to be the case—one has acquired (by virtue of these background beliefs) a conclusive reason for believing what is expressed in these observations. If the background beliefs are themselves unjustified (to the satisfaction of a sceptic), then, of course, one might be persuaded (by a sceptic) to abandon one's claim to have seen by having the lack of justification called to one's attention; but the abandonment of the claim to have seen, by virtue of the rejection of unsupported background beliefs, does not entail that *when one had those background beliefs*, and was taking their truth for granted, one did not see what one thought one had seen. It implies only that *now* one no longer has any reason to think one saw it.

So we have here a rather peculiar case. The so-called 'inductive gap' *can* be bridged by observation. We can arrive at general truths, those entailed by our observations, without a justification for those assumptions which make possible these observations. I use the word 'we' rather loosely here since I, and I take it the reader also, tries not to make assumptions which we have no reason to think true. Hence, *we* seldom, if ever, bridge the inductive gap in this way since we are unwilling to assume things without *some* justification. And even if we were willing, what would be the likelihood that our assumption was true?

Therefore, the reason this procedure does not represent a significant means of by-passing the more laborious inductive techniques is that (1) we are generally unwilling (or unable) to assume something which we have no reason to think true, and (2) even if we were willing and able, the probability would be overwhelmingly great that what we assumed would be false. And either of these features, our unwillingness to make an assumption, or the falsity of what we assumed, would prevent us from making the appropriate observation and, hence, arriving at knowledge of general truths. Empiricism is still the best method to acquire true beliefs. What this discussion has shown is that the failure to satisfy the demands of empiricism does not bar one from knowledge of general truths; failure to satisfy these demands simply diminishes the likelihood that one will arrive at such knowledge.

4. *Mathematics and Measurement*

Let us call a *quantity* any feature of an object, or system, which admits of numerical expression, and for which the assorted arithmetical identities represent actual relationships between, or operations upon, the objects or systems possessing this feature. This is by no means a precise statement, but it will give the reader some idea of what I wish to talk about: *viz.* such things as length, area, volume, velocity, torque, momentum, energy, force, field intensity, charge, and so on. I shall not be talking about such things as color (unless this is understood in terms of wavelength or frequency), shape, value, edibility, etc.

We say of a table that its color is brown and its height is 3'. If one were to judge from these constructions alone, it might appear that '3' in height' was, as was 'brown in color', a property of the table. Well, what is wrong with this? Nothing really; the term 'property' is generally used in a loose enough sense to cover both. But if one mistakes this assimilation for something more than it really is, several misleading consequences follow. For example, if we can see, by looking at the table, what color it is, why can't we see, by looking at the table, what its height is? And here we have the beginning of a typical philosophical puzzle. For, generally speaking, a table that is 3' in height does not look any different than one that is 3' plus a small fraction of an inch, not at least with respect to its height. I can, perhaps, see that a table is *about* 3' in height, but to see that it is *exactly* 3', and this *is* the property it has, is a bit beyond anything I can determine by simply looking at the table. To see that a table is 3' in height seems to suggest that we can see that it is not 3' plus $\frac{1}{128}''$ or any other small fraction we may wish to choose. And this is not true.

When we are dealing with quantities we seem to have an infinite number of values which the quantity can assume, and if we admit irrational numbers, the possible values become greater than the first order of infinity. Are such distinctions possible? Let L be the smallest distance discriminable by the human eye. Suppose, now, that one table is 3′ in height and another 3′ plus $L/2$. Obviously, we cannot see the difference. Yet the claim to see that something is 3′ high (implying, as it does, that it is 3′ high) is logically inconsistent with its being 3′ plus $L/2$ in height. If we cannot distinguish, visually, between the state of affairs we claim to see, and a state of affairs that is incompatible with it, what significance is there to our claim to be able to see what the height of something is? Or does our seeing that something is 3′ high not imply that it is 3′ high? Does it, perhaps, imply only that it is *about* 3′ high, or 3′ high allowing a reasonable margin of error? If this is so, why not just admit that the various values which such quantities can assume (as expressed numerically) are beyond the scope of observation. '3′ in height', and any one of the other infinite number of values which this quantity can assume, are not themselves observable. In this sense 'height' and every other quantity is not observable; for no *one* of its possible values can be observed to the discrimination of that infinite number of other possible values lying within the 'reasonable margin of error'. Quantities, in so far as they are given mathematical expression, are unobservable.[1]

This argument, or something like it, seems to be the basis for some of the apprehension philosophers feel when they are confronted with the scientist's observations; for, of course, the height or length of something is precisely the sort of thing which is treated as an observation. The apprehension gives rise to such distinctions as, on the one hand, the technical notion of 'velocity' and, on the other, the ordinary counterpart to this, 'speed' or 'motion'.[2] The idea seems to be that the latter, the 'ordinary counterpart', is an observable phenomenon while the former is a technical or theoretical construct, and, hence, un-

[1] Something close to this argument is expressed by Hempel on pp. 29-30 of *Fundamentals of Concept Formation in Empirical Science* (Chicago, 1952).

[2] I neglect, here, the fact that 'velocity' is a vector and 'speed' a scalar (i.e. velocity has a direction), since I do not believe it is *this* difference which anyone thinks to be crucial in distinguishing between the observability of the two quantities.

observable. Let us, however, back up a moment and look at some of these matters in more detail; part of the confusion, and I believe that such arguments do embody several confusions, can be dispelled by a clearer understanding of some preliminary distinctions.

Leaving aside for the moment the question of whether we can see *what* the value of a magnitude is, I think it is quite clear that we can, frequently, see that one table is higher than another, that one man is taller than another, and that one pencil is longer than another. Some differences in length (height, distance, etc.) are easily distinguishable; others are not. This same point holds for many other quantities, even when they are understood in their most technical and rigorous sense; we can feel a temperature or pressure difference, see when something has increased its momentum or kinetic energy, feel a variation in current intensity. Any pedestrian who cannot see that a fast-moving automobile's velocity is greater than his own velocity either does not understand the concept 'velocity' or, to use the standard complaint, needs his eyes examined. Of course, I may not be able to see how fast the automobile is going (what its velocity is), but this certainly does not prevent me from seeing that it is going faster than we are (that its velocity is greater than our own velocity). I cannot tell you, off-hand, what is the square root of 214; neither can I tell you, off-hand, what is the square root of 340; but I can tell you, off-hand, that the root of the former is smaller than that of the latter. And it is not because I do rapid calculations.

Also, it must be understood that when we assign numbers to the instances of a quantity we are locating these instances by means of their *relations* to standard values of the magnitude—generally the unit value. Whatever procedure or operation we use to assign the number '3' to a length, we can be sure that, if length is a quantity, this operation thereby establishes a relationship (in terms of the procedures of measurement) of this length to any other instance of the magnitude which has a number assigned it and, specifically, to the unit value. Measurement is a procedure for assigning numbers to the instances of a quantity by *comparing* the instance to certain standard instances; the comparison, once carried out, then establishes an entire network of relations between the measured instance and every other instance of the quantity to which a number has been assigned; for each number was assigned on the basis of the same (or a similar) procedure of comparison. All this occurs, of course, once it has been determined that the feature being measured *is a quantity*—i.e. that the procedure for assigning numbers does satisfy certain conditions of additivity and so on.

I have scarcely hinted at the complexities that are involved in a complete analysis of measurement.[1] I am not, however, interested in the complexities themselves, only in some of the more obvious aspects of measurement. I have already said that we can see the difference in length between a 3' desk and something that is appreciably different in length—say, a foot-rule. I can see that the desk is longer than the foot-rule. What *more* is involved in seeing that the desk is 3' long? Well, one would suppose, if a person could see that the desk was three times as long as the foot-rule, then he would, given a minimal understanding of what he was doing, have seen that the desk was 3' long. Or, if he had something which he knew (proto-knowledge) to be 6' long, then, if he saw that the desk was exactly half as long, he would see that it was 3'. Even if he had a yardstick, which he knew (proto-knowledge) to be 3', and could see that the desk was precisely the same length as the yardstick, then he would achieve the same result. This is another way of suggesting that to see what the length of something is, to see that the length is so-and-so, is to see that it bears a certain determinate relation to other objects whose length is known—either because they have been conventionally designated as a standard or because they have been themselves already compared to some standard and have received, thereby, a numerical value. Seeing what the *value* of a quantity is is seeing that a certain determinate physical relationship obtains between the item which has this value and other known items; it is a case of seeing that b is R to c, where c's value is known (proto-knowledge), not seeing that b is P. This is certainly not original; both scientists and philosophers of science have appreciated the relational nature of quantities for some time. I draw attention to it only for the purpose of stating a few corollaries.

The first of these corollaries is that we cannot be expected to see what the height or length of something is, how fast an object is moving, by looking exclusively at the objects themselves.

[1] For an extended treatment see Ellis, *Basic Concepts of Measurement* (Cambridge, 1966).

For these objects, taken by themselves, do not look any characteristic way when they possess one value of this quantity rather than a variety of other values. I can't see how high a table is by contemplating the table any more than I can determine a man's position by scrutinizing the expression on his face; I must see these things in their relation to other things since both the height and the position of an object is constituted by a system of determinate relations which the object bears to other objects. Yardsticks and kindred devices do not replace observation; they do not remedy an otherwise chronic visual defect. They are an essential part of what is seen when we see, *primarily*, what the length of something is.

Once this matter is understood, one is prepared to confront the real issue of this section. Granting that to see what the length of something is is to see that it bears certain determinate relations to articles of known length, is it possible to see, with anything like the required precision, what these *determinate* relations are? The state of affairs expressed in clause (iii)—conditions are such that the table and the yardstick would not look the way they do (relative to one another) unless they were equal in length—is scarcely realizable. For we can always find some small fraction, say $\frac{1}{1000}$, such that, in these background conditions, the table and the yardstick would look the same way although the table was 1 and $\frac{1}{1000}$ times the length of the yardstick. The precision implied by the numerical expression of a quantity (involving, as it does, fractions to any desirable degree of minuteness) is a precision which surpasses our powers of discrimination.

Let us admit that 'length' is a precise concept if this is understood to mean that the numerical expression of it permits any desired degree of accuracy; if we don't ask what it is that is supposed to differ in length, we can make the difference in length as small as we please. '·00000000000001 inch' does represent a difference in length, a difference which the human eye is incapable of discriminating. And if such differences can be determined with special instruments, we can always add a few hundred zeros to make this impossible. The result is still, in the abstract, a difference in length. But does the resulting difference *still* represent a possible difference in length, say, between two tables? Between the height of two men? Between the distance of *any* two objects from a common object?

To see *what* the value of a quantity is, one must possess a level of discrimination sufficient unto seeing *that* the magnitude takes one particular value instead of any of *the other values that it might have taken*. But, and this is the important consideration, 'the values it might have taken' are not, in every context, regardless of what is being measured, *all* of those which can be expressed within that compact series of rational fractions. That is, because we use a system of numbers to express the length of something does not imply that every number available in that system represents a different length *for that sort of thing*. What sense would it make to express the length of a table in micro-inches? I am not asking: What practical purpose would it serve? Rather, I am asking whether it would be meaningful to suppose that two tables differed in length by one micro-inch (and this is what would be implied by expressing its length in micro-inches, even *with* a margin of error). It is not that we do not, normally, take the trouble to find out, with this degree of precision, what the length of a table is. Tables just do not have lengths of this sort. To suppose that two tables could differ by only one micro-inch is to suppose that the edges between which one measures are smooth planes—smooth to an accuracy of one micro-inch at least. When objects do have their faces plane to this degree of accuracy, then it makes sense to ask about the distance, in micro-inches, between the faces. But for many objects it does not make sense. To suppose that we could, with sufficiently delicate instruments, measure the length of our kitchen table to an accuracy of one micro-inch is comparable to supposing that we could ascertain, within one foot, California's height above sea level. Our inability to do the latter is not the fault of our measuring instruments; it's the fault of California. And the failure of tables to have lengths in micro-inches is not a result of our indifference, nor is it the fault of our crude everyday measuring instruments; the trouble lies in the tables. We could, of course, measure *something* to an accuracy of one micro-inch if we had the proper instruments; for example, I might measure the distance between the two most widely separated molecules in the desk with this sort of accuracy. But who would suppose that *these* are the edges of the desk? Splitting hairs, literally, is quite acceptable scientific practice when one is measuring the width of hairs; but it hardly represents scientific rigor when measuring the height of a man.

Suppose someone wants to know *exactly* when you were born. A fanatic on precision, he wants to know down to the last microsecond. You had thought, up to this time, that you knew exactly when you were born (5·42 a.m., December 9, 1932); the fanatic, however, shrugs this off with some remark about its being *approximate* or *rough*. He wants to know exactly. What shall we say? 'There was no one at the hospital with a sufficiently accurate timepiece'? 'No one bothered to get the exact time of birth'? Are these really the right answers? Of course not. Even given the right incentive, and given the requisite instruments, a *birth* is not something that happens in a micro-second. There is not a particular micro-second before which one was not born and after which one was born. But there may be a particular *minute* that satisfies these conditions, and to know this minute, the minute *during which* one was being born, is to know *exactly* when one was born.

Another fellow, anxious about his diet, wants to know exactly how much he weighs. The best scales he can find only provide him with a rough or approximate figure in pounds and ounces. Dissatisfied, he finally discovers the super-scale which is capable of registering *any* difference in weight (never mind how it works or what its dial looks like). Elated with the prospect of finally discovering his exact weight, he prepares to climb on the scale. But, knowing a little physics, he realizes that the farther something is from the center of the earth, the less it will weigh. He has a problem. Shall he open or close his eyes (this will make a difference)? How shall he hold his arms? Should he swallow before he gets on? Perhaps wash his hands? How much? Clean his fingernails? How shall he part his hair? Shall he stand up straight or assume his normal slouch? I think we can safely leave this fellow standing in front of the scale; for *this* instrument is not going to help find his exact weight. It might tell him what the difference is between his weight standing up straight and his weight slouching, his weight when his eyes are open and his weight when his eyes are closed, etc. But which of these is *his exact weight*? All of them and none of them. The *weight of a person* does not increase and decrease as he flutters his eyelids; the concept 'weight of a person' is not a concept which can significantly descend to these levels of precision. A person's *exact* weight has a meaning, but its meaning is in terms of pounds and fractions of a pound, and when you know your weight to the tenth of a pound, you know your *exact* weight. We have reached, here, what in other contexts is called the 'shot effect' or the 'grainy structure' of what is being measured. The same phenomenon occurs, for example, when one tries to measure the current intensity with a device that is *overly* sensitive; for such a device is capable of revealing not only the net drift of electrons (the current intensity) but also the random *thermal* movements of these particles. But these random thermal movements can hardly be significantly identified with fluctuations in the current intensity. Such an instrument does not permit us to measure the current intensity more accurately; it permits us, if anything, to start measuring something else *besides* the current intensity. And this is another way of saying that 'current intensity' also has limits to the precision with which it can meaningfully be expressed. The notion of 'a significant digit', a common expression in measurement, means precisely what it says: that there are certain levels of accuracy beyond which it is meaningless to proceed.

To say of a given measurement that it is not exact, or that it can be made more precise by exercising greater care, or by utilizing advanced techniques, is to imply that *what is being measured* has its boundaries, so to speak, more precisely defined than the precision achieved in the measurement. If I am measuring the distance between *A* and *B*, the precision which can be meaningfully demanded of such a measurement is limited to the precision with which the boundaries of *A* and *B* are understood. The distance between two people is one thing; the distance between the wave peaks in monochromatic light is another thing. The failure to apply the precision attainable in the latter to measurements of the former is not the fault of a public that is indifferent to precise data; it is bred by an inherent feature of what we are measuring. To use angstrom units to express the distance between people is to suggest that one angstrom unit constitutes a difference in the distance between people. And this is to suggest the false idea that the distance between people changes as one of the parties wrinkles his nose. Yardsticks are not just a convenient device for measuring these distances; a good yardstick represents *all* the precision which it is possible to achieve. This same feature is carried over to even the most 'reputable' measurements. Intermolecular distances can be expressed in angstrom units because molecules, where they end and where they begin, have tolerances on this order of magnitude. But to suppose that even these measurements are approximate, never representing the exact, true, or real distance in question *because,* theoretically, we can always talk about measurement with an accuracy one billionth that of what we have already achieved, is to forget that this implies that the molecule, where it begins and where it ends, and hence where its center is, is significantly specifiable within these tolerances.

What this discussion reveals is that whether we are capable of observing the exact value of a quantity or not depends not only on the sensitivity of the instrument which we employ in making the measurement but also on the level of precision which it is meaningful to attribute to that which is being measured. The quantity itself, considered in the abstract, can be expressed to any number of decimal points we please; but this does not mean that when we are measuring its value for *this,* or its value for *that,* that any failure to achieve a precision to any number of decimal points we please reflects a failure to achieve the kind of precision that is possible. For this will depend on *this* and *that.* This is why we cannot say, in the abstract, whether the exact value of a quantity is observable or not; whether we can observe what the value of a quantity is depends on *what it is* that has a value of that quantity and, then, on what comparison devices are available for discovering this value. What it is we are measuring will determine the level of accuracy which it is meaningful to ascribe to any measurement; the comparison device will determine whether we can distinguish between the various values at this level of precision. *Together* they determine whether we can *see* what the value of the quantity is. I cannot use a foot-rule to measure the thickness of a hair or the thickness of a sheet of paper; a micrometer might be better, but even it may not be capable of the distinctions which can be meaningfully ascribed to such a thickness. This is not to say, however, that nothing is capable of making the appropriate discriminations and allowing us to see what the exact values are. Nor does it mean that whenever a machinist or a carpenter uses a foot-rule or a micrometer, they would have been better advised to use some more sophisticated instrument in order to arrive at a more *precise* figure. For in many cases (not *all*) there are no more precise figures than the ones they have already obtained.

One other point should be mentioned in this regard. Once we have expressed a measurement in numerical terms, it becomes possible to operate on this number in various ways. We can take its square root, divide it by 3, and so on. The result of these arithmetical operations often result in numbers that can only be expressed with a great many decimal places (this may be infinite). For example, when we divide 1 by 3, the answer is .33333 . . . When we take the square root of 2, we get 1·414 . . . Occasionally these numerical operations have a corresponding significance in the situation or state of affairs which has been measured. For example, the length of the diagonal of a 1′ square is $\sqrt{2}$′. When the unit length is exactly three times the length of a given piece of material, the piece is then .33333333 . . . units in length. Now, if we can see (as I have been urging) that the side of a square table is exactly 1′, doesn't this imply that the diagonal of that table is 1·414 . . . (to as many decimal places as one cares to express it). Doesn't this, in turn, imply that it must make *sense* to express the dimensions of a table in these precise terms (e.g. to the 40th decimal place)? We just can't measure it with this accuracy, that is all. And if we can't, we can never really see exactly what the value of the dimension is.

The answer to this line of argument is simply that every operation on the numbers which express a quantity does not give a number which is significantly attributable to what has been measured. Not every solution to a differential equation represents a possible state of affairs for that process whose development is represented by the equation. I can divide the number '1' by any number I please; this does not mean that one billionth of an inch represents a difference in the distance between two stars. What properties of the numbers representing a quantity can be significantly attributed to a situation in which that quantity appears depend on that situation. I can use the integral and differential calculus to solve problems in hydrodynamics; this does not mean that water, or water flow, can be divided without limit. For, eventually, I reach a point where smaller magnitudes cannot possibly represent water any more; I have gotten beyond the dimensions of a water molecule. To take all these mathematical operations as literal reflections of corresponding processes or states of affairs whose development they purport to describe is to mistake their purpose. Is the diagonal of a

3'-square table, then, $3\sqrt{2}$? Yes, because when we are talking about the dimensions of tables, three times the square root of 2 is, at the most, $3 \times 1\cdot414'$. For most tables the third decimal place is the *last* significant digit for such a dimension.

When scientists carry out correction procedures, or qualify their repeated measurements with 'margins of error', a question may be legitimately raised about whether the resulting information constitutes an *observation* or not. In a sense, I believe this is a semantic point. I do not believe that the resulting information can be understood as a primary or a secondary observation as I have defined these terms. Such a technique bears a marked similarity to seeing how the stock market is doing by *computing* the value of the Dow-Jones Industrial Average. That is, we are reaching a point in the use of the term 'observation' and, correspondingly, in our use of the verb 'to see' that bears very little, if any, relation to our sense of sight. I do not wish to legislate out of existence, even if I could, these uses of the terms 'observation' or 'to see'. I think, however, it is fairly clear that these uses do not represent the sort of *visual achievement* with which this book is concerned. We would, of course, have to examine such cases if we were examining the use of the verb 'to see' and the *use* of the noun 'observation'. But this is a goal to which I never aspired. Rather, my aim has been to explore the ways in which man's visual abilities contribute to his acquisition of knowledge about the world around him, and, for this purpose, some, but surely not all, uses of the terms 'to see' and 'observation' are relevant. What a scientist calls an 'observation' may well go beyond what we can, in my sense of the term, see to be the case in either an epistemically primary or an epistemically secondary way.[1] But, as we have already noted, so does our ordinary use of the verb 'to see' go beyond any of the more restricted characterizations I have supplied. This, I think, is to be expected. I did not set to out explain what might be meant by a blind man seeing how to use his cane; nor am I interested in a mathematician seeing what the solution to an equation is. I am interested in such epistemic achievements only in so far as they are essentially visual, in so far, that is, as they represent a coming to know by

[1] This was the point of my earlier remark that scientists may consider my characterization of 'observation' *too* narrow.

having seen it to be the case. And for this purpose not everything that is called an observation is relevant.

I think, then, that the 'mathematization' of concepts does not, by itself, constitute an insuperable barrier to our seeing what the value of a quantity is, even when this is understood as seeing what the *exact* value is. What often makes the *exact* value of a quantity unobservable is not that it can, in the abstract, be expressed to any number of decimal places we please; but, rather, that the articles which possess this quantity actually have their borders, so to speak, significantly specifiable within tolerances which exceed the precision of available measuring devices. The question 'Is length (mass, velocity, etc.), in its technical scientific sense, an observable feature of things or not?' *cannot* be answered. We must first know: 'The length (mass, velocity, etc.) *of what?*' Once we know this, it is time to ask what kinds of instruments are available, if instruments are required at all, which embody the degree of accuracy appropriate to what it is that is being measured. Then, but only then, is it possible to say, not whether 'length' ('mass', 'velocity', etc.) is observable or not, but whether *the length of this, the mass of that,* and *the velocity of those* are observable or not, and, if they are, whether the observations are primary or secondary in nature.

5. *Micro-Theories*

This book will conclude on the same note with which it began: a discussion of non-epistemic seeing. Specifically, I wish to examine a view according to which the emergence of a scientific theory about the constitution of matter, or the constitution of whatever it is that we do see, reveals what it is that we *have been seeing* all along—without realizing it, of course. That is, this view alleges that a theory which explains a body's behavior by appealing to its constituent structure thereby provides an appreciation of what it is that we have been seeing when we have seen that body: *viz.* a collection of those constituents which the theory appeals to in explaining the body's behavior. The way of seeing which is in question here is obviously non-epistemic, for it would be absurd to suppose that we saw, epistemically, what the constituents of a body were without realizing what they were.

In one sense, a fairly trivial sense, the acquisition of a piece of information about an item provides one with an improved appreciation of what it is one is seeing when, and if, one sees that item. I do not *begin* to see the hors d'oeuvres only when I am informed by one of my dinner companions that these are, indeed, the hors d'oeuvres and not, as I feared, the main course. I have simply found out something about what I see, but what I found out was true of it prior to my enlightenment. Of course, once this knowledge is acquired about what we see non-epistemically, then we are in a position to *apply* this knowledge (as proto-knowledge) in epistemic seeing. Once I have found out that these are the hors d'oeuvres, however I may have done this, I can see that the serving is quite adequate for the four people at the table. In my state of ignorance this was something I did not see; in fact, I believed just the reverse. In this chapter I wish to discuss only the first point: whether certain theories reveal what it is that we have been seeing in a non-epistemic way. How this appreciation can be translated into a widened ability to see things epistemically has already been described in earlier chapters.

I wish, in particular, to discuss those theories which rely on what I shall call 'constituent analysis'. By this I mean that the theory achieves its explanatory and predictive results, whatever these might be, by referring to the fine structure, the constituents and their interrelations, of those items whose behavior is to be accounted for. The atomic theory of matter provides the most familiar instance of this sort of theory, and I shall take it as my chief illustration throughout the discussion. But we also have light, in so far as it is regarded as a train of waves or a stream of photons, organisms as a complex system of cells, and even economic or historical methodologies which attempt to explain the large-scale phenomena in terms of its constituents and their mutual interaction. In point of fact, *any* conceptualization which regards the whole as a composite of parts for the purpose of explaining the character and behavior of the whole will fall under what I have to say about constituent analysis. Moreover, there can be *levels* of constituent analysis; we can regard an automobile as made up of parts, the fenders, tires, axles, etc. Or we may think of the automobile as made up of molecules, all of the molecules which make up the fenders, tires, etc. Or, again, we can talk of its atomic constituents, the parts of the molecule, as it were; and, finally, the constituents of the atom—electrons, protons, and so on. Each level represents a constituent analysis in my sense, and what I have to say will, I hope, be true of each such level.

I think one of the unquestioned features of all scientific theories is that they attempt to explain, and a theory which represents a constituent analysis attempts to explain the behavior or properties of whatever it is that has these constituents. For example, water evaporates, and it evaporates more quickly the higher its temperature. This phenomenon can be explained by referring to the molecular constituents of the water and the manner in which they behave. An increase in temperature is an 'increase' in the mean kinetic energy of the water molecules; since their average kinetic energy is greater, a greater number of molecules, on the average, will have an energy in excess of what it takes to overcome the surface tension of the liquid and escape. Of course, this is a rough characterization, but even in these rough terms the 'explanatory force' of the theory is clear enough. When we add the dozens of other phenomena which such a theory is capable of explaining we have, by this fact alone, an impressive array of evidence in favor of the theory's truth.

But I am interested, not so much in what such theories explain, as that they explain and the presuppositions embodied in such explanations. For it seems clear that such explanations are predicated on the *identification,* in some sense, of the material whose behavior is to be explained with the system of constituents whose mutual interaction provides the explanation. The explanation I sketched above was an explanation *because* the water was considered *to be,* in some sense of this verb, an aggregate of molecules. It is not that the water provided the receptacle, as it were, for an aggregate of molecules in the way a balloon functions as the receptacle for the enclosed air. Rather, the water somehow *is* the system of molecules. To construe the relationship any other way is to undermine the very explanations which the theory attempts to give. Unless the water is a system of molecules, I do not understand *why* the escape of more molecules issues in an increased rate of evaporation. Why should fewer molecules result in less water? Does the escape of molecules *cause* the water to diminish in the way that the escape of the air from a balloon causes the balloon to diminish its volume? But when the air from a balloon is gone, we still have the balloon, but when the water molecules are gone there is no water left. Clearly, I think, these speculations are misdirected. The escape of molecules does not *cause* a diminution in the quantity of remaining water; for if we were to understand it this way, we should *still* need an explanation of the causal connection between the molecular behavior and the behavior of the water. Rather, the escape of the molecules *is* the evaporation of the water because the water *is* such a system of molecules.

I think this is fairly obvious to most people. We don't have a table and, then, a system of molecules which props it up like a heap of marbles under a handkerchief. The table is not the veneer on a porous system of minute particles. If it were, I, for one, would no longer understand why, say, a rapid oxidation of this system of constituents resulted in the desk going up in smoke—any more than I could understand why the handkerchief disappeared just because you took away all the marbles.

If this were all there was to say, we might conclude immediately that to see a table *is* to see a collection of molecules (or whatever the theoretical constituents of tables are supposed to be). For if the table is such a collection, then, in accordance with the argument form elaborated in Chapter II, when we see the table we must see such a collection, just as I see a rare antique, whether I know it or not, because what I admittedly do see (the chair) *is* a rare antique. And the conclusion to this line of argument is that we, knowingly or not, see collections of molecules, systems of atomic particles, and/or assemblies of whatever it is that happens to constitute the objects which we do see. A scientific theory merely brings us to an appreciation of what we have been seeing all along (in a non-epistemic way, of course). I have already indicated why I refuse to apply this 'principle of substitutivity' to these and similar cases. I pointed out that the 'is' of 'a table is a collection of molecules' does not support the kind of weight we are accustomed to putting on it in such contexts. Neither does the 'is' of 'that tiny speck on the horizon is an airplane (or a flock of geese)'. Generally speaking, when we say that P is Q, it may be legitimately concluded that if P has a certain property, say S, then Q also has S. If that animal is a giraffe, then if that animal is only eight feet tall, then some giraffe is only eight feet tall. And if that animal has brown spots, some giraffe has brown spots. However, reasonable as it is to say that our table in the study is solid and has four legs, does it make sense to say that some collection of molecules is solid and has four legs? When I varnish

248

the table, do I varnish some collection of molecules? When I carve my initials in the table, do I carve my initials in some collection of molecules? We could, of course, blithely answer these questions in the affirmative, secure in our knowledge that the table is, after all, a collection of molecules, but I think to do so would be to sacrifice an insight into the relationship between 'wholes' and their 'parts' and the way this relationship is connected with what we see. Let me, in order to clarify this connection, first state as precisely as I can the sense in which 'collection' must be understood in the equation of a table with a collection of molecules (or whatever constituents one chooses to analyse the table into).

A whole is not the *class* or *set* of its constituents as these terms are used in logic or mathematics; for a class or set of elements remains the same as long as its membership remains unchanged, no matter how little *organization* exists among its members. A whole, on the other hand, is something which exhibits an organization of its constituents; it is these constituents in so far as they bear certain mutual relations to each other. The whole disappears when this organization vanishes; the class of constituents, though, remains unchanged.

But *how much* organization of the parts is implied by the identification of the whole with an organized set of its parts? Consider an automobile which is made up of various parts. If we 'freeze' the auto at a given instant, all of its parts have perfectly determinate relations to one another. The piston in cylinder three is at its closest point to the spark plug; the glove compartment door is closed; the accelerator pedal is up; the needle on the gas gauge is at the half-full point; and so on indefinitely. Now, this system of relationships defines a certain organization among the parts of the auto; it is a perfectly *determinate* organization in the sense that any change in the relationships which the parts bear to one another generates a *different* organization. Let us call such a perfectly determinate organization *a particular configuration of the constituents*. It seems fairly clear that an automobile cannot be identified with any particular configuration of its parts; for this would imply that to open the door, say, of the auto would be to generate a different auto, since such an action changes the particular configuration of parts into a *new* and *different* configuration.

A constituent analysis represents an identification of the whole, *not* with the class of its constituents, *not* with any particular configuration of its constituents, but with these constituents organized in a fashion looser than that of a particular configuration but tighter than that of a class. The whole is a *system* of parts, a set of parts organized in such a way that any particular configuration of those parts is but an embodiment of that less determinate organization defining the system. A whole consisting of parts is always these parts as they exemplify a minimal level of organization, and it is the maintenance of this minimal level of organization that constitutes the persistence of the system and, hence, of the whole which is to be identified with the system. The system remains the same (the minimal level of organization persists) throughout the succession of particular configurations; for each of these particular configurations embody, as a minimum, that level of organization defining the system. The system is the horse and jockey with the latter *on* the former. Particular configurations find the jockey now up in the saddle, now down, now fighting to retain control of the horse, now sitting back easily; all of these configurations contain the minimal level of organization requisite to the system: *viz.* the jockey's being *on* the horse.

I shall, henceforth, speak of a *system* of constituents. A table is, in this sense, a system of molecules; a certain minimal organization among the molecules is requisite to the maintenance of the table's integrity. Unless the molecules formed a solid, with the necessary bonding relationships which this implies, the table would not have those features expected of tables; i.e. it wouldn't be a table. Particular configurations of the constituent molecules represent the various momentary states of the table.

Generally speaking, whenever one is speaking of a collection of constituents instead of the whole, different criteria of identification and re-identification become operative. I can, for instance, put a new fender on my auto; it is still the same automobile, it just has a new fender. The parts of the auto are not the same parts it had yesterday, but it is still the same automobile I have owned for three years. It has changed, yes, but it, so to speak, endured throughout the change. Of course, this exchange of parts is a process which is subject to a great deal of vagueness. The exchange of parts must be done gradually, over a period of time, without loss in the continuity of the remaining system; if these conditions are satisfied, a complete exchange of parts can occur without a destruction of the whole. For example, the human body is alleged to suffer a complete exchange of its cellular constituents every seven years; this discovery does not imply that we have a different body every seven years. All this implies is that the human body is not a collection of invariant constituents, constituents which are never replaced or never lost. Rather, it is a system of ever-changing collections. The system persists throughout such alterations; the minimal organization remains, and as long as this remains, the whole with which it is identified remains.

There is another source of ambiguity when we come to speaking of collections of constituents. At a given instant we can say that the table is a collection of molecules, but, even here, given the different degrees of vagueness associated with the concepts 'chair' and 'collection', we can expect no exact 'fit' between the chair and the collection of molecules which compose it at a given instant. We cannot, perhaps, say of every given molecule whether it is or is not part of the chair at that moment; hence, the system must remain as vaguely defined (at an instant) as the chair with which it is to be identified at that instant. But to say that the chair, for this reason, even at an instant, is not a system of its constituents is like saying that the Milky Way is not a system of stars because we cannot, for every star, decide in some non-arbitrary way whether it is in or out of the Milky Way. What we are doing here is *tailoring* the system of constituents to meet all the requirements of the whole: we are using the whole as our pattern in selecting the constituents and in specifying their organization. We are using the criteria of identification for the whole in selecting the system of constituents with which the whole is to be identified.

So much for our elucidation of the concept 'system'. I think it is fairly clear that if an item is to be identified with any function of its constituents, it must be with a system of these constituents. But are we any better off in reference to the initial objection? Does it make any better sense to say that a system of particles is solid, that we varnish such a system, or carve our initials in it? We are still left with an apparent conceptual disparity between the whole and the system of parts with which we wish to identify it.

To indulge in a little science fiction for the moment, suppose that to everyone's surprise the red spot on Mars turns out to be a herd of Martian cattle wandering over the Martian landscape.

Is this impossible? Well, given what we know about Mars, it probably is, but we can always change the example to an astronaut sailing over Farmer Parnell's fields. That little semicircular dark patch which he sees in the middle of the green landscape happens to be Mr. Parnell's herd of Black Angus cows. Now, I think that most of my readers will agree that a herd of cows is not something that can be black; the *cows* might be black, and, hence, we might have a herd of black cows, but to say that the herd itself is black is either nonsense or it means that it is a herd of black cows. Now, our astronaut does not see the individual cows in the herd; this is a level of resolution of which he is incapable. He sees, if indeed he sees anything, a black semi-circular patch which is (in some sense) a herd of cows—i.e. some cows collected together into a fairly close spatial proximity to one another. If, now, we say that our astronaut sees the herd of cows (it looks like a black semicircular patch to him), although we cannot say it is black, although it doesn't make much sense to say it is black, in the requisite sense, the herd may, nevertheless, *look black*. The result should not be too surprising; for at a sufficiently great distance a crowd might look like a gray dot, a forest like a green patch, and a swarm of locusts like a black cloud. Moreover, each of these items, a crowd, a forest, and a swarm, is a system of people, of trees, and of locusts respectively, just as a herd of cattle is a system of cattle in the sense in which I have defined this term.

The moral of this digression is that, although it may not make sense to say of a system of molecules that it *is* brown, there seems to be nothing objectionable in saying that it *looks* brown. Furthermore, if we apply the same analysis to other features, there seems to be nothing preventing us from saying that a system of molecules feels hard and smooth, looks rectangular or table-shaped, and, in general, appears to us in all the ways that are characteristic of a table. We can say this much without committing ourselves to the view that the system of molecules *is* brown, table-shaped, smooth, and hard, or even that it makes sense to suppose the system has such properties.

Once this concession is gained, what more need be said to establish the visibility of a system of molecules? Nothing. For in order to see something non-epistemically it is not necessary that one see *that* it has the properties it appears to have, it is not necessary that it *have* the properties it appears to have, it is not even necessary that it *makes sense* to suppose it has the properties it appears to have (does it make sense to suppose that Farmer Parnell's herd of cows *is* black and semicircular? Yet, the astronaut does see the herd; it looks black and semicircular). All that is necessary to see$_n$ something is that it *look some way* to the percipient, that the percipient visually differentiate this something from its immediate environment. And the system of molecules (and the herd of cows) meet this requirement. In a way this is inevitable. For, recall, the system of molecules (or constituents) which was to be identified with the object (of which they were constituents) was *tailored* to meet all the criteria of identification and re-identification of the object itself; hence this system of constituents must (if it is to be a satisfactory system of constituents) appear to us in all the ways that we are accustomed to having the object appear to us. If the system of molecules (which was to be identified with a brown table) did not (according to the theory which involved a reference to such constituents) *look brown,* then the theory would be, in this respect, unsatisfactory, and this system of constituents could not be taken as the (basic) constituents of the table.

I conclude, therefore, that when we see a table we see a system of molecules (assuming, of course, that the molecular theory of matter is true). I conclude this, not by an application of the 'principle of substitutivity', but by the fact that the sense of the verb 'to be' in the equation of a table with a system of molecules is a sense of the verb which allows us to say that when we see the table, the system of scientific constituents with which it is to be identified must look some way to us. It is in one respect the same sense of the verb which is at work in 'That speck on the horizon is an airplane'. Here, also, we cannot conclude that we see the airplane *because* we see the speck and the speck is an airplane (according to our principle of substitutivity). But we can conclude that we see the airplane because the sense in which the speck *is* an airplane is a sense which allows us to conclude that if we do see the speck the airplane must look some way to us and, specifically, it must look like a tiny speck on the horizon. And if it looks some way to us, then we see the airplane. Just as the brown table functions as our 'pattern' in selecting the appropriate system of molecules with which it is to be identified, that tiny speck on the horizon functions as our pattern in selecting what it is to be identified with. This tiny speck *is* just above the rooftops. What, over there on the horizon, looks (from this distance and angle) like a speck just above the rooftops? The brown table *is* solid. What system of constituents, and what mutual organization among them, would account for this feeling of solidity? What system of particles, and what postulated organization among them, would (if the table were identified with such a system) account for the assorted ways the table *appears* to us?

In one respect we are left with a somewhat incomplete position. Although I wish to say that there is a perfectly legitimate sense of the verb 'to be' such that an object *is* a system of its constituents, and that whenever we see the object we see a system of its constituents, I have refrained from committing myself to the view that the system of constituents can be significantly said to have *all* those properties, to enter into *all* those relationships, that can be significantly ascribed to the object itself. I have refrained out of deference to the 'oddity' which some philosophers seem to detect in those statements which transfer the properties of the whole to a system of its parts, and out of the conviction that this further commitment was not necessary to establish the visibility of the system of constituents. And since my chief interest in this section was to come to a decision on this latter point, the discussion might well be dropped without going further. However, one or two brief comments on this issue may be of some use in clarifying the relationship between the system of constituents which *looks* brown, but which cannot be said to *be* brown (without 'oddity'), and the whole which may not only look brown but be brown.

Let us grant, for the sake of argument, that it is odd, to the point of absurdity, to say that a system of molecules is hard or solid, or that we eat a system of molecules, or go to the barber to have a number of such systems removed or reduced in size. Such utterances assuredly sound funny, but what are we to conclude from it? Are we to conclude that nothing which is red *is* a system of molecules? That food is not? That the hairs on our chin are not? Consider the case of a man who turns to you in the middle of a Shakespearean play and asks whether it was really John that killed Desdemona. What can you say? 'No, Othello did it'? Your neighbor looks at his program and sceptically replies that, according to it, John is playing Othello tonight. And when he asks you to point to John, in verification of this piece of information, you always point to Othello. This is a ludicrous confusion, of course, but I do not think it any more ludicrous than wondering why it isn't the system of molecules that is red because, according to the program in the physics book, the red object is a system of molecules. John, playing the part of Othello, looks a certain way to the audience; in a certain sense he is supposed to look like he is killing (the person playing) Desdemona. But John is not killing Desdemona; Othello is. Although we can rest assured that if the program is correct, whenever we see Othello on the stage we are also seeing John, this does not mean that *everything* we can sensibly say about Othello we can sensibly say about John or vice versa. Similarly, if the physics books are correct, whenever we see a red object we see a system of molecules; this does not mean, however, that everything that can significantly be said about the one can be significantly said about the other. The system of molecules looks red, yes, that is the way it is supposed to look; but to cross a 'category' boundary by saying that the system of molecules *is* red is to generate the same sort of confusion as is generated by the crossing of the boundary between people and the roles they play. The role of a physical object is a role which molecules sometimes play, and they play it whenever they exhibit the requisite organization.

My analogy may, I fear, be misleading in one respect. I do not wish to suggest that the world of physical objects, the world of tables and chairs, rocks and houses, is some kind of phenomenal show, some kind of sensible gloss, over the 'real' world of molecules. I do not wish to suggest that tigers and teapots are 'the tiny specks on the horizon' and scientific investigation reveals what such things 'really' are. We cannot say that Othello did not *really* kill Desdemona because John is playing the part of Othello, and John, as we all know, did not kill anyone. Similarly, one cannot say that an object is not *really* red (round, soft, solid . . .), or that there really is no table because the system of constituents with which it may be identified is not hard (brown, solid, . . .). Nor can one say, as some are wont to say, that theoretical science has shown us that our everyday world of objects and events are not real; for this is tantamount to saying that theoretical science has shown us that there are no systems of elements which appear to us in the ways that tables and chairs are expected to appear. It is tantamount to this because, within the scientific context, this is what a table and chair amount to. No amount of delving into John's psychological problems, or his murderous intentions, is relevant to whether Othello, the character he was playing, killed Desdemona or not; and no amount of theoretical speculation about the constituents of an object is relevant to whether an object is really red. For an object being red, or its not being red, or its being an object at all, is presupposed in *having* a system of constituents for the explanation of such facts.

I conclude, then, that scientific practice is relevant to what we see in several different ways. It gives us a greater appreciation of what we do see, and have seen all along, by providing us with alternative specifications of what we do see. In this respect it does not broaden the scope of what we see; rather, it simply enhances our appreciation of what there is to be seen, and, in the process, reveals what it is that cannot be seen; for in learning that what we do see *is* a system of certain elements, we thereby learn that the elements themselves, taken individually, are something we have not seen and, perhaps, cannot see. Whether we can see the elements, however, is not a question which can be answered in the abstract; its answer depends on the nature of the elements themselves, our power of discrimination, and the instruments available for enhancing these powers.

Scientific practice also reveals that observation, what we can see to be the case, is as sensitive to theoretical developments as are the theoretical developments to the observations on which they depend. There is here a reciprocal relationship. A theory is, to a large extent, dependent for its viability on the observations which either conform, or fail to conform, to its theoretical predictions, and on those observations for the explanation of which the theory was introduced. But once the theory has achieved a status where it is no longer in the process of confirmation no longer being tested against observation, no longer given only qualified acceptance (which is not the same as irrevocable acceptance), then it is free to augment the range of observation. It gets swallowed up, so to speak, in proto-knowledge and new background beliefs and a new plateau of observation is achieved.

This procedure should come as no surprise; we find it taking place in everyone's perceptual history. What we know is dependent, to a greater or less degree, on what we have seen to be the case; but what we are capable of seeing, epistemically, is expanded by the accumulation of more information. The greater our experience, the more inclined we are to take certain things for granted; the more inclined we are to take things for granted (providing always, of course, that they are true), the more pregnant with information become the things we can see to be the case; and this more rapid accumulation of information accelerates our expanding perceptual horizons. It is, indeed, a snowball effect. This final chapter has exhibited nothing new in this respect; it has simply tried to sketch the progress of the snowball through scientific practice, and with it the evolution of scientific observation.

INDEX

abstract nouns, 13ff.
after images, 22, 45, 63ff., 66, 92
appearances, 64ff.
  total appearance v. partial
    aspects, 85–6, 89ff.
Armstrong, D. M., 16
associated description, 54
Austin, John, 55n.
awareness, direct, 70ff.
Ayer, A. J., 44

background belief, 113, 145
  differences in, 176–7
  for secondary seeing, 158
  justification of, 130, 133ff., 159,
    232–3
  manifesting of, 118–20, 158–9
  overspecification of, 117n.
  restrictions on, 89–91, 112ff.,
    141n.
  underspecification of, 116, 182,
    187–8
background condition, 82, 112ff.,
  187n.
  for relations, 141, 144
  for secondary seeing, 153n., 158
Barense, Jack, 56n.
belief, 6, 17n.
belief content, positive, 5ff.
  negative, 5, 12
Benacerraf, Paul, 60
Blanshard, 55

Campbell, N. R., 221n.
causal conditions for seeing$_n$,
  50ff., 68ff.

causal theory of perception, 51ff.
certainty, 132ff.
Chisholm, Roderick, 13n., 23n., 52
class (set), 249
collateral information, 18–19
collections, 58ff., 247ff.
colorblindness, 84, 177
configuration, 249
constituent analysis, 246
Cooper, Maj. Leroy Gordon, 26n.

demosing, 191
differentiation, visual, 20, 23ff.
  of events, 31ff.
dispositions, 192–3
dreams, 46n.

eidetic images, 149
Ellis, B., 237n.
equivocation, 57
events, 14ff., 31ff., 42, 163ff.
existence condition on seeing$_n$,
  43ff.
  suspension of, 47ff.
existential clauses, 108, 146–9
explanation, 247–8
  of how we see$_n$, 51–4
extensional contexts, 55

facts, 163–4
feelings, 184
force, as an observable, 200

general v. particular, 223–4
generalization of background belief, 114, 141n., 174, 182, 187–8

259

given, the, 75
Gregory, R. L., 15n.
Grice, H. P., 22n.

hallucination, 44ff., 70ff., 100ff.,
109
Hamlyn, D. W., 16
Hanson, N. R., 37
Hempel, 235n.
Herbst, Peter, 164n.
Hirst, R. J., 55, 72n.

identity, 58ff., 253–5
identification, 247
criteria for, 250
and seeing$_n$, 16–17
image, double, 48
eidetic, 149
imagination, 7ff., 46n.
implication, truth, 35ff.
utterance, 35ff., 80n.
incorrigible beliefs, 30
induction, 232–4
inference, 159–60
intensional contexts, 55
interpretation, 159–60
inverted spectrum, 178

justification of background beliefs, 135
justificatory contexts, 81, 141

knowing one knows, 137ff.

laws, scientific, 208ff.
Lees, Robert B., 14
Linsky, Leonard, 55n., 57n.
look
as if, 20
as though, 20, 92
like, 20ff.
some way, 20ff., 253
the look of something, 64ff.

Malcolm, Norman, 62n.
mass, as an observable, 212ff.
measurement, 234–7
mistakes
and direct perception, 62–6
about after-images, etc. 92–3
in background beliefs, 88–9,
128
in proto-beliefs, 101–4
Moore, G. E., 21n., 44, 62n.
mosing, 191

nominals, interrogative, 14, 54
relative clause, 14, 54, 56
noticing, 15

observable, 99–100, 203ff.
observation, 205–8
terms, 211ff.
generalized, 225–34
observe, 204–5
other minds, 189–90

parts, spatial, 27ff.
temporal, 31ff.
–whole relationship, 249ff.
percepts, 65, 71
Perky, Cheves West, 8n.
potential for demosing, 193, 195
proto-knowledge, 96ff., 128, 223–
5
differences in, 173–5, 177, 197–8
for relations, 145–9
for secondary seeing, 160, 212
specialized, 174–5, 181–2, 187–
9, 223
for existentials, 108, 146–9

quantities, 234ff.
Quine, W. V., 54

reasons, 120–4
conclusive, 124ff., 138